School Public Relations

Building Confidence in Education

National School Public Relations Association

School Public Relations: Building Confidence in Education

National School Public Relations Association
15948 Derwood Road
Rockville, MD 20855

ISBN 0-87545-126-8
Item 222-10069

This publication presents a variety of viewpoints and practices. The views and practices expressed or implied in this book should not be interpreted as official positions of the National School Public Relations Association.

Contents

Introduction

By Rich Bagin, APR

Momentum is building on the need and value of the school public relations / communication function. Interest in what the PR function can do for school districts has never been higher.

School leaders are finally grasping the fact that effective communication at all levels is a critical component to school district and student success. Superintendents, board members, and their school colleagues are beginning to understand how powerful communication can be when it is strategically integrated into the everyday operations of a school district.

Here are some examples:

- **Test scores and achievement rise when parents, families, and volunteers are involved in the teaching and learning process.** An abundance of studies prove just that. But the studies fail to mention that effective, ongoing, two-way communication is the elixir that makes that involvement and subsequent achievement happen.

Professional communication makes the difference.

■ **Communication is essential in developing trust and credibility between parents and their schools.**

■ **Communication also can play a key role in keeping attendance numbers and achievement up.** Students need to attend regularly to achieve.

■ **Districts with ongoing communication programs have a much stronger chance of passing a finance or bond election.** We all know what happens to programs and buildings when finance elections fail. It's the beginning of a downhill slide.

■ **Communication makes your school district richer in various ways.** In some areas, marketing to recruit students has helped both financially and programmatically. An NSPRA research project found that if you invest $105,000 on better communication, you only need to recruit 15 kindergarten students at $7,000 per student funding to recoup these costs.

The real financial bonus is that if those students graduate from your system, that initial investment blossoms into more than $1 million. Programmatically, recruiting students also helps boost enrollment in advanced courses. If you help

recruit five more students for the AP Physics course, it will be offered. Otherwise, the class will be canceled because it will not be financially feasible to offer it to just a few students.

■ **Two NSPRA studies of practicing superintendents and the search consultants who place them agree that communication is among the top three skills required of today's superintendent.** And we add that if superintendents who implement comprehensive programs communicate effectively, they normally increase their tenure in districts. Recent studies have also proven that increased tenures mean stronger achievement in our schools.

The days of just "getting good press" as the key objective of a program are over.

This totally revised edition of *School Public Relations… Building Confidence in Education* is designed to give you an overview of what the communication function can do for your district. The days of just "getting good press" as the key objective of a program are over. This book's 26 chapters give you practical advice and considerations for building a program in your schools.

This resource would not be possible without the contributions of some of NSPRA's best professionals who authored each chapter in the book. Our profession is indebted to the following pros:

■ Sandra Cokeley, APR

■ Marsha Chappelow, Ph.D.

■ Bob Noyed, APR

■ Janelle Albertson, APR

■ Bill Banach, Ed.D., APR

■ Stephanie Bateman

■ Susan Hardy Brooks, APR

■ Tim Carroll, APR

■ Jennifer Wayman Reeve, APR

■ Lew Armistead, APR

■ Jim Cummings, APR

■ Ed Moore, APR

■ Tom Salter

■ Rick Kaufman, APR

■ Harry Roberts, APR

■ Sylvia Link, APR

■ Tom DeLapp

■ Buddy Price

■ Nora Carr, APR

■ Karen Kleinz, APR

■ Ron Koehler, APR

■ Jim Dunn, APR

■ Larry Wiget, Ed.D., APR

■ Gay Campbell, APR

■ Mark Havens, APR

■ Joe Krumm, APR

Special thanks to Bob Noyed, APR, Director of Communications for the Wayzata Public Schools (MN) and the 2006–07 NSPRA President, who worked with each author in developing this book. He also served as its primary editor.

The Center for Clear Communication, Inc., of Rockville, MD also receives a great deal of thanks and respect for its pro-bono contribution of graphics, production, and editing of the publication.

Without the work of these two professionals, this book would still be another great idea waiting to happen.

NSPRA is proud to publish this comprehensive and practical resource for all school leaders. It serves as a blueprint on how to build a comprehensive communication program for your schools. Read it and reap!

Rich Bagin, APR
NSPRA Executive Director

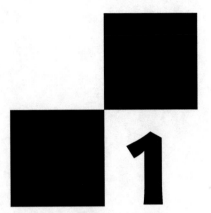

Overview

What Is PR? Understanding the Need for Effective School Communication

By Sandra Cokeley, APR

When many people hear the term *public relations*, their thoughts immediately turn to slick, carefully crafted cover-ups that are designed to protect an organization or person, typically in times of trouble. They ask questions like, "What really happened?" and "What aren't you telling me?"

They try to read between the lines and interpret body language to get at what they believe is "the real truth." More often than not, they turn to the rumor mill — their "trusted source."

At the same time, we all have our own perception of each of the thousands of organizations, events, and people we meet. We have opinions about whether we like them, respect them, and believe them.

We have opinions about the quality of their work, and whether it is a product or a service. We decide over and over again if we want to spend our time, energy, and money with them. Most important, we have decided how much we trust them.

These perceptions are formed from a vast array of inputs. They can include:

■ Personal interactions

■ Research

■ Use of a product or service

■ Written or printed references

■ Newspaper and media stories

■ Electronic interface

■ Third-party hearsay or the rumor mill

Guiding perceptions and opinions resulting from each of these experiences and many others is the art and science of public relations.

Defining Public Relations

Public relations has early roots in ancient Greek theorists writing about public will. Denny Grisword, the former publisher of *Public Relations News*, wrote one of the first definitions of public relations:

> Public relations is a management function which tabulates public attitudes, defines the policies and procedures of an organization with the interest, and executes a program of action to earn public understanding and acceptance.

The National School Public Relations Association (NSPRA) defines school public relations as follows:

> Educational public relations is a planned and systematic management function to help

improve the programs and services of an educational organization. It relies on a comprehensive, two-way communication process involving both internal and external publics, with a goal of stimulating a better understanding of the role, objectives, accomplishments, and needs of the organization.

Educational public relations programs assist in interpreting public attitudes, identify and help shape policies and procedures in the public interest, and carry on involvement and information activities which earn public understanding and support.

While the definition has not changed much from its early roots, public relations has become a highly complex and critically essential force for organizations and corporations of all sizes. It is an established profession complete with its own international credential, the Accreditation in Public Relations (APR), and numerous codes of ethics. Both undergraduate and graduate degree programs are available in public relations.

The public relations function is organized through job titles at all levels from entry to senior, departments within organizations, one-person departments, full-service public relations firms, specialty area firms such as media relations or direct mail, consultants at all levels and in all areas, and countless other scenarios.

According to the 2004 U.S. Bureau of Labor Statistic, public relations specialists held about 188,000 jobs and advertising, marketing, promotions, public relations and sales managers held about 646,000 jobs.

In its description of the nature of public relations work, the Bureau of Labor Statistics states,

> An organization's reputation, profitability, and even its continued existence can depend on the degree to which its targeted 'publics' support its goals and policies. Public relations specialists — also referred to as communications specialists and media specialists, among other titles — serve as advocates for businesses, nonprofit associations, universities, hospitals, and other organizations, and build and maintain positive relationships with the public. As managers recognize the importance of good public relations to the success of their organizations, they increasingly rely on public relations specialists for advice on the strategy and policy of such programs.

What PR Is Not

Any discussion on what something is, especially something that can be as subjective and intangible as the social science of public relations, deserves a discussion on what it is not. Unfortunately, public relations is sometimes misused — intentionally and unintentionally. While not meant to be exhaustive or complete, here is a list of what school public relations is not:

▦ A tactic to get your superintendent's name in the paper as often as possible

▦ A "carefully-word-smithed-not-the-whole-truth" explanation for a problem or occurrence

▦ An afterthought without considering how the audience will receive your message

▦ A ploy to win favors with key community leaders

▦ A contest for column inches with the local charter school

▦ "No comment" statements to the media

▦ A secret campaign to get your school board president re-elected

▦ A scare tactic to provoke certain sentiment for your district's support

Making the Case for School PR

Typically, the public school system is one of the largest investments a community makes. The community's investment through tax support of the schools can be well into the hundreds of millions of dollars, depending on the size of the district. Its annual investment in teacher salaries, textbooks, computers, supplies, and equipment is significant. School taxes are often the lion's share of local taxes. Most important, the primary purpose and focus of a school district — to educate the children to grow into productive, contributing members of society — is tantamount.

Public schools must be accountable to the students and families they serve. They are equally accountable to their faculty and staff, district residents, taxpayers, community officials, business partners and others. These stakeholders have the right to be informed about their public schools. They have the right to straightforward, effective communication designed to meet their needs. And they have the right to become involved and engaged with their schools.

Dr. Curtis Culwell, superintendent of the Garland Independent School District in Garland, Texas, states:

> School leaders have to understand that public education is going to continue to struggle for the hearts and minds of the public. So much disinformation is out there, and some of it is intentional. Superintendents need help telling the school district's success story. It is critical to their success.

This thought is supported by the teachings of the late Dr. Edward Bernays, known as the Father of Public Relations. Bernays, one of our country's leading public relations counselors for more than 60 years, advocated strongly for school public relations as an act of social responsibility. According to Bernays:

> School districts must intensify existing favorable attitudes toward education, convert those who are on the fence, and negate attitudes that are negative.

> Schools don't hesitate to hire accountants or lawyers, so why shouldn't they hire counsel that understands public relationships — many of which have nothing to do with the teaching process?

Maximizing School PR

At its best, school public relations is a formalized, planned, structured discipline at the senior leader level in a school district. Ideally, it is led by a trained and credentialed public relations director who works closely with the board of education, school superintendent and other top administrators.

School communications plans should be based on research and support the district's educational, financial, social, and other goals. Perhaps the best list of essential factors for a school public relations program is the core beliefs of NSPRA. According to these core beliefs, school public relations:

■ Is a crucial management function essential to the success of education

■ Is rooted in honesty, integrity, accuracy, and ethical behavior and is always in the public's interest

■ Serves as the conscience and soul of the organization

■ Strives to build consensus and reach common ground

■ Is a fiscally responsible investment

■ Provides counsel and service to all segments of the staff and community

■ Is the shared responsibility of everyone in education and their communities

■ Develops two-way, meaningful, trusting relationships with all audiences

■ Requires continuous professional growth to meet the accelerated pace of societal and technological changes

■ Enables education to function at its best by bringing schools and communities together

An effective communication plan follows the RACE model — research, analyze, communicate, and evaluate. A more detailed description of this model is presented in *Section 2: Communication Planning*. What is important to understand in the greater context of effective communication is that this model supports effective two-way communication.

Public relations is the critical link between a school district and its stakeholders. As much as public relations works to communicate out from the organization to its students, parents, faculty, staff, and community, it must work equally hard, if not harder, to understand these stakeholders. It is the responsibility of the public relations function to know their beliefs, opinions, expectations, and preferences.

Listening is one of the most critical components of effective public relations. Information and ideas gleaned from the listening process should be shared with the senior leadership as they make decisions and plan and deliver programs so staff, parent, and community input are incorporated.

> In the eyes of the public, everyone who works for a school district is an official ambassador for the organization.

Sharing the Load

While supporting a structured, formal communication program led by a trained and experienced professional is essential, school districts must make sure that all employees have a role in the public relations program. As has often been said before, public relations is everyone's business.

Parents and community residents can come into contact with a school district in literally hundreds of ways. Relationships between school personnel and the public form the foundation of trust. Because of this, every school employee must understand the need and importance of effective public relations practices.

In the eyes of the public, everyone who works for a school district is an official ambassador for the organization. Helping employees understand their role as ambassadors and equipping them with the information and skills they need to fulfill this role is part of establishing an effective public relations program.

Choosing the Right Structure

The size, scope, and budget of school public relations departments vary as much as the size, scope, and budget of school districts. Public relations departments fulfill the roles of counselor, strategic advisor, advocate, lobbyist, copy editor, researcher, reporter, graphic designer, photographer, speechwriter, special event organizer, pollster, facilitator, interpreter, webmaster, staff developer, television director, talk show host, customer service expert, liaison, complaint manager, and countless others. A department or job description should be designed to meet the district's specific needs and maximize the resources available to support the function.

A school public relations program can expand in many different ways. For larger districts, full departments with copywriters, photographers, and webmasters are the norm. Others have fully staffed cable television departments because that media works well in their community. Some have their own print shops to minimize costs in high-volume print districts. Some rely on a blend of staff and consultants who specialize in specific areas at agreed-upon time schedules to maximize cost-efficiency. In some states, regional educational service agencies provide communication services on a contractual basis.

Regardless of the size and structure, all school public relations programs should be guided by a solid public relations plan that supports the district's goals and objectives.

Effective PR Is a Must

An effective school public relations program is a must for both large and small districts. Even during times of tight budgets, the investment can pay off for the district. The benefits of investing in a public relations program can include:

- Improved student achievement

- Increased parent involvement in their children's education

- Increased support of school budgets and bond referendums through positive votes

- Increased community support for district programs, events, and issues

- Effectively managed crises, minimizing negative impact

- Increased trust through transparent, honest communication

- Improved relations with legislators and civic leaders

- Increased volunteer contributions, including participation on committees and task forces

- Increased business partnerships

- Increased alumni involvement

- Increased recruiting pools for hiring

- Greater faculty and staff retention

In reality, the percentage of a district's total annual budget into its communication program is typically less than one half of one percent. Taxpayers, parents, community members, and all stakeholders deserve to know how the other 99.95% is being handled, which is part of the role of an effective school public relations program.

Effective school public relations is clear. It is understandable, and it is certainly doable. Most important, it is the right thing to do. The rest of this book will give you practical ideas and strategies for making effective public relations a reality in all school districts.

In summary, school districts have a responsibility to communicate with their constituents. They are obligated to foster honest and transparent two-way information flows, both in good times and in bad. This critical responsibility should be in the hands of a trained professional.

Sandra Cokeley, APR

Sandra Cokeley, APR, is the director of quality and community relations for the Pearl River School District, Pearl River, New York. Along with serving as a member of the senior leadership team, she manages the district's improvement processes and wrote the district's winning 1994 NYS Excelsior Award application and 2001 Malcolm Baldrige National Quality Award application. Her district was one of Baldrige's first education winners.

In addition, she coordinates the district's community relations functions including internal communications, media relations, print and electronic communications, and the adult education program.

Cokeley holds a Bachelor of Arts degree from Dominican College and is accredited in public relations (APR). She is past president of the New York State School Public Relations Association and former northeast vice president for the NSPRA. She currently serves as NSPRA's representative on the Universal Accreditation Board and is past chairperson of the Education Advisory Committee for the American Society for Quality.

Cokeley maintains a private consulting practice and presents regularly on community relations and quality in public education. She is co-author of *Malcolm and Me: How to Use the Baldrige Process to Improve Your School*, published by Scarecrow Press.

Relationships: The Goal of Effective Communication

By Marsha Chappelow, Ph.D.

Relationships, relationships, relationships is the mantra for any school public relations professional. It is much like, "Location, location, location," is the mantra for the realtor who tells homebuyers what the most important priority of their investment is. The school PR professional acts like the realtor when advising the superintendent and the school board about the priority of their district's investment in communication.

Successful school districts today must invest in communication tools or options for both internal and external audiences. However, if the investment only focuses on tools like publications, web sites, e-mail service, or telephone notification systems and does not concentrate on building both internal and external relationships, then the investment in the tools will never really have the intended impact for successful communication.

> **Communication tools do not build relationships — people build relationships.**

If school district leaders do not build solid, trusting relationships with internal and external stakeholders, the district will never make the connections with its various stakeholders that are needed to be successful in the long term. Communication tools do not build relationships — people build relationships. Building relationships take time, effort, and commitment by the school district.

The seventh edition of the *Oxford Dictionary* defines the words *relation* and *relationship* with the same definition:

> The way in which two people, groups, or countries behave towards each other or deal with each other.

Relationships in school districts mean much more to the entire community than this basic definition. "Relationships constitute the essence of school public relations. It is through relationships that schools form their identity, formulate their culture, involve diverse stakeholders, and affect student learning," according to Mary and Dan O'Hair in their research about strategic relationship management in school public relations in the *Journal of School Public Relations* (2006).

Meaningful, authentic relationships with a district's various publics must be developed and maintained by the school

district's leadership with the school PR professional acting as the strategic advisor and manager of this process. This is not an easy task. The O'Hair's research (2006) points out:

> Relationships are an elusive asset to manage. Relationships must be constantly developed, nurtured, managed, maintained, de-escalated, exited or rekindled.

In the first edition of NSPRA's *School Public Relations: Building Confidence in Public Education* (1999), no single chapter was solely devoted to building relationships, even though references to this important activity were included in other chapters of the book. What has changed since the first edition was published? Now more community members are disconnected from public schools than even eight years ago. These disconnections exist for many reasons, including:

■ Fewer residents have children in school.

■ Charter schools and other alternatives have increased.

■ District budgets have decreased while expectations have increased.

■ The federal government has increased unfunded mandates.

■ Technology has increased.

■ Fewer people are becoming teachers.

■ More women are in the work force.

Building relationships starts with district leadership.

While these changes are not necessarily negative, they all have had some impact on public education and its relationships with its various publics. J.A. Ledingham in the *Journal of Public Relations Research* (2003) states:

> The major shift occurring in the discipline, then, involves recognition that the appropriate domain of public relations is, in fact, relationships. Sustaining of public relationships requires not only communicating but organizational and public behaviors, a concept central to the relationship management perspective.

If a shift in the perspective of public relations has occurred, then school district leaders must decide where to put their time, their efforts and their public's funding. This is not an impossible task for a school district; however, it must be well planned and strategically managed in each school district and community. It is actually a very simple concept.

"When we're invested in something personally, we tend to have a better opinion of it," says David Matthews, president of the Kettering Foundation in *American School Board Journal* (September 2006).

> What people are looking for is not information, but relationships.

Building relationships starts first with district leadership — the school board and the superintendent with their strategic advisor, the school PR professional.

Role of the Board and Superintendent

If the goal of effective communication in school districts is building and maintaining relationships for the immediate and foreseeable future, then establishing a district culture for this to happen is of utmost importance. This culture starts with district leadership — the school board and the superintendent.

School boards have two primary functions in the operation of the school district. The school board:

■ Hires the superintendent to manage and lead the district

■ Sets policy for the district to operate

Hiring a superintendent is the first step in establishing a culture of communication and especially to developing and maintaining relationships with both internal and external publics of the district. According to one of the surveys of NSPRA's Communication Accountability Project (CAP), the three top reasons superintendents lose their jobs are:

■ Poor board relations

■ Communication failure

■ Poor people skills

So if communication and relationship-building in a school district are to be successful, the school board must hire a superintendent who is able to maintain relationships already built by the district or is able to build or rebuild relationships with the staff and community.

The board's selection of a superintendent sets a school district up to be successful or not in establishing a culture for relationship-building because superintendents are role models for staff and a leader in the community. Superintendents are the most visible leaders to the staff and most visible district leaders in the community. They set the tone of the communication and show the commitment to communication for the district.

The role of the superintendent in establishing a culture of communication is crucial for successful communication and relationships with staff and the community. Through many communication audits conducted by NSPRA leaders, NSPRA has identified the following attributes as being a key part of the superintendent's role in building relationships:

■ **Superintendents must "walk the talk."** In other words, it is no longer enough for the staff and general public to have superintendents say that communication is important. They must demonstrate that communication is important through their behavior and actions. This consistency helps to build the trust needed for solid relationships with the staff and community.

■ **Superintendents value staff and community perspectives on issues and solutions.** Public engagement processes are an important part of the input process and are not just for show. Community engagement is part of a meaningful process when issues arise in a district. Many will look at the superintendent's leadership and communication priorities if the public engagement process is not a valued and authentic part of the communication process in a district.

■ **Superintendents are physically visible and actively participate in staff, school, and community events, regardless of the size of the school district.** The visibility of the superintendent continues to be of importance to staff members and the community. Either group easily notes it if the superintendent is not visible.

■ **Superintendents must set the tone and expectation of transparency for the school district culture.** In education, business, financial and personnel decisions, the operations and processes should become demystified and transparent to the district's internal and external stakeholders. This again will build trust in relationships, but the superintendent must be the leader of this effort.

These four areas done solely by the superintendent contribute to building strong relationships, both internally and externally, for the district as a whole with its various publics.

Policies for Communication

The second function of the school board is to set policies for the school district. These policies may be both philosophical and operational; they form the foundation for procedures and guidelines for the students, staff, parents, and community members.

Policies are the first step in setting expectations for developing and maintaining a district culture in all areas of the district. Policies are especially important in establishing the role of the communication in building relationships for the school district.

Five key policy areas are related to building effective relationships:

■ Role of communication in the school district

■ Professional behavior of school board members

■ Open records and public access to information

■ Media relations

■ Community involvement

While these areas may be titled differently depending on how board policies are written in each state, they are important to have in some form because issues will invariably arise in these areas.

Policies can always be changed as new situations or issues arise in a district, but having at least some policy foundation in these areas will give the district leadership a starting point for discussion and review.

Establishing a communication policy is seen as a commitment.

The role of communication

Policies that establish the role of communication in a district lay the groundwork for effective communication. These policies set the school board's expectations for district administration and staff members' actions and let community members know what they can expect in communication from the district.

Some districts are more specific than others, but the point is to have some kind of policy about the existence of communication and its importance with the board and the district. Since a lack of communication has become a common complaint for many public school districts today, having an effective communication policy is even more important now than in the past.

Establishing a communication policy is seen as a commitment. What kind of commitment for communication is the district making to its community?

Some items that could be discussed in this policy include:

■ Importance of school/home connection to student achievement

■ Two-way communication

■ Communication tools

■ Communication function

■ Accurate and timely communication

■ Relationships with various publics

It is no longer enough to say that communication is important. If communication is to be successful, district board policies should set expectations for behavior and actions of the board and district staff.

Professional behavior of school board members

For a variety of reasons, in recent years many districts have instituted policies for professional behavior of school board members. Some reasons for enacting this type of policy include:

■ Lack of professional behavior at school board meetings

■ Board members' promoting special interests even if a decision has been made

■ Lack of denoting a spokesperson for the board on district issues

Many boards have developed policies or a code of ethics for board members and have shared them in new board member orientations. No matter if it is a policy, a code, or guidelines, the importance of this topic to district communication is that it helps individual board members see how important their behavior and actions are in building trust and relationships with both staff and the community as leaders and representatives of the district and its leadership.

Clearly establish what information is open to the public and what information is considered to be private.

Open records and public access to information

The third area of board policies to establish is open records and public access to information. This policy area is established by state statute so it will differ from state to state. A sample policy for this can be easily obtained from any state school board association.

The bigger issue with this policy is understanding the policy and communicating it to school board members and administration. In many states, information has become more open to the public in recent years. It is critical to clearly establish what information is open to the public and what information is considered to be private. Receiving negative publicity about not following this policy set by state statute can affect the trust level for the district and the development and maintenance of relationships with various groups both now and in the future.

Media relations

To help the district as well as the media, especially in times of crisis or emergency, school boards should set expectations in policy for procedures for working with the media. A policy may include general information establishing the communication office as the first contact. Administrative guidelines may outline specific procedures.

Setting a policy for media relations sets expectations for district leadership and staff and helps them to understand their roles better in media situations. This policy will help a district build its relationship with its media by setting up procedures so that the media can obtain timely and accurate information. It also helps the district build relationships with its public through using its media outlets.

Community involvement

While some districts include community involvement in a general communication policy, having a separate policy highlights the importance of the community in the decision-making process. It also establishes ways for the community to be involved in the district such as standing board advisory committees, open forum at board meetings, and public engagement processes.

Many times community members want to know how they can become involved in a school district. While this policy should not be a list of involvement activities, it is a way for a school board to state the importance, purpose, and parameters of community involvement in its processes of making district decisions.

These five areas of policies may be combined or subdivided by school boards and communication professionals, depending on their policy style. Policies in communication are important because they set expectations for the board, staff, and the community; develop a district culture; and maintain transparency for school district operations and procedures. Setting policies about communication in a district helps develop trust which is crucial to developing relationships for the district.

How to Build Effective Internal and External Relationships

Many activities discussed in other chapters of this book will help a district develop effective relationships with various internal and external groups. The individual skills of each member of the district leadership team will also add to developing and maintaining relationships. The examples of activities given below for staff, parents, and the community have the possibility of going beyond the expected impact of a school district communication program. These activities can enhance a district's relationships, both internally and externally, for the long term. Depending on the needs of a school district, some examples may be more appropriate than others.

Activities that will enhance relationships between the district and staff members include:

■ **Regularly scheduled meetings to discuss concerns or issues with the administration and teacher association leadership** — These meetings should take place monthly, not just when conflicts occur. This activity can help promote better understanding of each group's perspectives when issues do arise in the district.

■ **Regularly scheduled meetings with a classified employee council representing different support staff groups** — This activity helps promote better understanding of perspectives from different employee groups when issues do arise in the district or within the support staff.

■ **Regular weekly communication from the superintendent to all staff members** — It is important to inform your internal audiences about issues so they do not hear about them first from the media or neighbors.

■ **An internal key communicator network** — This is the same philosophy as an external key communicator group, only it is with identified internal staff members. These individuals are the "go to" staff members who may not hold leadership positions, but who will be sought out by colleagues for perspective on key issues. This communication can be done through meetings or through an e-mail network.

Some activities can enhance relationships between the district and parents and community members, including:

■ **Board advisory committees** — These are opportunities for involvement and input in areas such as finance, technology, curriculum, student services, and other areas, depending on the needs of the district. These are standing committees of the school board and may include board members. These committees are a way for the district to gain expertise and find resources from others in the community and to share information about the district, its procedures, and issues. These committees can help make the district and its operations more transparent to its stakeholders.

- **A school district foundation** — The district can be a partner with this effort. Again, expertise from community individuals can be used in the foundation which also assists the district's students and staff with additional funding for projects. These people also become more educated about the district's operations and issues by discussing funding projects for various educational programs. Since funding is the main priority, anyone who is involved will develop a different type of relationship with the district than other parent or community groups.

- **A public engagement process** — Whatever engagement model a school district decides best fits its needs, public engagement should be done regularly, not just when controversial issues arise in the district. Any public engagement process must be meaningful to the participants and seen as an important part of the decision-making process.

- **An external key communicator network** — A district should identify key parent and community leaders who are sought out by others as sources of information. The district will then give these identified people accurate school district information that they can share with other parents and community members.

- **A senior citizen volunteer program** — The important aspect of the relationship between the district and senior citizens is to get these individuals into the district's schools so they can see the students and learning in action. Since these community members no longer have children in school, it is important for them to actually see what students do in schools today. Including groups like senior citizens who are not normally included in school activities can be the beginning of a strong relationship with an important group of the community.

- **A school-business partnership program** — A needs assessment may be appropriate to see how the district's businesses want to be involved with the district. Activities may range from school partnerships to a business advisory council. Having a relationship with the businesses in a district's community is important to have on several levels. These representatives can give business advice to the district, they can be a resource for district issues, and they can share accurate district information with other business and community members.

Final Thoughts

For a school district to be successful in educating students, it must first build relationships with its many internal and external publics. Building relationships is an important part of district and school communication.

Relationship-building activities can take many different forms in a district with its staff and community. However, the school board and superintendent are the primary leaders and role models of communication and building relationships for any district. They lead the district to develop a culture of effective communication along with the strategic assistance from the communication professional. For strong relationships and communication to be built and maintained, a district must strategically develop a plan and set expectations.

As Matthews from the Kettering Foundation in the *American School Board Journal* (September 2006) further observes,

> The problems public education faces are not going to be solved by more public relations or simply trying to create a better image. We have to find a better way to connect the public and its public schools.

The first step of this connection is through a district strategically building relationships with its many publics on an ongoing basis.

◼ Marsha Chappelow, Ph.D.

Marsha Chappelow, Ph.D., has 18 years of experience in school communication in her 33 years in public education. She is currently the assistant superintendent for human resources and communications in the Ladue Schools in St. Louis, Missouri. Before going to Ladue, Chappelow served as the assistant superintendent of communication services in the Blue Valley Schools for 15 years and developed the district's communications program. She also has experience as a classroom teacher and building administrator as well as the curriculum/instruction and business/finance areas in a school district.

Chappelow will serve as NSPRA President in 2007–2008. She also served as a co-chair for NSPRA's Communications Accountability Project (CAP) and served as the South Central Region Vice President in 1999–2002.

Chappelow has been active at NSPRA Seminars with individual presentations, as a panel moderator, and panel participant. She has also participated as an auditor in NSPRA Communication Audits.

Professional Continuum: From Technician to Strategic Advisor

By Bob Noyed, APR

When many people think of a position like "director of communication," they think of duties like writing, editing, media relations, photography, and other technical skills. These skills are certainly part of any communication position, but for many school public relations professionals, they represent only a small portion of the job description.

Along with many traditional technical skills, many people serving in positions like a director of communication also serve in a role as strategic advisor to the superintendent, school board, and other key leaders. When school public relations professionals serve as strategic advisors, they do not simply "communicate" a decision or issue, but they also play a role in shaping issues and decisions.

A strategic advisor helps think through issues at the front end.

A strategic advisor helps the superintendent and other key leaders think about implications of decisions and how district stakeholders will respond to the decision. A strategic advisor helps think about potential reactions to a decision and helps craft strategies that will lessen the impact of the decision. In other words, a strategic advisor helps think through issues at the front end rather than just putting out fires at the back end.

A school public relations professional cannot just simply declare, "I'm a strategic advisor," and expect the superintendent and other key leaders to immediately respond. To be seen as a trusted strategic advisor, a strong relationship must first be in place.

The superintendent must be able to trust the thinking and actions of the school public relations professional. There must be a sense that you understand the larger issues that affect the school district. The relationship between you and the superintendent must be solid. A strong sense of loyalty must be present.

This relationship does not happen over night, but can be built over time. When a strong relationship between the superintendent and school public relations professional is present, the overall communication program of the district gets elevated to a more strategic level. The communication program does not just focus on sharing information, but it also features strategies that are in line with the overall strategic direction of the district.

An effective strategic advisor is not always the source of the answer, but should be the source of the questions that lead to options or answers. A strategic advisor is someone who demonstrates the following abilities:

■ Thinks about and presents perspectives on future possibilities

■ Thinks about and presents context for discussions

■ Thinks about and presents perspectives on how issues and decisions interrelate or disconnect

■ Thinks about and presents perspectives on issues from a systemic approach, not just from a communication perspective

■ Can translate thought into action

■ Presents options for consideration

■ Asks "what if" and "why" questions to discover deeper meaning

Along the Professional Continuum

When school districts create a public relations position, most of the emphasis is placed on writing, editing, photography and other technical skills. This position is usually created to write material for newsletters, web sites, brochures, and news releases.

The statement, "We need to get more good news out about our school district," is often heard by superintendents and school board members when creating a public relations position.

Even when positions begin at this level, the way to make the most of the position is to move along the following professional continuum to become a strategic advisor:

The labels along the continuum are not job titles, but reflect how school public relations professionals would spend their time if their position was framed in this way. The following descriptions further point out what someone might do at each point along the continuum:

Technician

Technicians would spend most of their time creating materials. Writing, editing, graphic design, photography, and other technical skills would be the most used.

Public information coordinator

Public information coordinators would spend most of their time "getting the good news" out about the district. Writing news releases and newsletters are two examples of tasks that would be most emphasized.

Communication manager

Communication managers would have a comprehensive role in the overall district's communication effort. Most of their time would be spent communicating decisions and issues seen as important by the superintendent and other key leaders.

Strategic advisor

Strategic advisors would be responsible for the overall communication effort, but would also be engaged with other key leaders in helping to make and shape decisions.

Even those who spend most of their time in a strategic advisor role are still likely to use some technical skills in their work. For example, you may be involved in discussions about district budget reductions and then be assigned to write the materials on the reductions to be communicated.

Strategic advisors do not abandon technical skills or the duties in the other roles along the continuum, but spend most of their time in the strategic advisor role. Over time, this role becomes dominant.

Differences along the continuum

As a school public relations position shifts to a greater emphasis on the strategic advisor role, clear differences affect the person in the position. The following are a few of the differences that occur when shifting along the continuum from a technician role to a strategic advisor role:

■ **Lower individual risk vs. higher individual risk.** People in technician roles are asked to produce materials and are not involved in decision-making. They do not risk being identified with a decision that is not warmly accepted. However, because strategic advisors are likely involved in considering options and assisting with decisions, they can be connected to decisions and take on more risk in their position. In other words, risk increases as responsibility and authority increases.

■ **Task oriented vs. system oriented.** People in technician roles are asked to complete tasks — design the newsletter, post material on the web site, or edit the brochure. Their work is usually divided into individual tasks or projects. Strategic advisors often deal with issues that are multifaceted and that affect the entire system or organization.

■ **Less complex projects vs. more complex situations.** As noted above, people in technician roles usually have work that is organized in simple, well-defined projects.

Strategic advisors often deal with situations that might include numerous projects or tasks. These complex situations are often evolving and require ongoing attention and management.

■ **Reacts to change vs. initiates change.** People in technician roles are usually told that a change is being made and then must adjust to the change. While strategic advisors may also react to changes, they are more likely to be in a position to create or initiate change because of their role in the decision-making process.

School public relations professionals bring a different perspective because they have not followed the traditional track of their colleagues.

Expanding Your Role

As was stated earlier, becoming a strategic advisor does not happen quickly. If you are seeking a more strategic role, you must develop a strong relationship with the superintendent and other key leaders. In addition, it is essential to recognize other key components of becoming a strategic advisor.

Consider and practice these core beliefs on your journey to expanding your role as a strategic advisor:

■ **Your greatest value to your organization is not just as a "communicator," but as a strategic advisor.** Effective two-way communication is critical for any public relations plan to be successful, but the effectiveness of the program becomes elevated when the school public relations professional is involved in shaping the messages rather than just sharing them.

■ **You bring a perspective that is not usually represented among other leaders in your organization.** Most members of school district management teams followed a similar track of first working as teachers and then moving up through the organizational chart. With some exceptions, most school public relations professionals today come from backgrounds such as mass communication, marketing, journalism, or public relations. Because of this difference, school public relations professionals bring a different perspective because they have not followed the traditional track of their colleagues.

■ **Part of your role as a school public relations professional must be teaching others in your organization the value of the public relations function.** Because your colleagues followed a different path to arrive as a member of the school management team, they may not completely understand what a school public relations professional can bring to the organization. You need to teach others not only what you can do, but also the value of the public relations function to the success of the organization.

■ **Expanding your role as a strategic advisor requires you to think differently and see the big picture.** As a strategic advisor, you will be involved in issues that affect all parts of the organization. You do not have to be an expert in other areas, but you must understand other functions of the organization such as curriculum, instruction, special education, business, transportation, and human resources. Your understanding of all aspects of the organization and the "big picture" — how these aspects interrelate — is integral to being effective in the strategic advisor role.

■ **Some of the best work by a strategic advisor is never seen or understood by a broad audience.** People in technician roles produce materials and products that are seen and read by a broad audience. If you are spending most of your time in a strategic advisor role, your work may not necessarily be seen by most stakeholders. Your work is demonstrated by the questions you ask, the options you offer, and the advice you give. Your fellow colleagues will likely notice your contributions, but you will have fewer tangible products when you function in this role.

Demonstrate Leadership Characteristics

School public relations professionals who are seen as strategic advisors are often viewed as key leaders in the organization. Leadership is not just demonstrated by the superintendent, but should also be part of what you need to do to expand your role. While this chapter is not meant to provide inspirational messages on becoming a leader, there are things that you can do to demonstrate greater leadership.

Characteristics to consider in demonstrating greater leadership in your organization

Leaders...

■ identify problems and offer solutions

■ remove obstacles

■ help others improve and excel

■ see the big picture

■ help others see the big picture

■ take action

■ think

■ respond to the future

■ connect issues

■ work several steps ahead

■ make others better

■ learn

■ are generally more proactive and less reactive

Understanding and embracing each of these characteristics will help increase your worth and value to your organization.

Assess Your Position in the Organizational Structure

While you always have opportunities to play the role of a strategic advisor in informal ways, having a formalized role in the organizational structure makes it easier. Becoming a strategic advisor includes having a "seat at the table" and having opportunities to exercise your influence with the superintendent and other key leaders.

Before assessing your relationships with the superintendent and other key leaders, it is helpful to assess the status of your position in the organizational structure. Consider these questions when you assess your position and determine the status of the public relations function in your organization:

■ Do you report directly to the superintendent?

■ Do you serve on the superintendent's cabinet or senior management team?

■ Do you have direct and regular access to the superintendent?

■ How often are you asked to discuss important issues with other district leaders?

■ Do you represent the district on external committees or groups?

■ Do you have clerical and logistical support?

■ At what point do you know about important district issues?

■ Along with public relations and communication functions, what other duties have been assigned to you?

■ Is the public relations function a regular target for budget reductions?

Your answers to these questions will help chart a course of improvement and should identify ideas that can help you re-position yourself in the organizational structure.

Having a strong relationship with the superintendent makes it easier for you to function in a more strategic role.

Your Relationship with the Superintendent

As stated earlier, one of the key pieces in being seen as a strategic advisor is the relationship you have with the superintendent. Having a strong relationship with the superintendent makes it easier for you to function in a more strategic role.

Consider these questions when you assess your relationship with the superintendent:

■ Does your superintendent like you? How do you know?

■ Does your superintendent trust you? How do you know?

■ Do you like your superintendent? Do you trust your superintendent?

■ How well do you know your superintendent? How well does your superintendent know you?

■ Are you comfortable telling your superintendent when he or she is wrong?

■ How well does the superintendent understand the value of the public relations function?

■ What does the superintendent ask you to contribute?

■ How often are you asked for your perspective or opinion?

■ Are you part of the superintendent's "inner circle"?

■ Does the superintendent come to you when the heat is on him or her?

Each situation is going to be different, but there are strategies that every school public relations professional can implement to create a better relationship with the superintendent.

The following are a few tips to help you improve your relationship with your superintendent:

■ **Decide if it's worth it.** Most times a relationship can be improved or repaired. However, it may be necessary to determine if it makes sense for you (and the superintendent) to invest in the relationship or if it is time to move on.

■ **Schedule a meeting to define your role.** Schedule a meeting to find out what the superintendent is looking for from you, how you fit into the organization, and what you can do to be more effective. This is also an opportunity for you to talk about what else you can add to the organization and how you can work more strategically.

■ **Know what they know.** Learn about the superintendent's areas of interest and expertise so you can relate to what they are talking about.

■ **Provide perspective on key issues.** Even if it is not requested, provide perspective on key issues so the superintendent sees that you understand the district from a systemic perspective.

■ **Be a rabid dog and a loyal friend.** Behind closed doors, ask tough questions to help the superintendent think through critical issues. But once the decision is made and it is ready to share with stakeholders, be a strong and loyal supporter.

■ **Make it their idea.** Let others take credit for the good things that come from the district, and be comfortable with playing a "behind the scenes" role.

■ **Weave into the strategic plan.** Help the superintendent see how your work and thinking can advance the district's strategic initiatives and how the district's communication program can help to advance the district's strategic direction.

Assess Your Relationship with Other Key Leaders

Along with the superintendent, other key leaders usually play an important role in leading the district. Consider these questions when you assess your relationship with the other key leaders in your district:

■ How often do other district administrators come to you for help?

■ What do other district administrators ask you to contribute?

■ How would you describe your relationship with each of the other district administrators?

■ How often do building principals come to you for help?

- What kind of assistance do building principals ask from you?

- What kind of assistance do you give principals?

- Do you have better relationships with some principals?

- When do principals and other administrators call you for help?

- Do other district leaders trust you? Do you trust them?

Here are a few tips for improving your relationship with the other key leaders in your district:

- **Learn their jobs.** Especially for principals, spend time in their schools and let them know that you understand what their jobs are like.

- **Make their lives easier.** Give principals and administrators tools, resources, and information that will help them more easily deal with issues and do their work.

- **Use them as resources.** Go to other administrators and allow them to teach you about their areas.

- **Show them how you can help.** Many administrators don't know what you can add to the district, so give them examples.

- **Be accessible.** Be available to help others at a moment's notice.

Demonstrate Strategic Thinking

The previous sections of the chapter provided more of a philosophical background on assuming the role as a strategic advisor. While it is critical to understand the importance of becoming a strategic advisor, you can use several specific strategies to not just demonstrate your strategic thinking abilities, but to also help the district make decisions and advance its strategic directions. Two of the strategies are presented below.

Executive Summary Outline for Decision-making

The first strategy to try is the *Executive Summary Outline for Decision-making*. You can use this outline to present information to your superintendent, but you can also use it to organize information that is presented as part of a school board meeting.

The sections of the outline help organize thinking around a specific issue or recommendation.

When preparing an executive summary on a specific decision, include these major categories:

- **Initiator.** People responsible for the recommendation

- **Recommendation.** Statement of concept being proposed

■ **Objectives.** Statements of the purpose of the recommendation or why you are making the specific recommendation

■ **Options considered.** Description of other concepts considered in presenting the recommendation

■ **Strategic criteria.** Description of the criteria used in making the recommendation and how it fits with the overall direction of the school district

■ **Benefits.** Description of how this recommendation will improve the school district

■ **Potential reactions.** Description of the human responses, both positive and negative, that may come from implementing the recommendation

■ **Associated risks.** Description of the risks in approving and not approving the recommendation

■ **Preventative actions.** Description of what can be done to minimize the effect of associated risks and potential reactions

By organizing your thoughts according to the *Executive Summary Outline*, you will be better able to present a detailed perspective. In addition, the information included in the outline will also be helpful when it is time to communicate about the issue.

Communication Protocol Outline

The second strategy to demonstrate your strategic thinking abilities is by using a *Communication Protocol Outline*. A communication protocol is a set of questions to follow when considering how to communicate issues and decisions. Like the *Executive Summary Outline,* it provides a structure to think through an issue and to organize your thoughts. The protocol is also a tool that is helpful to stimulate others' thinking.

Consider these questions when you determine how to communicate important issues and decisions that arise in your district:

■ **What is the issue or problem?** Discuss and clearly identify the core issue or problem to be addressed.

■ **How will the issue be framed?** Consider how the district will outline or frame the issue or problem and how it will be presented to stakeholders.

■ **How does this issue or problem affect other issues?** Consider how a particular issue or problem will affect other issues in the district.

■ **What stakeholder groups need to know about this issue?** Identify the stakeholder groups that are the primary audiences for this issue.

■ **What are the key messages that we will communicate about the issue?** Identify the key ideas that we want stakeholders to know about this issue.

■ **How will this issue be communicated?** Identify the methods and strategies to be used to communicate to identified stakeholders.

■ **What is the timeline to publicly release or respond to this issue?** Develop a timeline for communicating about this issue.

■ **Who is the main spokesperson on this issue?** Identify a person who will serve as the main spokesperson on this issue with the board, media, and other groups.

While it is not essential to cover every step of the protocol each time an issue is discussed, it is important to carefully consider how an issue will be communicated and how stakeholders will respond to how an issue is framed.

Both of these strategic tools will stimulate thinking that will take in "big picture" issues and will encourage you and others to think about future implications of a decision.

As was stated earlier, strategic advisors must consider how issues interrelate and must think about the implications of decisions. These are key and critical components of being an effective strategic advisor.

■ Bob Noyed, APR

Bob Noyed, APR, is the director of communication for the Wayzata Public Schools, Wayzata, Minnesota. He has more than 22 years of experience as a school public relations professional and educational leader. Noyed has worked directly with superintendents, school board members, principals, and other school administrators, and understands the obstacles, challenges, and opportunities in public schools.

Noyed served as the 2006–2007 NSPRA President and as the North Central Region Vice President from 1999–2002. He is the 2005 recipient of NSPRA's Barry Gaskins Mentor Legacy Award, recognizing his work in mentoring new public relations professionals and providing leadership in professional development.

He co-authored NSPRA's best selling CD *Unlocking Sensational Service: Tools for tapping the people power in your schools* and also co-created the NSPRA New Professionals Program, which began in July 2001 and continues to be one of NSPRA's most popular professional development workshops. He also edited two editions of NSPRA's *Scenario Collection*.

Noyed is a frequent presenter at NSPRA Seminars and at local, state, and national conferences. He has also written numerous materials on school public relations topics.

2

Communication Planning

Understanding the PR Process

By Janelle Albertson, APR

An old song lyric says, "If you don't know where you're going, any road will take you there."

The same can be said about a school district's approach to its public relations program. To be effective, your public relations program must be focused and that means you need a plan.

Having a thoughtful, systematic, two-way communications plan will help ensure that your organization is speaking with one clear voice and you are using data to make strategic communication decisions.

One of the most effective models in communication planning is the four-step process known as the RACE model.

The steps of the RACE model

Research

Analyze

Communicate

Evaluate

This chapter will provide an overview of the process. The next four chapters focus on each step in greater detail.

Step 1: Research

To start, you have to clearly identify the problem or issue that needs to be researched. That is, you have to answer, "What's happening now?" and "What's causing the problem?" These are the first steps to conducting research. In this phase, you conduct an investigation and collect data. As one researcher put it:

> Without data, you're just another person with an opinion.

Research is simply a way of providing context by gathering information to describe what's happening now and then to question basic assumptions and determine potential consequences. In this phase, public relations professionals take a comprehensive look at the situation, examine the prevalent attitudes, and outline the difficulties they uncover.

Many seasoned public relations professionals conduct a situation analysis as one method of research. They ask, "What is the issue?" and they probe using guiding questions that may include:

■ What threats and opportunities do we face?

■ What bothers us about this issue or situation?

■ What is the seriousness of the issue?

■ What is the potential?

■ Who is involved or affected?

■ How are they involved or affected?

■ How do others perceive this situation or issue?

■ When is this a problem?

■ Where is this a problem?

Other formal methods of research help clarify the issue at hand and help illuminate clues as to how to solve the problems. Some of the most common research methods are:

■ Surveys

■ Interviews

■ Objective and systematic data collection

■ Collection of representative samples

■ Focus groups

Equally as helpful are the informal methods of research such as:

■ Hosting community forums

■ Conducting study circles

■ Enlisting the opinions of personal contacts

■ Listening to key communicators

■ Gleaning information from telephone or mail logs

■ Eliciting feedback using postcards or response cards

Step 2: Analyze and Plan

Once the data have been gathered, the next step is to analyze the information. The data from the research step will help define the problem or opportunity and articulate the impact (or potential impact) to the organization.

This is where strategic thinking comes in. Given what you know about the current situation, determine your desired outcome. Realistically, what would you rather have your current situation look like? Answers to these questions form your goal or set of goals.

When you're writing your plan, create SMART goals, which are:

- **S**pecific
- **M**easurable
- **A**ction-oriented
- **R**ealistic
- **T**ime-oriented

If you skip this step, the strategies you select to address may not focus on the problem. Without careful analysis, you may be throwing solutions at the situation and waiting to see what works. When you take time to map out your plan, you're being proactive. You're helping to shape your own headline. You're taking some control and making tomorrow's decisions today.

With your goals in mind, considering several guiding questions will move you toward accomplishing your goals or shaping your intended outcome. These questions should prompt the development of your plan's objectives. Examples of guiding questions include:

- What's getting in the way of accomplishing our goals?

- What is the benefit of implementing this plan as it relates to the general goals or mission of the organization?

- Who, or what groups, are involved?

- What behaviors need to change relative to each target audiences?

- How can we influence a change in these behaviors?

- When are these changes in behaviors needed?

- What changes in the social, economic, technological, or financial environment do we anticipate? What impact will those changes have on our target audiences? Our organization? Do we need to include plans for any anticipated changes?

- What systems need to be changed to create the most advantageous environment?

- What new systems must be created to create the most advantageous environment?

- Are there laws, ordinances, rules, or expectations that need to be altered, eliminated, or created?

- What are the human, financial, and political costs of implementing the plan?

■ What training is needed to implement the plan?

■ Do we have the right players at the table to develop and implement this plan?

Answers to these guiding questions can help shape your plan's objectives and target audiences.

as well as face-to-face communication and public engagement strategies.

In addition to communicating messages and initiating public engagement strategies, it's important to include in your plan things like a detailed budget, the staffing needed to execute your plan, responsibility assignments, and the timelines for carrying out your plan.

Step 3: Communicate

In this phase, outline what your organization is going to say and do related to the identified situation. For every major action or activity developed in the previous phase, the plan also needs to address these questions:

■ Who needs to know?

■ What do they need to know?

■ Why do they need to know?

■ When do they need to know?

■ How are we going to tell them?

■ What do we want them to do with the information they receive?

■ What actions or behaviors are we aiming to prompt?

Remember that this phase should include a strategic mix of one-way and two-way communication. It's not just about what information the organization wants to push out. Rather, it's a give and take of information. It includes printed materials

Step 4: Evaluate

Once you've carried out your plan, it is important to evaluate the strategies that were implemented to see what worked and what did not work. It is in this phase that you go back to your SMART goals and check your progress.

Here are some guiding questions to help prompt developing the evaluation component of your plan:

■ Did we accomplish our goals?

■ Did we make progress in accomplishing our goals?

■ What changed as a result of executing our plan?

■ Did we monitor along the way? If so, did we make adjustments and were they useful?

■ What changes did our target audiences see or realize?

■ Is there a need to refine our goals, make changes in our plan, and continue down this path?

- Did we adequately prepare to implement our plan?

- What feedback do we need from various groups to help us better understand the changes we made?

- What were the unintended consequences?

- What did the cost/benefit analysis reveal?

- Was this plan and its implementation an efficient use of our resources, compared with alternative uses of the resources?

Janelle Albertson, APR

Janelle Albertson, APR, is a seasoned public relations veteran with varied leadership experience at both the state and local levels. She currently serves as the chief communications officer for the Adams 12 Five Star Schools in Thornton, Colorado.

As an active member of various professional organizations, Albertson has held executive board positions, including president, with the Kansas School Public Relations Association, International Association of Business Communicators in Kansas and Denver, and the Colorado School Public Relations Association.

She served as the NSPRA Southwest Region Vice President from 2004–2007. Albertson is regularly invited to speak at conferences and has earned a variety of national and state awards for her communications work.

Research: Don't Start Your PR Effort Without It

By William J. Banach, Ed.D., APR

Research is simply a matter of asking questions, and reflecting on the answers.

We need to improve communication. Let's put out a newsletter.

Everybody is connected to the web. That's why we need a web site.

The school finance election is just three months away. The ballot proposal will never pass unless we get busy informing parents about the issues.

In all three cases, people are trying to do the right thing. And, in all three cases, they are likely to stumble along the way. The primary reason is that they have not asked the right questions — that is, they have not done their research. They know where they want to go, yet they are generally clueless about how to get there.

Improving communication is a noble goal. But putting out a newsletter in a community where reading is not embraced is a bad strategy. On the other hand, in a community of readers, putting out an attractive, informative newsletter may be a great idea. Research can tell you about literacy levels in your community.

Most people who get lost have a map — they just don't use it.

While it seems as if everybody is online, many are not. But what about those who *are* online — what are they doing there? Are they chatting with friends, checking sports scores, shopping, or looking for school news? And, what kinds of school news are they seeking? Research will tell you about "the market" for a web site and what should be on it.

And, while there is nothing wrong with having parents informed about a ballot issue, are there enough parents to carry the election if only one-third of them vote? Given that parents are a minority population in most communities, a better strategy might be to create an informed electorate composed of parents and those without school-age children. Research will tell you how many positive voters you need and their demographic composition.

Most people who get lost have a map — they just don't use it. They drive off without really knowing how they are going to get where they are going. These are the people you see at the gas station asking directions.

This is often what school districts (and businesses!) do when it comes to communication (and virtually every other significant initiative) — they drive off. In many cases, they are so sure of where they are going that they don't question where they are and they don't seek help determining their direction.

That is why they will eventually get lost or take a long time to get where they are going.

Research allows people to see where they are and where they want to end. Given their current position and their intended destination, research enables them to develop a plan for getting where they want to go. In addition, thorough researchers might check two web sites for driving directions, and then reference what they discover with information from online sources such as their state's department of transportation (road construction alerts), local news outlets (traffic reports), and, perhaps, a weather web site (driving conditions). This research will help them confirm or amend their travel strategies.

Research:
The First and Most Important Step

Research is the first and most important step in the communication process. It is also the most frequently ignored.

When you visit the doctor, a nurse weighs you, takes your temperature, and checks your blood pressure. These assessments take place before you see the doctor, no matter the reason for your visit. The doctor orders this research because the data will provide clues and the clues can lead to a more accurate diagnosis and more effective treatment.

If your legal counsel proposed a strategy without knowing your situation and without asking any questions, you would expect a less than desired outcome.

If your dentist started drilling your teeth before checking for cavities or taking x-rays, you would quickly leave the chair.

Before investing time and energy in any PR initiative, do some research. Find out what should be in your newsletter, know how a web site should be organized and how frequently it should be updated, and develop a clear picture of who will vote in your next financial election.

Doing research first makes so much sense that not doing it first is nonsense.

Research Is Only Good if You Use It

A map is worthless if you don't use it. The same is true of research.

Quite frequently, we simply ignore the research that we have. Examples include:

■ We have learned that you shouldn't print over artwork because that makes it difficult to read the print and to see the artwork. Yet almost every district newsletter and annual report will have something printed over artwork.

■ We know that parents are a minority category in almost every community (and a significant minority in many), yet we focus the vast majority of our communication resources on them.

■ We know that some school-related information interests some people, but not everyone. The intricacies of school finance are not of interest to most people, yet it is the primary subject in most newsletter columns written by or for superintendents.

■ We know that you can't please all the people all the time, yet we continue to spend most of our time dealing with those who will never be pleased or support our schools.

■ We know who is online, why they are there, and what kinds of information they are accessing. We ignore this research and provide our electronic audience with recycled newsletter copy, difficult navigation schemes, poor graphics, and little opportunity of interaction.

The point here is that it is just as important to act on research as it is to conduct research.

What You Should Know About Your Community

Environmental scans are conducted in the hope of gathering information that will allow an organization to seize an opportunity or to resolve an issue before it reaches crisis proportions. Environmental scanning is research conducted with the goal of creating strategic advantage for an organization.

Similarly, the purpose of marketing research is to learn as much as possible about the customer so the customer's needs and wants can be addressed effectively and efficiently. The goal of the research is to provide an edge in creating and keeping a customer.

It seems logical that PR initiatives should also be research based if they are to change perceptions and influence behaviors, which is the purpose of public relations.

As an example, the following are some basic things every PR practitioner should know about a community and how these things can be researched:

What to know: What is the general condition of the community?

How to do the research:

Observe. Get in your car and drive around. Look at the condition of the houses, the nature and appearance of the businesses, the kinds of cars that people are driving, and the appearance of the people. Stop at the Chamber of Commerce or the city, township, and county offices. Ask the people there for information. Ask for information that is collected about the demographics and make-up of the community. Then go online. Type the name of your community into a search engine. The research is there for the clicking! You can also learn a great deal about your community from current census data.

What to know: Information about your school staff

How to do the research:

Go to the personnel or human resources office. Ask the people there about numbers — how many staff? How many teachers, custodians, secretaries, and other employee groups are in the district? How many males and females? How many retirements did the district have last year? How many new staff members were added this year? How many staff members are at each grade level? These are just a few of the questions to consider to learn more about the staff in your district.

To this point, we really haven't done any research. We have just dug up data that exists and moved it around a little. We have simply taken out the map and looked at it.

Digging deeper requires that you consider what people in your community need and want and gain some insights into what they believe, value, and think. There are at least two ways to dig deeper — surveys and focus panels.

Essential Steps of Surveys

Surveys are effective research tools. Done properly, they give you representative feedback from large populations by interviewing a sample of people. They are relatively easy to do if you follow the necessary steps.

Interestingly, the first step in the survey process is often the most difficult — deciding what you want to know. Careful consideration of this question is critical. Sometimes what you think you want to know is not what you need to know. For example, you may want to know if voters will support a bond issue for a new swimming pool. What you need to know is what people value in an education and how a swimming pool relates to what they value.

To help you think about whether a survey is something you should consider, it is important to consider the following essential steps of conducting a survey:

1. Determine what you want to learn from the survey

"Everything" is not a good answer. Your survey has to have some focus. You may want to know how people regard the schools (an A, B, C rating, for example), where they get their school information, what kinds of school information they want, and what their thoughts are on selected educational programs or services. Other surveys may focus on the components of a financial issue, school district priorities, or another specific topic. If this is the first survey ever conducted in your school district, resist the pressure to ask questions about everything.

2. Determine if you can get the information you want without doing a survey

Basic Survey Rule Number One: Don't ask a question if you can look up the answer. Surveys are only necessary if the information is not available from another source.

3. Determine the target audience for the survey

If you want to learn something from parents, the target audience for the survey should be parents. But is the real target parents of preschoolers, parents of elementary students, or parents of secondary school students? The answer to Step 1 usually determines the target audience, but it is important to be specific with segments of your target audience.

4. **Determine the type of survey method you'll use**

    There are three basic ways to conduct a survey — personal interview, written survey and telephone interview. Online surveys are also becoming more popular and can be an efficient way to gather information.

5. **Decide how accurate you want your survey to be**

    Do you need to attain a 95% level of confidence (being sure of the results 95% of the time or 9.5 times out of 10) or can you get by with a 90% level of confidence (being sure of the results 90% of the time or 9 times out of 10)? This is an important question to consider because it determines how many surveys you need complete.

6. **Develop a timeline for the survey project**

    Start with the end in mind. Decide when you need the results. Then work backward from that date to make sure everything is done on time.

7. **List the resources you need to do the survey**

    Even the least expensive survey requires resources — your time, postage, meetings, data processing, and printing reports. Develop a realistic budget.

8. **Draw the sample**

    Decide who is going to be surveyed and the method you will use to ensure representativeness.

9. **Outline the survey's content areas and write the first-draft questions**

    Here's where you begin to focus. Keep reflecting on Step 1 as you do this.

10. **Refine the questions' wording and design the questionnaire's format**

    This is the final draft. It likely has followed one or more "rough" drafts.

11. **Pretest the draft questionnaire**

    Try out the questionnaire on people just like those in your target population.

12. **Use the pretest findings to develop the final questionnaire**

    Ask those who participated in the pretest if they understood the questions, if any questions or words were confusing, etc. Use their input and your observations to develop the final questionnaire.

13. **Recruit and train interviewers**

    If you are doing personal or telephone interviews, you need interviewers, and you will need to train them.

14. Conduct the interviews or send out the written surveys

Here, you are actually "doing" the survey.

15. Tabulate the data

Code the responses and prepare them for computer scoring. (You can do this by hand but people will think you are silly. Worse, you'll never be able to use all the data you have collected.)

16. Analyze the results

Figure out what you've learned. Be careful not to editorialize. If you find yourself saying, "I think this means…", you are editorializing.

17. Report the new knowledge

People — especially those who have been interviewed — like to know what you discovered. Let people know what you learned.

18. Use the results

To return again to our analogy, a map doesn't do you any good unless you use it.

Driving around your community and observing is listening with your eyes. Looking at data in the clerk's office is listening with your mind. Talking with principals is listening to their thinking. A survey is simply a systematic way of listening to the opinions and perceptions of selected populations.

Focus Panels

Focus panels and various engagement techniques give you opportunities to listen to people. As such, they provide useful "research."

Focus panels gained favor because they are relatively easy to conduct and they can provide valuable insights. For example, if parents don't understand how well their children are doing in school, assemble a focus panel (or 2 or 3) by inviting parents to discuss the subject and give you their insights. There should be about 6–8 parents on each panel. (Invite 8–10 to cover no-shows.)

Tell the parents that you need their help. Tell them you want to improve the ways schools report student progress. Show them what you are doing now and ask questions. For example, ask how many are familiar with the weekly progress reports, what information they find most useful, what could be deleted from the report, what should be added, or other related questions.

Show them all the ways you report student progress and ask questions about each of them. Then ask for observations and ideas related to reporting student progress. The information they provide should give you insights into what is missing from your student reporting system.

Engagement Techniques

Engagement techniques — particularly community engagement techniques — are another useful listening tool. It has become increasingly important for educators to engage their community — perhaps building by building — if they are to effectively address their needs and wants.

People can be engaged in a variety of ways. What all of them have in common is that they produce better understanding of what an education should look like and what it will take to provide it. This is research, face-to-face.

Engagement helps school people respond to their marketplace, and it provides a forum that can be used to build a constituency for public education. Engagement is important, not only because it provides educators with valuable information, but also because it brings communities together in the best interest of its children. *Public Engagement* in Section 4 of this book has more in-depth information on public engagement strategies.

Research: It's Common Sense

Baseball pundit Yogi Berra said:

> It's amazing what you can observe by just looking around.

He was right. We might add that it is astounding what you can hear if you just listen.

Research is simply looking around and listening. Research can be as simple as reading a report or having a conversation — or it can be as elaborate as conducting a survey or engaging a community. Research is fundamental to a successful school communication program. In fact, it may be the essence of a successful educational program.

Research is the first thing to do when starting a communication program. It is, in fact, something educators must learn to do in a variety of ways all the time. Everything you can learn about people will help you be more responsive to them. People support organizations that are responsive. In the case of schools, this is how you use research to ensure that students receive the best education possible.

Note: For a step-by-step guide to conducting education survey, refer to *The ABC Complete Book of School Surveys*, a workbook available from NSPRA.

William J. Banach, Ed.D., APR

Bill Banach is CEO of Banach, Banach & Cassidy, a Michigan-based social forecasting and communication research firm. He helps his public- and private-sector clients think about the implications of change and capitalize on the opportunities that change presents. Banach is nationally recognized for his issues management and social forecasting programs.

Banach created the Institute for Future Studies and is on the editorial board of the *Journal of School Public Relations* and the *Journal for Effective Schools*.

He is a past president of the National School Public Relations Association, and recipient of the Association's Presidents Award, the highest honor of the educational communication profession.

Banach authored *The ABC Series*, four books focused on educational planning and marketing, the *Survey Research Primer*, and *The ABCs of Teacher-Parent Communication*.

His articles have appeared in more than 100 journals and magazines, and he served as the host of *America's Learning*, a weekly, hour-long program on National Public Radio.

Analysis and Planning: Getting Your PR Act Together

By Stephanie Bateman

The adage, "If you fail to plan, you plan to fail," can easily be applied to public relations. Sometimes called *assessment*, the planning component joins research, communication, and evaluation as one of the four major cornerstones of the public relations process. And even though PR professionals are often pressed for time, this step should *not* be omitted.

The time spent planning on the front end of the public relations effort reduces the amount of back peddling necessary later in the process. Sure, it takes extra time, and pressure may be on to complete specific activities quickly, but skipping this step is like starting a cross-country road trip without a map.

That's all PR planning is: a road map that guides your communication strategies and allows you to achieve your goals and objectives. The planning component of public relations is about thinking ahead and anticipating potential pitfalls. The benefits of communication planning are enormous and include:

■ Planning enables districts to achieve the goals and objectives identified as critical to student success.

■ Planning allows PR professionals to position their districts as *the* provider of quality educational services in the community.

■ Planning can help strengthen positive opinions of the school district, neutralize some negative opinions of the school district, and move some neutral opinions to the positive column.

The downside of not planning also is enormous. Without planning, communication strategies may not be as successful as possible. Without the structure and guidance of a well thought-out plan, it is possible to implement strategies that do not deliver the best message and the most appropriate target audience.

Communication planning begins after research has been thoroughly analyzed. Surveys, focus groups, phone logs, and anecdotal comments all provide valuable information about the strengths, weaknesses, and challenges a school or district faces. This analysis helps identify the most effective strategies and messages.

In addition to being grounded in research, an effective communication plan should:

■ Support the district's goals and initiatives

■ Include specific objectives and strategies

■ Identify target audiences

■ Consider all available and needed resources

■ Be measurable

Support District and Board Goals and Initiatives

An effective communication plan should support a school district's major objectives — not just the communication needs of the day. The strategic direction of a district should be supported by a strategic communication plan. For example, district and board goals about school atmosphere and parent and community support have broad implications for the public relations department as well as for local school principals. Having a district-wide communication plan allows the public relations department to play a significant role in achieving these goals.

Likewise, planning the communication's strategies for every major initiative the administration undertakes is also necessary. If the curriculum department decides to overhaul report cards, the transportation department proposes a new bus facility near a residential community, or the district partners with local law officials to crack down on truants, the communication opportunities and pitfalls must be considered as the projects are developed and before the implementation occurs.

The objective must be clearly stated, specific, and measurable.

Identify Specific Objectives and Strategies

Every public relations campaign should have a clearly stated purpose as well as specific objectives to keep it focused. The plan should not be driven by activities but by what must be accomplished to achieve your objectives. Start with the end in mind and create a plan that will move toward meeting the goal.

It is also important to think about what behavior change is desired as a result of implementing the plan's strategies. Is the plan focused on getting parents to vote "*Yes*" for a bond issue, sign up for parent-teacher conferences, or support more daily homework assignments?

Whatever it is, the objective must be clearly stated, specific, and measurable.

Consider this scenario:

Your district recently developed a new technical magnet program for high school students. The communication department is asked to immediately share information with the community about the program that will generate a large number of applicants.

Your communication team quickly begins to bombard the print and electronic media with news releases and media advisories about the new program. News releases announce the program, district staff members are scheduled for media interviews, and the newspaper's editorial staff is persuaded to write an editorial praising the district for developing the "cutting-edge" program.

Everyone is happy with the campaign. Information was shared in numerous ways, but it is important to measure the effectiveness of each strategy in generating applicants for the program.

Sharing information is not enough — did the effort meet the intended goal?

Identify Target Audiences

A plan not only needs to identify what must be accomplished, but it must also include specific target audiences. You must clearly identify your target audiences to effectively implement your communication strategies.

If the goal is to raise the level of parent support, a strategy might be to increase the number of parent-teacher conferences. With this goal, target audiences may include:

■ Parents who have previously attended parent-teacher conferences

■ Parents who have not attended in the past

■ PTA

■ Teachers and school staff

■ The business community

■ Civic and faith-based organizations

■ News media

By identifying specific target audiences, it is then possible to focus messages at specific groups. The information you share with parents who regularly attend conferences will likely be different from the messages you send to parents who have never attended those conferences. Identifying these audiences helps target your message and increase the likelihood of success of the public relations effort.

Identify Necessary Resources

All too often communication professionals are challenged to create "silk purses out of sows' ears" on a moment's notice with no additional funds or staff support. Mounting a successful public relations campaign requires the right resources, which include money, staff, and the time to execute the strategies.

Whether the effort is toward a creating campaign to build support for a major change in school boundaries or announcing a school-community partnership, resources must be allocated to complete the task. When considering the resources necessary to implement a public relations plan, think about the following:

■ What will be needed to implement the plan?

■ What is the estimated cost?

■ How much time is needed?

■ What expertise will be needed?

■ Are funds available to effectively implement the plan?

There's nothing worse than brainstorming then proposing great ideas that cannot be effectively executed because of a lack of resources.

Measure Success

The planning process is not complete without a tool for measurement. Did the communication strategies move the district toward its stated goals and objectives?

It is impossible to answer this question without a way to measure the impact of each strategy. Here's an example of a plan that includes measurable objectives.

The Jefferson County Public School District in Kentucky has used a "systems" approach for more than a decade to structure work of all of its major departments to help the district achieve its goals. In the area of communication, staff members are responsible for meeting four quality/performance indicators identified in three of the board's goals.

The communication system compares baseline data from 10 years ago (collected through the district's annual survey of parents, students, and staff) with data from the current school year's survey.

The communication system covers four areas:

■ employee satisfaction

■ parent satisfaction

■ community engagement

■ market share

The plan includes specific goals, measurable objectives, and strategies. Communication team members (and their units) assume responsibility for the strategies and establish timelines for the activities they create. While the goals have not changed in 10 years, the measurable objectives have.

Each year, the superintendent — with the communication team — reviews the data from the annual survey to assess the effectiveness of the strategies and activities. After the review, the team revises and refocuses the plan for the next school year.

However, instead of crossing an objective off the list when it is achieved, the bar for success is raised higher, reflecting the district's belief in continuous improvement for the administrative staff as well as for students.

On the next page is one section of the Jefferson County Public School District's communication services "system."

Communications Services System for Jefferson County Public Schools

Quality Indicators

1. Parent Satisfaction

Baseline data	Current data
1997-98 Parent/guardian overall grade of JCPS – 2.6	2005-06 Parent/guardian overall grade of JCPS – 2.9
1997-98 Parent/guardian overall quality of education – 4.3	2005-06 Parent/guardian overall quality of education – 4.3
1995-96 PTA members – 73,262	2005-06 PTA members – 60,841
1998-99 Parent/Teacher conferences – 117,006	2005-06 Parent/Teacher Conferences – 135,310

Goals	Measurable objectives	Strategies/activities
Increase parent satisfaction with JCPS	Increase parents' overall rating of JCPS to 3.0 by 2007.	Keep parents informed about JCPS programs, services. Activities include publishing *Parent Connections*, *Annual Report*, and other publications; production of *Our Kids®* TV show, PSAs, and videos; working with news media; and operating the FactLine.
		Develop a customer-service program to improve the school-visit experience. Activities include creating a vision, standards, and training modules.
		Review effectiveness of district communication annually with target audiences. Activities include using focus groups from target audiences to review effectiveness.

Goals	Measurable objectives	Strategies/activities
	Increase parents' overall rating of the quality of education to 4.4 by 2007.	Explain the significance of the GE Foundation grant and the need to revamp the science and mathematics curricula. Activities include publishing news and information for employees and parents in district publications, maintaining a dedicated page on the web site, and collaborating with grant partners on project work.
		Provide public opportunities for student and school recognition. Activities include Board meetings, student recognition nights, PTA Reflections ceremony, media, etc.
		Assist schools in producing school newsletters and other publications that describe and explain school programs.
Increase parent involvement	Increase the number of parent/teacher conferences to 137,000 by May 2006.	Promote the importance of parent/teacher conferences to secondary audiences as well as to parents. Activities include letters from the superintendent to local CEO's, churches, influential leaders requesting their support and encouragement.
	Increase PTA membership 2% by May 2006.	Implement a plan for more principal leadership in PTA participation and membership
		Support and assist the PTA with its operations. Activities include publicizing membership campaign, CAP (Clothing Assistance Program), parent trainings, and value of a PTA in every school.

■ **Stephanie Bateman**

Stephanie Madison Bateman is the director of communications and publications for Jefferson County Public Schools (JCPS), Louisville, Kentucky. She is responsible for developing and implementing creative strategies for internal and external communication including the annual report, video projects, print advertising, and local school marketing plans. Bateman currently produces and hosts the school district's monthly television show, *Our Kids*. She also is a frequent presenter at the Kentucky and National School Public Relations Association Seminars.

Bateman has created several internal public relations tools for JCPS staff including the *Principal's Planner*, *Best Foot Forward* marketing guide, and the *JCPS In Style Guide* for district publications. She also developed the concept for *Parent Connections*, a monthly newsletter for JCPS parents, and several award-winning advertising campaigns. She is a member of the Kentucky and National School Public Relations Associations.

Bateman has 31 years of experience as a journalist and public relations professional. She received her Bachelor and Master of Arts degrees from Western Kentucky University.

She started her career as a radio news anchor for WHAS-FM and transitioned into public relations with the KFC Corporation before joining the school district in 1979. Bateman also produced and hosted a public affairs program for the Fox affiliate, WDRB-TV; worked as a freelance journalist; and taught communications and English courses as a part-time University of Louisville faculty member.

Communication and Implementation: Applying Effective Strategies

By Susan Hardy Brooks, APR

Now that you have completed the difficult work of conducting your research, analysis, and planning, your focus should turn to the communication and implementation stage of developing your strategic communication plan. You have identified your communication goals and audiences, and now it is time to do something with them. The practical part of the process is figuring out what behaviors you want to motivate among your audiences in order to achieve your goals.

People often skip research and planning and go straight to implementation or action. Skipping critical steps in the planning process results in activities that may be characterized as "busy work." In the end, these types of activities don't contribute to the strategic goals of your school district and don't add value to your role as a PR professional.

You really do need to know *who* and *why* before you develop tools or implement strategies. Research, analysis, and planning are vital to figuring out *how*, which includes identifying and implementing your strategies.

Key Messages Are Key Elements of Success

Key messages give you a powerful way to strengthen the impact of your communication strategies on your audiences. Key messages provide continuity and extend your reach by connecting what your audiences already know with what you want them to know or do. School PR professionals use key messages to provide perspective, context, and a point of view. Key messages help you break through the communication clutter and improve your success in communicating.

Several ways will help you identify the most important messages you want your audiences to hear and remember. A few good sources of information for key message development include:

■ Strategic plan vision, mission, values, and goals

■ Focus group comments

■ Previous media coverage, publications, and speeches

The best place to look for key messages is often your district's strategic plan. Typically, internal and external groups

have labored for months over the content in the strategic plan. People already feel ownership in the statements within the plan, and the wording reflects the top priorities of the district. After all, key messages should reflect the essence of an organization's mission, beliefs, and goals.

Key messages should always be based on promises you can keep as a district.

Key messages can also come from research you gather in focus groups or surveys. In focus groups and surveys, people are often asked what they believe are the district's strengths and weaknesses. These findings can give you ideas about the messages you should use. The findings can also identify gaps between people's perceptions and facts about the organization. You can develop key messages as part of a strategy to begin closing gaps in perception.

For example, if several focus groups say that ABC School District has caring teachers, then a key message about "caring teachers in a caring environment" will likely resonate with your audiences. If survey respondents indicate that they view the curriculum as needing improvement when, in fact, the curriculum is nationally recognized for quality and innovation, then a key message about "securing students' futures with the best curriculum in the region" will work to close the perception gap. Of course, key messages have to be true to be effective. Key messages should always be based on promises you can keep as a district.

Sometimes you can look in archives of recent news releases, speeches, and promotional materials for high-impact statements that you can use as key messages. Powerful quotes can become powerful key messages to use in a variety of ways.

Applying Key Messages

Once you define your key messages, you can use them in a variety of ways. For example, if increasing student test scores is one of your district's goals, then a key message like "Committed to Student Success" could reflect that goal. Here are some ways you can use key messages:

■ Tag lines with logos, as e-mail signatures and on web sites

■ Speeches to external and internal groups

■ Themes for news releases and publications

■ Internal publications, staff meetings, and in-service training sessions

■ School marquees, signs, and bulletin boards

You can also develop key messages for particular programs, campaigns, or initiatives. The Oregon School Boards Association (OSBA), for example, has developed key messages for their members to use for Annual Yearly Progress (AYP) under No Child Left

Behind (NCLB). By being proactive with its members, OSBA is equipping educators with clear, concise statements about an often-misunderstood program.

You can consistently apply the best key messages with all of the audiences you reach and in all of the tools you use. The same wording doesn't always have to be used and every key message may not apply in every situation. Flexibility in applying your key messages allows you to tailor the key messages to the particular audience. Sometimes it is the concept or theme of the message that carries through.

For example, Kent State University's *Guide to Key Messages* provides specific examples of how key messages are used as underlying themes in speeches, publications, and advertising for the university. A similar guide could be developed for a school district based on its key messages. According the guide, Kent State's key messages include:

■ Imagine a university that changes people's lives.

■ Imagine a university that makes ideas work.

■ Imagine a university that is worth caring about.

Flexible, yet consistent key messages are powerful elements in your overall communication strategy.

The guide also includes the following examples of how the university's key messages can be used:

■ In a speech given at a reception for students who have been admitted to the School of Journalism and Mass Communication, the director of the school includes information about the graduates of Kent State who have won Pulitzer Prizes. (*Imagine a university that changes people's lives.*)

■ The Office of Technology Transfer and Economic Development produces a directory of business and university partnerships that is available online and in print. The directory is distributed at trade shows, professional meetings and to the media. (*Imagine a university that makes ideas work.*)

■ The *Beacon Journal* publishes a story about a Kent State graduate donating $500,000 to the School of Journalism and Mass Communication to help students prepare to communicate in the digital age. (*Imagine a university that is worth caring about.*)

Key messages can be used verbatim as tag lines or statements, or they can provide underlying themes for communicating with various audiences. Flexible, yet consistent key messages are powerful elements in your overall communication strategy.

Creating an Action Plan

Now that you have identified some over-arching key messages, it is time to create your action plan: the strategies you will use to reach your audiences with your key messages and motivate them to act.

At this point, you can do several things to make sure your plan has the energy and resources behind it to make it effective. To avoid hitting any roadblocks at this stage of the game, make sure that you have secured support from the superintendent, board, and executive team. Their buy-in is critical because it is difficult to implement projects or processes without people and resources — two things district leaders control. You also want to be sure that everyone at the top agrees on the direction of the public relations, marketing, and communication effort.

You can approach the development of your action plan in several ways. You can do it alone sitting at your computer and coming up with implementation ideas. Another way is to put together a cross-functional "action team" team representing various internal groups in the district (a principal, a central office person, teachers, a support person, and a student, for instance) to identify implementation strategies. You can also put together an external advisory team made up of public relations and advertising professionals in the community.

The advantage of doing it yourself is that you can get it done quickly. The disadvantage is that no one except you bears any responsibility for implementing the plan.

The advantage of working with an internal action team is that you can create buy-in and ownership among various internal audiences because representatives of their interests have been involved in the process. The disadvantage is that you have to educate the team on the real work of public relations and the process can take a lot longer.

The advantage of establishing an external advisory team is that you can tap some of the best thinking in the private sector about what strategies will work. It might also be possible to get some in-kind support from members of the team. The disadvantage is that some participants on the team may be after a contract with your district and that may cloud their judgment about the tools and strategies the school district needs to be effective.

Whatever approach you take, keep reminding yourself and your team that the plan is a flexible document and that nothing you decide has to be set in concrete.

Tactics, Tools, and Timelines

For each strategic communication goal, you will need to identify the following:

■ **Tactics** — specific strategies for achieving your goals

■ **Tools** — collateral materials that will support your tactics such as web sites, publications, direct mail or e-mail campaigns, etc.

■ **Timelines** — estimated start and finish dates for the tactics

Imagine that a school district created the following strategic communication goal:

> To ensure that ABC School District is understood and valued as a vital community asset that provides a great return on investment for public dollars.

To address this goal, tactics and tools would be necessary. The following are two examples:

Tactic	Tools for this tactic
Conduct and distribute a study on ABC School District's economic impact on the community with the help of a local college or university economics or marketing program. (Complete research by 9/1/08)	▨ Prepare a print publication and PowerPoint presentation that explains the highlights of the study. (10/1/08) ▨ Host a news conference to announce the results of the study. (10/15/08) ▨ Host a series of series of *Return on Investment* sessions with community business leaders. (11/1/08 – 4/1/09)
Increase understanding and support for ABC School District's overall rankings on state and national test scores among parents.	▨ Create a web page about testing that features test preparation information, rankings, and links to state and national testing organizations. (9/1/08) ▨ Send postcards to parents announcing the web address for testing information. (10/1/08) ▨ Prepare a series of articles about testing and the meaning of test scores for building-level newsletters and the media. (1/15/09 – 4/15/-09) ▨ Host *Measuring UP* seminars for parents to explain the testing process, how to prepare children for the tests, and what the individual, school, and district results really mean. (3/1/09 – 4/15/09)

Usually, 5 to 7 goals are more than enough to include in your strategic communication plan. If you identify too many communication goals, the implementation strategies can become unmanageable.

Another example of communication strategies comes from the Rockwood Schools, Wildwood, Missouri. Rockwood's communication team chose to identify overall goals that reflected the desired outcomes for internal and external audiences.

The goals included the following:

Rockwood's Overall Goals

Audience	Goals
Internal	▓ Take pride and ownership in the district
	▓ Keep informed on key issues
	▓ Exhibit district values of caring, integrity, and collaboration
	▓ Feel responsible to share their understanding of the objectives of the district with parents, students, and community
External	▓ Feel involved and engaged in public schools
	▓ Exhibit community pride and trust in schools and the school district
	▓ Support Rockwood schools
	▓ Choose the Rockwood School District because of the quality of education provided to students

Objectives	▓ Increase opportunities for public input and response
	▓ Increase opportunities to share district information with community
	▓ Expand external key communicators' network
	▓ Provide a coordinated community relations effort that focuses on key goals for the district
Strategies	▓ Implement an external key communicator group and share information to promote student achievement
	▓ Facilitate dialogue among community and district administrators, religious leaders, business groups, legislators, and private and parochial schools
	▓ Promote Board of Education meetings through increased information sources
	▓ Provide district representation for community programs such as Chambers of Commerce, business partnerships, and senior citizen meetings
	▓ Promote district knowledge and participation in Rockwood Schools Foundation

Next, the Rockwood team developed objectives and strategies for each segment of the communication function, such as community relations, media relations, internal communication, and others. In the community relations section, the Rockwood communication plan included the following objectives and strategies:

The format for Rockwood's communication plan is somewhat different from the previous example, but just as effective. The point is that you should create a plan that works best for your school district. A cookie-cutter or textbook version of someone else's plan will not work.

Communicating Your Success

Once you have identified your goals, tactics, and tools, you are better able to build your budget request for the resources you'll need to implement the plan. With a plan in place, you will have strong justification for getting the financial and human resources you need to be effective.

As you implement your plan, be sure to keep your superintendent, leadership team, and board informed of your progress and schedule regular updates with your communication committee. The updates should include ongoing evaluation of your work. Remember the saying, "What gets measured gets done."

For more on evaluation methods and benchmarks, see the next chapter.

■ Susan Hardy Brooks, APR

Susan Hardy Brooks, APR, has counseled school leaders on a range of marketing communication issues and strategies for more than 28 years. Since starting her company, Hardy Brooks Public Relations in 1998, she has provided strategic communication counsel to more than 50 clients in the private and public sectors, including K-12 school districts, community colleges, universities, state education agencies, and other organizations that support public education.

From 1981 to 1998, Hardy Brooks served as marketing director for three career technology centers, including Metro Tech, Canadian Valley Tech, and Francis Tuttle. She served as Francis Tuttle's marketing director for 10 years.

Hardy Brooks is currently serving as Executive Director of The Citizens' Policy Center, a public policy research and education organization (think tank) dedicated to creating better opportunities for individuals and families. Support for public education is among the Center's top priorities.

Hardy Brooks is serving as NSPRA South Central Vice-President from 2005–2008. She has presented public relations and marketing workshops in 25 states. Her strategies have been featured in *pr reporter*, NSPRA's *Network* newsletter, *Techniques* magazine, and several other national journals. She is a frequent presenter at state and national marketing conferences and has received more than 100 awards for her marketing campaigns, publications, projects, and events.

Hardy Brooks has a master's degree in education administration from the University of Oklahoma and a bachelor's degree in journalism from Oklahoma Baptist University. She is accredited in public relations (APR) by the Universal Accreditation Board.

Evaluation: Completing the Loop

By Tim Carroll, APR

Evaluation is a simple concept to understand, but difficult to achieve for most school public relations practitioners. Evaluating people and programs within a district establishes the basis for many instructional and administrative decisions. Still, public relations practitioners often downplay or completely overlook evaluating their own programs.

Evaluation is one of the primary steps in all public relations planning cycles. The RACE formula requires evaluating the communication activities to determine their effectiveness. Otherwise, time and resources may be wasted on projects that failed to achieve their goal or were totally ineffective.

Evaluating public relations programs and activities is essential for many other reasons besides scoring public relations "hits and misses." These include:

■ **Budget tightening as school boards seek accountability from all program**

areas. Evaluating public relations programs can show how their investment pays off.

■ **Financially pressed school districts are cutting back on what they may see as "nonessential" expenditures.** If the public relations budget is cut, evaluation will help you set priorities and develop ways to work within your budget.

■ **The continuing emphasis on achieving organizational goals includes public relations activities.** Evaluation can show how your efforts help achieve the organization's mission and goals.

■ **Proper evaluation of the public relations program will also help you organize and prioritize day-to-day activities.**

Beyond benefits to the school district, a solid evaluation program helps build credibility and job security for the public relations position. In the education field, where accountability and measurement are so important, accountability is also respected in the non-instructional departments of the organization.

Purpose of Evaluation

Evaluation or assessment may be as simple as a follow-up phone conversation or as complex as a communication audit. In either case, the purpose is to gauge the effectiveness of a public relations activity or program.

Whenever possible, evaluation should be designed to provide measurable data that will help practitioners:

■ add or delete existing public relations activities

■ determine if the public relations program achieved its intended results

■ determine if the results were worth the time and money invested

■ bring greater management visibility to the public relations program's accomplishments

Evaluation Methods

Numerous formal and informal methods may be used to evaluate a school public relations program or activity. Ten common methods, in descending order from formal to informal, include:

1. Communication audit

2. Evaluation by objective

3. Scientific random surveys or questionnaires

4. Actual results, e.g., election returns

5. Personal interviews

6. Telephone surveys

7. Focus groups

8. Monitoring news media coverage

9. Maintaining a log of public relations staff's time

10. Counting citizen attendance at public events

Each method can be effectively used to evaluate public relations programs and activities. More detail on several methods is included in the sections that follow.

Communication audit

The most comprehensive evaluation tool available to practitioners is the communication audit. An audit is a detailed analysis of a district's internal and external communication program.

The audit is designed to take snapshots of the district's communication needs, policies, activities, capabilities, and programs. It involves staff and community leaders with a goal of setting recommendations from a communication expert that the administrative team and school board should act on.

A comprehensive audit will uncover communication gaps and suggest the following possible areas:

- Prioritized short- and long-term goals

- Themes and issues to be emphasized

- Prioritized list of publics

- Perspective on the community pulse on key issues

- Communication techniques that are working

- New communication techniques that warrant implementation

- Staffing needs

- Budget reallocation

- Benchmarks for future evaluation

Major topics covered in a school district communication audit include:

- Communication philosophy, policies, management's openness, management's support of communication, and the role of the public relations office

- Community demographics — analysis of current and projected populations

- Objectives and goals of the school district and the extent to which the annual public relations plan supports the objectives and goals

- Organization and staffing of the public relations office

- Review of the existing public relations program, its products, activities, and general plans for internal and external public relations

- Public and staff feelings about the present public relations program

- Needs and expectations expressed by focus group participants

Five steps in an audit

1   Research and review current program and data on school community

2   Find out what "we" think, talk to key management, and assess the school district's strengths and weaknesses in public relations, instruction, and management

3   Find out what "they" think — ask key internal and external publics their opinions on communication strengths

4   Evaluate the difference between what "we" and "they" said. Develop a public relations balance sheet of assets, liabilities, strengths, and weaknesses

5   Recommend how to close any gaps uncovered by the audit

While an audit may highlight the district's success stories, its primary purpose is to point to areas and make recommendations that can make the district's public relations program more effective.

The results should be used to develop new public relations plans, strategies, and objectives which, when correctly drafted, can assist in the annual evaluation of the public relations program. NSPRA offers a communication audit service.

Evaluating by objective

Newsletters or web pages pale in importance to the overall mission of a school district, which is to give students the best possible education. That is why public relations practitioners must constantly be aware that their efforts must support the district's mission. Perhaps the toughest evaluation question for practitioner is:

> What did I do today to help children learn?

As a part of the district's team to support teachers and building administrators, the best strategy for the public relations professional is to create measurable public relations objectives that are tied to organizational goals. The evaluation should then measure how you accomplished those goals.

A school district goal that calls for improved standardized test scores can be mirrored with a public relations objective to:

> Assist teachers in educating parents about the purpose and interpretation of test results.

Some people view the public relations objective approach to evaluation as just a game of "numbers for numbers sake," but used effectively, it can enhance the credibility and management status of the public relations program.

The advice from public relations people using this approach is to move as much as you can toward measurable objectives. A public relations objective to "improve internal morale and communication" is so vague that it will be very difficult to know if you were successful. Is morale better? How did communication improve internally?

Most day-to-day public relations activities can be measured and tied to organizational goals.

A better objective might read, "build staff morale through increased participation in co-curricular and social activities." Evaluating this objective is much easier because the number of participants and activities can be counted. Many aspects of public relations, such as goodwill, persuasion, and human relations are difficult to capture and measure.

Most day-to-day public relations activities, however, can be measured and tied to organizational goals. These activities include:

■ publications

■ media relations

■ special events

■ electronic communication projects

Ultimately, it's important to show how public relations activities "helped children learn." Writing measurable objectives and evaluating the program against them will build accountability and greater value into any public relations program.

Surveys and questionnaires

Public relations effectiveness can be measured through survey instruments specifically designed for that purpose. The same information can be gathered by combining public relations evaluation questions into a broader needs assessment of the staff and community. The process for assembling and conducting surveys and other research is described in *Research: Don't Start Your PR Effort Without it*.

Surveys and opinion polls are most often used for evaluation aspects of the public relations program which cannot be measured in an easier way. Public attitude toward your school district or a particular school issue, for example, can best be determined by an opinion poll. Surveys can be used as a post-test for gauging progress against an initial research activity or pre-test.

Focus groups

A focus group is little more than a discussion group brought together to express opinions about specific aspects of your organization or its public relations activities. An objective third party who keeps the discussion focused and relevant facilitates the group.

Focus groups are most effective when they represent the thinking of larger populations, such as teachers or parents. The size and selection of each focus group are also important to the activity's success. Think of the focus group as a dinner party where guests with similar interest or backgrounds are invited. The conversation is much more spontaneous and meaningful.

> You can ask a bear to dance, but the bear says when to stop!

This sage advice also applies to focus groups. When you ask for people's time and opinions, be prepared to respond to their concerns or suggestions.

The purpose of focus groups is not to pat the organization on the back. It is to solicit thoughts and opinions from district stakeholders on areas where the program or school district can improve.

Evaluation benchmarks

Another effective way to evaluate public relations efforts is to measure them against accepted benchmarks. NSPRA and many other national and state organizations offer self-assessment checklists to begin the evaluation process.

Checklist evaluations are just one part of the total evaluation process. They offer a reminder of what you should be doing (or not doing), but do not measure effectiveness or quality.

Still, a checklist is a good first step because if forces you to examine some aspects of your program that might otherwise be overlooked. Literally

hundreds of questions can be used for self-evaluation.

Here are 16 questions to consider:

1. Does your district have a written, clear policy regarding public relations?

2. Does the policy express the purpose of the public relations program and provide for the funding and resources necessary to carry it out?

3. Is the public relations program part of the management function and does the person directing the public relations efforts have the necessary skills and training to do so?

4. Does the public relations professional report directly to the superintendent?

5. Is there a written plan or strategy for carrying out public relations activities? If so, do the goals of the plan support the school district's overall mission and goals?

6. Does the program provide effective means of internal communication?

7. Does the public relations professional conduct in-service training in school-community relations for other staff?

8. Does the program use a variety of communication channels?

9. Does the program have a procedure for identifying opinion leaders and

key groups and maintaining two-way communication with them?

10. Are school district publications reviewed annually to determine relevance, fairness, and overall effectiveness?

11. Does the public relations program encourage, receive, analyze, and utilize feedback on its activities?

12. Is there a systematic process for the employees to communicate with the news media? Does the public relations office monitor media coverage for accuracy and saturation?

13. Does the public relations professional monitor external communication from all campuses and departments, including newsletters, cable TV, and Internet sites?

14. Does the public relations professional actively participate in state and national professional organizations and staff development related to public relations?

15. Does the public relations professional spend more than half of his or her time in activities that foster two-way communication?

16. Is there continuous and systematic evaluation of the public relations program?

Answers to these questions will certainly indicate if you have the proper climate, organization, and implementation of an effective school public relations program.

They will not, however, tell you if you are succeeding. Only your publics can tell you that.

Listening:

The Greatest Communication Skill

Getting out of the office and listening to what your many publics have to say about your organization is key to the evaluation process.

Give people opportunities to speak about school issues that concern them. Drop the defensive posture many school officials take, and seek common ground on how your constituents can help in efforts to improve your public schools.

Skillful listening is where the best school public relations professionals begin their work. Once refined, that skill will help build relationships, provide counsel, and assume an important role in managing the school district.

■ ■ **Tim Carroll, APR**

Tim Carroll, APR, has served as director of information services with the Allen (TX) Independent School District since 1995. For the previous 14 years, he was public information director with the Penn-Harris-Madison School Corp. in Osceola, Indiana.

A member of the NSPRA since 1982, Carroll is past president of the Indiana Chapter of NSPRA and served as the chapter's executive director for three years. He is accredited in

public relations (APR) by the Universal Accreditation Board and earned his accreditation in 1987.

Carroll has taught public relations courses as an adjunct faculty member at Texas A&M University — Commerce and Indiana University-South Bend. He is also a former seventh grade teacher.

He holds a master's degree in school public relations from Rowan University in New Jersey and a degree in journalism and education from Murray (KY) State University.

Carroll also manages Carroll Communications, providing school public relations and consulting services.

Effective Communication Plans: How to Get Started

By Jennifer Wayman Reeve, APR

If you've just weathered a crisis or failed in a tax election, you may be painfully aware of the need for an organized system of public relations for your school district. If not, you may be lulled into thinking you don't need to spend money on "PR" because everything is going okay. Don't be fooled.

Public relations is as essential to student achievement in your school district as well-articulated curriculum, and neither should be left to chance.

Public relations is not just something you employ when things aren't going well. And, it isn't just an add-on to a school district's educational programs. Public relations — planned or not — is the way a school district relates to its many publics, and it is an integral part of all school district programs and services.

A good public relations program creates an environment in which the district can achieve its goals. It also demonstrates a school district's accountability to the taxpayers — or shareholders — of the school district.

School districts that have the support of their communities pass needed tax elections. Boards and administrators that employ systems to discover and manage issues often can spot a crisis before it happens. School leaders who work to keep employees informed and involved generally have happier employees who enjoy their jobs and work hard to do their part in educating students.

Just as regular exercise promotes a healthy body, an ongoing program of public relations promotes a healthy school district.

It has been said that all school districts have public relations, whether they intend to or not. Everyone has a perception or opinion about the schools. It may come from personal experience (no matter how many years ago) or it may come from communicating with friends or family members who have direct contact with the schools.

For an increasing number of people, their only perception of the school system is provided by the news media. That's a scary thought, especially if there is no formal communication with the media through a public relations professional. This is why a school district must plan and carry out a public relations program that not only bolsters the district's image, but helps build relationships, community confidence, and support.

Everyone who has close contact with the schools — employees, parents, students — communicates messages about

personal experiences they have with the schools. The wise and responsible school district tries to ensure that contacts with the schools, and therefore the messages communicated, are positive ones. How? By investing time and money in a sound program of public relations.

> **School public relations requires a planned system of two-way communication.**

Can We Afford It?

Many school boards and administrators fear spending taxpayer money on public relations. This fear can be quickly dispelled if they realize what a good public relations program is ... and is not.

It is wrong to spend taxpayer dollars on efforts to cover up bad decisions or to "spin" the school district's story into a false positive light. But that's not what school public relations is all about.

Good school public relations supports the mission of the school district. An effective school PR program creates a positive environment for student achievement by helping the school district align its goals with the expectations the public has for its schools.

Thus, school public relations requires a planned system of two-way communication — a system that listens to the district's publics and is accountable to those publics.

While public relations programs are criticized as a frivolous expenditure by some, quite frankly, most districts can't afford *not* to spend money on public relations. Often, school districts that do not have planned public relations programs end up spending more taxpayer dollars to iron out problems or fix mistakes than they would on proactive public relations efforts.

Not communicating with the public is a tremendous disservice to the people you serve. Additionally, imagine a business with the number of customers (*students*), employees (*teachers and staff*), and shareholders (*taxpayers*) your school district has that does not have a public relations or marketing professional on staff.

While many school officials realize the need for a planned program of two-way communication, they often feel overwhelmed when thinking about how to begin. Don't worry.

Building an organized public relations program in your school district is not as daunting a task as it may seem. And that's just where to begin — by building on the strategies that are already working in your district.

One way to start building your PR program is to conduct a self-assessment.

Evaluate Your Current Efforts

Even if you don't have a planned public relations program, the board, superintendent, principals, and other school employees are certainly already doing some things to connect with internal and external publics.

One way to start building your PR program is to conduct a self-assessment to evaluate the effectiveness of your current communication activities.

You can use a variety of methods to assess and evaluate existing communication activities. For more information on these methods, see the previous chapter, *Evaluation: Completing the Loop*.

Establish a Public Relations Task Force

Some districts have used a public relations task force to get started. This group, made up of staff and community members, is charged with reviewing all of the methods that the district is using to communicate with its publics, evaluating how well these are working, and recommending areas for improvement.

The task force's final report is a starting point for the school district in building its public relations program. A task force is most effective when it includes members of the community with public relations or marketing expertise and when it is given a specific charge.

You may choose to combine the work of a task force and a communication audit by having the task force review audit findings and make recommendations as a result. A detailed description of a communication audit is included in the previous chapter.

An added value of a task force is that, after its initial work, it can become a public relations advisory committee which meets with the district's public relations professional several times each year to review the district's efforts and provide guidance.

The task force's final report is a starting point for the school district in building its public relations program.

Study Best Practices

Yet another way to begin a public relations program is to learn about other districts' successful programs and compare those to what you are doing in your district. Ask for a copy of their public relations plans.

Other good resources are NSPRA, a state chapter of NSPRA, and the NSPRA annual Seminar where the best practices from throughout the U.S. and Canada are showcased.

Begin with Board Policy

Before beginning your public relations program, you must obtain the school board's support. A school board policy that requires two-way communication with internal and external publics will reinforce the importance of the public relations program and set the tone for school district accountability.

Many other school board policies are essential to school public relations, including those that address the following:

▓ Communication within the school district

▓ How the public may obtain information from the school district

▓ What procedures are in place for the public to address the school board

▓ How the district will interact with the news media

▓ Commitment to customer service

Here are five key points that the school board should consider as it develops its own school district public relations policies:

▓ The district should commit to writing a clear and concise policy statement with respect to its public relations program.

- The policy statement should be approved through formal action by the school board, published in its policy manual, and reviewed by the board annually.

- The policy statement should express the purposes of the organization's public relations program and delegate authority for the program to appropriate administrators in the district.

- The provisions of the policy statement should be made known to the entire staff.

- The board's commitment to its public relations policy should be demonstrated by allocating adequate human and financial resources.

A board that models honest, straightforward communication will go a long way toward promoting positive relations between the district and the community.

The school board's role

The school board's role in governing the school district is both corporate and familial. This means that the board makes decisions as a corporate body, but also has a role in maintaining good relationships between the school district and its many publics.

As a corporate body, the board adopts policies that govern the school district, including those that direct the staff's public relations or school district accountability efforts. These policies should address the familial role of the school board. For example, the board should have policies that consider how it will communicate with the public as well as how it will listen to the public.

The board should also have policies or operating norms that address members' relationships and communication with one another, with the superintendent, and with district staff. A board that models honest, straightforward communication will go a long way toward promoting positive relations between the district and the community.

In addition, the school board has a role in defending its decision to create a public relations program. A board that understands the importance of good relationships between the school district and the community has a responsibility to communicate this priority to the staff and community.

When a public relations program is created, the school board should proactively communicate the reasons through a variety of channels.

Develop a Public Relations Program

After the board has adopted policies and you have assessed the current communication strategies, it is time to put a public relations program together. In doing this, consider the following:

■ What are the goals of the program?

■ What strategies and activities will meet the goals?

■ What is the school district's budget for public relations?

■ Who will be responsible for developing public relations strategies and carrying out action steps?

■ Will you create a public relations department or employ public relations staff?

■ How will success be measured?

Public relations is a strategic management function.

What the public relations should function do

First and foremost, your public relations program should help achieve the mission of the school district and meet school district goals. If it does not, it likely will be irrelevant and will be viewed as a frill.

More specifically, public relations is a strategic management function that:

■ Counsels district leadership on the communication aspects of district issues and programs

■ Employs strategies for communicating to and listening to staff and the community

■ Stimulates a better understanding of the role, objectives, accomplishments, and needs of the school district

■ Helps interpret public attitudes

■ Identifies and helps shape policies and procedures in the public interest

■ Carries out involvement and information activities which earn public understanding and support

How to begin your program

One of the first activities in developing a public relations program is to develop an overall public relations plan with goals that are aimed at achieving school district goals.

A planned public relations program guides your activities and helps ensure that they have a purpose. It helps the public relations professional resist the temptation to be all things to all people by implementing various "good ideas" that may not contribute much to overall district success. In short, a planned public relations program gives you the ability to say, "No."

And, while the overall public relations plan should be systematic, it should also be flexible. Anyone who works in a public school district knows to expect the unexpected. Crises are inevitable. Don't be discouraged if you are diverted from your plan from time to time. It should be fluid enough to allow you to respond to immediate and changeable needs.

Direct most of your resources, time, and effort on the audiences that will best help you achieve your goals.

The plan should be based on research, which has been presented in previous chapters. This research phase helps determine the main areas of focus. It is important to remember that the plan must be targeted at specific objectives to get the most effective use of your public relations dollar.

Targeting the public relations plan means directing most of your resources, time, and effort on the audiences that will best help you achieve your goals. For example, if one goal of your public relations program is to gain financial support from taxpayers who are not parents of school district students, you will want to target those in the community who are considered opinion leaders, such as community or business leaders.

While it is tempting to expend the most effort on reaching non-parent taxpayers who are traditionally uninvolved in school or community issues, you will get the most "bang for your buck" by communicating with those who are likely to support you and asking them to reach out to others they know.

NSPRA has variety of resource related to public relations planning including a workbook, *Planning Your School PR Investment*. This guide walks you step by step through the public relations planning process.

How much money to allocate

After developing your overall plan, carefully estimate what it will cost to implement each action step of your public relations program and also budget for some unexpected needs.

No hard and fast rule exists for how much money should be allocated to public relations efforts. It depends on the specific needs and goals of your district. The most important thing to remember is that if the district has placed a priority on communicating with staff and community, then the communication program should be funded as a specific item in the school district's budget.

The following list includes expenditures that may be allocated in a budget for school public relations:

■ Employee salary and benefits, if employing a public relations professional

■ Fees for consultants to help develop and implement a public relations program

■ Costs for conducting surveys or other research methods

■ Costs to design and maintain a web site

■ Costs to produce and print publications

■ Costs of postage for mailings

Each item listed in your public relations program should be analyzed for estimated cost and then budgeted so adequate funds are available to implement the plan. Some district public relations offices have become self-sufficient by charging a fee to other district departments and schools for using services. By doing this, the public relations office functions like a public relations firm for its internal "clients." To do this, each department and school would need to budget for public relations activities.

To employ or not to employ

Obviously, someone must be responsible for carrying out the public relations plan. Those responsibilities may fall to several people in the district, but one person should coordinate the entire effort.

The best scenario is for the school district to employ a full-time public relations professional who reports directly to the superintendent. These two individuals must work together very closely, particularly in the area of managing the school district's reputation. In a sense, the public relations

professional functions as the eyes and ears of the superintendent and serves as the social conscience of the school system.

Some districts do not have the financial resources to create a full-time position focused on public relations. Other options for staffing the public relations function include creating a part-time position, hiring consultants, or adding responsibility for public relations to an existing position.

What to Look for in a PR Professional

The most effective public relations professionals are skilled and experienced in disciplines such as human behavior and social sciences, research methods, communication, organizational development, marketing, and journalism. It is not necessary for the school public relations person to have a background as an educator. In fact, it is sometimes beneficial if that person does not have an education background, so he or she can bring a different perspective into district decision-making.

As stated earlier, the public relations professional should report directly to the superintendent and have a close relationship with the superintendent, yet this person's main job will be to think differently from the superintendent.

If it is the superintendent's job to work with facts, it is the public relations professional's job to work with the perceptions of those facts. The public relations professional adds a broad focus and a softer look at the organization, how its internal and external customers feel about the organization, and how their actions will likely follow those feelings.

The best public relations professionals have an unconventional outlook; they are creative, intuitive, perceptive, and they thrive on chaos, instead of being threatened by it.

In addition, the public relations professional should be valued for telling the superintendent things he or she may not want to hear. Superintendents often have many "yes people" around them. The public relations professional needs to be a team player, but distinctly not a "yes person." This means the person has to be willing to play the role of devil's advocate and not be afraid to respectfully question ideas and plans and decisions before they are finalized.

Accreditation ensures broad knowledge

School districts rarely employ people with qualifications similar to those needed in a public relations professional. So, how do you know whether candidates for the position are qualified?

One way to judge the public relations professional's knowledge level is to ask if the person is accredited by the Universal Accreditation Board. Accredited professionals may display a series of letters after their names to show their

accreditation. The designation of APR (Accredited Public Relations) is now universally used by many public relations organizations, including NSPRA. The letters mean that the person has passed rigorous written and oral examinations that test their knowledge and experience in the field of public relations.

One word of caution: Just because a person is accredited does not mean he or she is the right person for your school district. Conversely, not all competent public relations professionals are accredited. Accreditation is a voluntary process that some public relations professionals do not choose to complete. Accreditation is, however, one criteria to use when looking at candidates for a school public relations position

Strategist or technician?

In hiring a public relations professional, you have options. Should you hire a strategist or a technician? Ideally, you would staff your public relations department with both.

A public relations strategist tends to be a more experienced professional, often, but not always, accredited by the Universal Accreditation Board.

■ A **strategist** is adept at anticipating and managing issues, providing wise counsel to the superintendent and board, bringing the staff's and community's points of view into leadership discussions and public relations planning and crisis management.

■ A **technician** is adept at some or many of the tools for communication, such as writing, design, or Web page development.

With limited dollars, you will get more "bang for your buck" by hiring a strategist. You will get broad-based knowledge and experience, and often, strategists come with technical skills as well.

What to pay

Salaries for school district public relations professionals often mirror the salaries for private-sector or government-agency public relations staff in your community. To get high-quality applicants for your public relations position, the school district should pay accordingly.

In addition, the Educational Research Service annually conducts a salary survey of school public relations professionals across the United States, which is published in NSPRA's *Network* newsletter. This also provides helpful guidance for what to pay your PR professional.

Generally speaking, your PR strategist — who should be ranked as a top-level administrator in your school district — should have a salary comparable to other top leadership positions.

What If You Can't Afford a PR Professional?

Although employing a full-time public relations professional is ideal, not all school districts can afford such a position. In small school districts, in particular, the few administrators must wear many hats, and one of those hats for someone should be public relations.

In many school districts, the primary responsibility for school public relations falls to the superintendent. And, even if the district *does* employ a public relations professional, the superintendent should be the primary reputation management leader of the school district.

Superintendents should have as part of their job descriptions many public relations functions, including participating in community activities, fostering business partnerships, speaking to the public, serving as the district's primary spokesperson, communicating with employees, and more. However, because of their many other responsibilities, most superintendents can't do it all.

While the superintendent must set the overall tone and have ultimate responsibility for the district's public relations, several options exist for getting the day-to-day public relations activities accomplished without a full-time public relations professional.

One way is to employ a public relations professional on a part-time basis. Another is to combine public relations with another job function. Examples are volunteer coordinator, foundation director, grant writer, or even half-time teacher.

What you are looking for is a person who fits the qualifications described earlier in this chapter and who has public relations skills that complement the superintendent's skills.

One note of caution: Make sure you are truly creating two half-time positions, not two full-time positions for one person. Otherwise, turnover could be high. Additionally, you will want to be sure the person is qualified to handle the duties of the public relations professional.

Another option is to work with a public relations consultant. Many work independently and some have school district public relations experience. Their services range from public relations counsel for the board and superintendent to public relations planning, to public relations activities, such as research or newsletter development. A good way to find these people is to call NSPRA, your state NSPRA chapter president, or another school district's public relations staff.

Many public relations firms also work with school districts. They offer much the same services as an independent consultant, but with a firm, you generally have the benefit of more than one person's expertise. The downside can be a lack of school district experience and higher cost. However, some public relations firms offer pro bono service to non-profit clients.

Form a District Public Relations Committee

Whether or not you have a public relations professional on staff, it is a good idea to form a public relations advisory committee. In a school district that cannot afford to employ a professional, this committee could take an active, rather than purely advisory role. Beware of overloading the committee — you will be relying on the services of people with other full-time responsibilities, so you cannot reasonably expect them to accomplish a great number of projects.

In a district that does have a public relations professional on staff, the committee can help brainstorm new ways to meet public relations goals, help with issues management, and generally look at the district's public relations program with fresh eyes.

The committee should be broad-based, including board, staff and student representatives, and community members with communication expertise. Public relations and marketing firms, corporations and major media outlets are usually willing to participate in this form of community service and generally like to be asked for their opinions.

A few words of advice: Be careful to honor the committee's work, but be clear that it is an advisory committee and will not be making board or staff decisions. Also, do not overload this committee with meetings. Quarterly meetings are generally sufficient for this group to do its work.

Public Relations Is Everyone's Job

It is important to remember that all district staff members have some responsibility for effective school district public relations. This means that the public relations professional should spend some of his or her time educating district employees about their role in school public relations.

School principals are a critical link between the schools and the public, and they can make or break a school public relations program. While many board members and administrators would like

to think that the community relates to the school district as a whole, the fact is that parents and non-parents alike feel most connected to individual schools.

In fact, national public opinion research proves time and time again that, although people are generally unhappy with the overall state of education, they are generally satisfied with their child's school, their neighborhood school, or the schools with which they have personal experience.

That's why the principal's role as public relations leader for his or her school is so important. In fact, in this era of school choice, good public relations and even marketing for schools is paramount.

The principal should be responsible for a building-level public relations plan that includes communicating with staff and parents, as well as the community surrounding the school. In many districts, one of the responsibilities of the district public relations professional is to train principals in effective school communication and to assist schools with public relations planning and crisis communication.

NSPRA offers a number of resources to help principals with public relations, including *PRincipal Communicator,* a monthly newsletter, and *Practical PR for Principals,* a handbook of proven school public relations ideas, and *Principals in the Public: Engaging Community Support.*

Jennifer Reeve, APR

Jennifer Reeve, APR, is director of programs for the Colorado Association of School Boards, where she leads communication, conferences, member relations, and board development efforts and provides communication training and services for local school boards and district staff.

Reeve has also developed and managed public relations programs for a 17,500-student school district in Texas, a business-education partnership in Los Angeles, and a Board of Cooperative Educational Services in Colorado. She served as an associate at a private public relations firm in the Los Angeles area and as public information officer for the Corporation for Public Broadcasting in Washington, D.C.

Reeve holds a Bachelor of Arts degree in Journalism from Texas A&M University. She is accredited in public relations (APR) by the Universal Accreditation Board.

Reeve is a past President and past Southwest Region Vice President of the National School Public Relations Association.

Basic Communication Strategies

Media Relations

By Lew Armistead, APR

Any number of school public relations professionals, superintendents, principals, and other educators can probably think of 1,001 activities they would prefer rather than talking with a reporter. Too frequently talking with reporters can be a negative experience. Yet, when educators understand the most effective ways to work with reporters, editors, and news directors, not only will media relations be more positive, it will also deliver your message to people who might otherwise not receive it.

The key is developing a media relations program now rather than waiting until your next crisis when reporters will naturally gravitate in your direction. Working with the news media is much like the broad public relations function — we need to:

- Analyze our media relationships

- Develop a plan for success

■ Create messages that we want to deliver

■ Evaluate how we're doing

The most important step is developing relationships with reporters, just like relationship building is so essential in overall public relations. This chapter suggests ways you can create and strengthen those relationships.

Neglecting the media can be risky.

While many public relations initiatives will have a more positive, long-term impact on your school system's reputation than working with the news media, neglecting the media can be risky. With the increasing number of adults who no longer have children in school, educators are losing their natural, daily opportunities to communicate with the vast number of audiences who need to hear your message. Yet, many of these community members read their local newspaper or listen to radio and local television news. Many immigrants, who may have limited ability to understand English, tune in to non-English speaking radio stations for their news. And research has demonstrated that elected officials and business leaders — two important audiences — pay attention to the media.

Consider reaching out to reporters, educating them about the school system, alerting them to key issues, and encouraging frequent conversations. It's wise to ask reporters what would interest them; understanding the reporter's interests can help you create strategies on the best way to deliver your message. If your district has a school public relations professional, be sure to work with him or her.

Understanding the Basics of Media Relations

There are a number of "basics" to effective media relations which need to be understood and practiced. Yet, as communication becomes more complex, there are additional "new ideas" to consider. This chapter will refer to the "basics" quickly, and then move onto other areas.

The basics to a successful media relationship include:

■ **Be honest.** The only thing you have when approaching a reporter is the credibility you have developed in past dealings. To hide information, lie, or tell half-truths is the fastest way to destroy credibility.

■ **Get to know reporters.** Media relations can be adversarial, especially when a problem arises. It's much better to get to know reporters before a crisis occurs. Have lunch with reporters, share information about the school district or your school, invite them into your office to meet your staff, or have them be a guest presenter in a high school class.

When problems arise, you and the reporter are likely to have different goals. If you know and respect each other beforehand, communication will go more smoothly.

■ **Be willing to spend time to "educate" reporters when they first get the beat.** Too frequently media rotate the reporters who cover education, yet we still need to invest the time in introducing them to the district or school. Prepare a packet of information that includes a listing of your schools, key people, programs, accomplishments, and other facts. Keep the list updated so you simply have to make a copy the next time a new reporter comes aboard. You've probably already created much of this information and you can use the packet with other audiences.

■ **Learn and respect deadlines.** A reporter's deadlines are not usually flexible. People who complain that their message isn't included in a story when they communicate that message after the deadline are simply showing their ignorance about media relations.

■ **Forget education jargon, acronyms, and abbreviations.** Education is difficult enough to understand. Don't confuse reporters and their readers or listeners by using jargon that no one but your staff understands. If you use jargon, acronyms, or abbreviations, provide a simple, clear definition of the terms.

■ **Be willing to be interviewed.** There's a story about a superintendent who complained that a local reporter never printed his "side of the story." In his next breath, he said he hadn't bothered to return a reporter's call that morning. There's probably a connection. Educators shouldn't expect to have their message delivered if they are unwilling to talk about it with reporters.

■ **Treat all media equally.** It is likely that more than one newspaper and radio and television station cover your community. All should receive the same information at the same time. Playing favorites, even with the community newspaper that has been most supportive, will get you in trouble in the long run.

■ **If you don't know the answer to a reporter's question, say so.** Promise to get the answer for the reporter before the deadline and meet that commitment. You can also refer the reporter to your best expert on that topic, making sure you alert the expert before the reporter calls. If you try to fake the answer, you are heading for trouble.

■ **Keep your head about errors, but correct them.** When the media makes an error in a story about your district, evaluate the magnitude of the error. Misspelling your name is not as damaging as inaccurately reporting dollar amounts in the school district budget.

While all errors should be corrected, demanding a printed retraction for small mistakes will not build positive long-term relationships. When an error occurs, start with the reporter. Just as we counsel a parent to talk with the teacher if a problem in the classroom occurs, we should start with the reporter who made the error.

If the reporter is unresponsive, it's appropriate to move to his or her supervisor — that's the news editor or city editor for a newspaper and the news director or assignment editor for radio and TV. But always be professional.

■ **Remember that reporters don't write headlines.** That's done at the copy desk, so don't blame the reporter. The reporter might be just as upset over a poor headline as you are.

■ **Take advantage of the "last question."** When reporters have asked all of their questions, they may say, "Is there anything else you would like to say?" Take advantage of that opportunity. That is your chance to repeat all of your message points.

Media relations should be part of your overall public relations plan.

Moving Beyond the "Very Basic"

Just as communication is more complex today, so is media relations. Educators must become more strategic and look for more effective ways to deliver the district or school's message through the media.

Here are effective ideas to help you deliver your district's or school's message:

■ **Develop your messages any time you communicate with a reporter.** Just as it's essential to have key messages prepared in any communication activity, so is it in media relations. It makes no sense to participate in a news interview if you do not have something you want to communicate.

When a reporter requests an interview, ask about the topic and take time to develop message points. You may already have messages in mind for current issues that are being discussed, in which case you can move right into the interview. If not, ask if you can call the reporter back in 15 minutes, so you have time to determine your messages. But you can't wait forever because the reporter likely will be on deadline. Ask for only a few minutes.

■ **Develop a mini-plan for media relations.** Just as public relations works better with a plan, so does media relations. In fact, media relations should be part of your overall public relations plan.

Your plan could include the most important issues to communicate for the year and specific ways to communicate using the media. In developing a media relations plan, review the overall goals of your school district or school and determine how you can communicate those issues through the news media.

For example, if a goal this year is to double the number of school volunteers, your media relations plan might include:

■ News release announcing the search for volunteers that is sent to all media in the community

■ Op-ed article in the local newspaper discussing how volunteers can make a difference in a student's education

■ Series of public service announcements for radio stations encouraging volunteerism

■ Guest appearance by the school district's top volunteer on a local television public affairs show

■ **Submit op-ed articles.** Many newspapers publish op-ed articles or opinion pieces written by people who are not on the newspaper staff. These articles usually appear opposite the editorial page, hence the label *op-ed*.

A strategic communicator looks for opportunities to submit op-eds on important issues. Check your newspapers to see if op-eds are published. If so, ask who is in charge of them, and contact that person.

Find out general guidelines, including if they want the article submitted via e-mail, and suggest a topic. Don't ask for a guarantee that it will be used, simply a willingness to review the article. After sending your article to the paper, it's appropriate to make one follow-up phone call to ensure that it has been received. If your community has more than one paper, consider sending the op-ed to the largest one on an "exclusive" basis (meaning you are sending it only to one outlet). You can then suggest to the editor that the paper has two weeks to determine whether it will be used; and if not, you would like it back to send to another paper.

■ **Discuss ideas with local editorial boards.** Too many educators wait until a newspaper publishes a negative article and then they complain. The strategic communicator looks for school topics that might result in an editorial and asks to present the school or district's view to the paper's editorial board before it is written.

Newspapers have editorial boards that are responsible for determining the paper's stance in its editorials and those boards often meet with community members. Consider contacting your newspapers when issues arise and ask to speak to the editorial board.

Bring a few people, not more than five, representing different constituents (a board member, a teacher, a parent leader, a business partner, and the superintendent, for example) to the meeting, and have each present a different aspect of your argument. Leave summary information of your position and be willing to accept questions after the meeting.

■ **Consider appearing on radio or television interview shows.** Many communities have local versions of *Good Morning America* or *The TODAY Show*, and they are good opportunities to deliver your important messages. Local colleges and even school districts have some public affairs shows. Consider seeking interviews on these shows.

Become familiar with the show's format, the hosts, how questions are asked, and other aspects of the show. If the show is right for you, call the station, ask to speak with whomever places guests on that show, and pitch your message. If successful, don't forget to develop message points.

Remembering News Releases

For many years, the news release has been a staple of school public relations. Now, however, many practitioners shy away from the release in favor of other vehicles.

There may still be a role for the news release. (For a sample news release, see the next page.) Consider using releases on such topics as student, staff, and school awards. While not all of them will be used, they carry positive news and some may be printed.

It's wise to discuss with reporters whether they want news releases or would prefer information in other ways. If you are using releases, be sure to find out how reporters want them delivered — e-mail, fax, or regular mail.

Another useful technique is the radio public service announcement, and a sample follows.

Radio PSA Samples

Produced by the National Middle School Association

ANNOUNCER: There's nothing more valuable to a business than knowledgeable, productive employees. Students begin developing those skills in middle level schools. Businesses can invest in future productivity by investing in the academic growth of young adolescents. Teach a mini-lesson. Let students tour your facility. Phone your local middle level school and ask how your business can help young adolescents grow academically. Remember, students are 100% of our future.

A message from the National Middle School Association and this station.

ANNOUNCER: Parents and guardians can do more to help their young adolescent grow academically than just looking at their report card. Promote reading in your home. Set a time in your house when everyone reads, whether it's a book, newspaper, or magazine. This might be once a week, every other day, or even daily, as long as it's on a regular basis. Then, discuss as a family what you are reading. Remember, students are 100% of our future.

A message from the National Middle School Association and this station.

ANNOUNCER: One way for parents and guardians to build their young adolescent's future is to encourage their academic growth in middle level school. Get to know your child's teacher. Talk about the academic part of school each day with your youngster. Show an interest in his or her academic work. Explore what they are learning and let them know how that will help them in the future. Call your school to find out other ways to help kids achieve academically. Remember, students are 100% of our future.

A message from the National Middle School Association and this station.

ANNOUNCER: Success in school isn't determined just by the amount of time a student studies. Good health is also essential to academic growth. Did you realize one out of every five adolescents today has at least one serious health problem? Pay attention to your child's health because unhealthy students are more likely to fail or drop out of school. Call your school for information on meeting young adolescent's health needs. Remember, students are 100% of our future.

A message from the National Middle School Association and this station.

Sample News Release

Reprinted from NSPRA's *Principals Public Relations Handbook*

For Immediate Release   For further information contact:

May 14, 2007   Your Name, phone number

LOCAL STUDENT WINS STATE AWARD

Emily Howell, a senior at NSPRA High School, has been named Virginia Forensics Champion for 2007, competing against more than 1,000 high school students from throughout the commonwealth.

Howell earned the award last weekend at the annual State Forensics Championships in Richmond. More than 200 high school teams competed and awards were presented by Governor Charles Allen.

"Emily capped an outstanding four years in public speaking at NSPRA High School with this state honor," said Principal Rich Bagin. "She has been involved in debate and forensics for four years here under the sponsorship of Charles Kennedy, her speech teacher."

This is the second time in five years NSPRA High School has had the top forensics student in the commonwealth. Steve Bosnick won the same award in 2002.

In addition to participating in speech and debate, Howell is a member of the NSPRA High National Honor Society chapter and mathematics club, competed in varsity basketball, and has maintained a 3.56 grade point average. She plans to enroll at the University of Virginia next fall.

-30-

Delivering Your Message in a News Interview

While it's wise to plan how you can initiate ideas with the news media, you must also be ready to handle a news interview on short notice. You might be called for an interview if a problem in a school occurs, when a new program begins, or when test scores are announced. The key to success is preparation.

This advice is geared especially to television interviews, but much of it applies to radio and newspaper interviews as well. It can also be used for giving speeches, holding a conference, or writing a memo.

While there's no guarantee of success in any news interview and some are tougher than others, the prepared communicator has a much better chance of delivering a message that is important to the district. You can go a long way in controlling an interview if you prepare, and preparation should start as soon as you get a phone call asking you to participate in the interview. This call is likely to come from a reporter or news editor asking for a "stand-up" interview or it can come from a "booker" who asks for an "in-studio" interview.

When you are asked to go on camera, first decide whether to agree to the interview. Strategic communicators will ask themselves whether participating will help their overall communication goals. However, it's usually a good idea to give interviews so that your views will be heard.

If the story or show is stacked against the schools, you may want to decline the opportunity. In such a case, you are probably going to be "beaten up." But keep in mind that the story will air with or without your participation. You or your position may be "beaten up" more if you decline to participate and your views are not included.

The key to success is preparation.

While it's usually a good idea to agree to a news interview, you should not agree to whatever time the reporter suggests. The interview must be completed before the reporter's deadline so that your views will be included, but you also need time to prepare. Negotiate a time that would both be convenient for you and agreeable to the station. You may only be able to get an extra 20 minutes, but that's 20 minutes more preparation time.

After you agree to the interview, don't end the phone conversation. Try to gather as much information as possible and ask what the reporter or show's host will ask and what the interview will cover. Indicate that you want this information so you can have the facts they need. You will not receive a specific list of questions, but you should receive an indication of what will be covered.

Find out what information the reporter already has. If you are going onto a news interview show, make sure you know if

---

other guests will be appearing and whom they will be.

Designing Your Message Points

Once you have as much information as you can obtain, it's time to decide what messages you want to communicate during the interview. These are called *message points* in media parlance, and you should decide specifically what yours are before any interview. It is not strategically advantageous to do an interview if you don't know what you want to communicate. Focusing on your message points does not mean you won't answer a reporter's questions; it simply means you will try to also communicate your views.

Determine just a few message points because you will not have much time in a radio or television interview to communicate. Two or three message points are plenty for any interview.

Put your message points into "memorable language."

Write your messages so you can refer to them during the interview.

After determining your message points, put them into "memorable language," which is exactly that — language people are more likely to remember. In any electronic interview, you will have only a few seconds to deliver your message and your words are gone as soon as you say them. It's not like a newspaper story that can be re-read and even clipped. With television or radio, people hear your message once. If they are going to act on what they hear, they must easily understand and remember what you said.

For example, if one of your message points is,

> If reading achievement is going to improve at our school, we need the help of parents, grandparents, brothers, and sisters — everyone in the home — to make reading a priority.

That's a long statement for a listener to remember. Your memorable language translation might be,

> Reading must be a family affair.

Then go on to explain your message.

It's Time to Bridge

Once you have message points converted into memorable language, the next step is to learn and use *the bridging technique*. This means that whenever you are asked a question, you should answer quickly and then "bridge" to one of your message points.

For example, if reading scores have declined at your school and a reporter is interviewing you about that situation, he or she might ask,

> How far have scores dropped?

Your answer might be,

> Two points, and we are making reading a family affair in this school and community.

You have been truthful in your answer, but you have moved quickly away from the problem to a solution. Bridging words include *and*, *but*, *however* — whatever will make the transition.

If the reporter asks the same question in an effort to get a different answer, repeat the initial answer. Don't let reporters move you away from your messages if at all possible. You can and should be responsive to them, but you should also "stay on message."

Take a Few More Steps Before the Reporter Arrives

Once you've completed these three tasks, practice, practice, practice. Yes, it will take some time, but if the interview is important enough to do, take 10 or 15 minutes to "get it right."

Try to anticipate the reporter's questions, especially based on the information you have obtained from your first phone call. Then, think about which message points you want to deliver and how you would bridge to that message.

After all this preparation, you have one more chance to prepare for the typical interview. Whether it's a stand-up or in-studio interview, the microphone will be

placed on you and sound checks will be done before the interview begins. You will have time to ask the show's host or reporter,

> Now, give me an idea of what we'll be talking about.

Sometimes the thrust of the interview will have been altered or a different reporter will be assigned to the story. Take advantage of this time.

These guidelines will not guarantee success in every instance, but you'll have a much better chance of communicating your message through an interview than if you skip the preparation steps.

Don't Forget the Visual

While the message is the most important aspect of any interview, it can be destroyed in a television interview if you forget about the visual aspects. You want to be seen as a relaxed, caring, professional, and knowledgeable person. The following are visual aspects that you can use to support your message:

■ **Location.** The backdrop of the interview says something about you. On one hand, if you are interviewed behind your desk, you'll be seen as bureaucratic or as another piece of furniture in the office. On the other hand, an interview in the media center or a classroom gives the impression that you are student-oriented.

For every interview, consider what location is the most appropriate. If a suicide has just occurred on campus, your office may be very appropriate. If you're talking about improving reading skills, the library might be best. Decide what location to use, and then suggest that place to the reporter.

■ **Dress.** Dress conservatively. Fancy patterns will be confusing on television, and viewers will try to figure out what you are wearing instead of listening to your message. Simple patterns, solid-colored jackets, and small jewelry are best.

■ **Eyes.** Your eyes deliver a message. Eyes focused on the ground indicate that you are hiding something; eyes that are always on the move indicate nervousness. It's best to keep your eyes on the reporter or host, just as you would in a relaxed conversation.

■ **Stance.** For a stand-up interview, pick a stance that is comfortable for you, but stand still. If you move around, you will be seen as nervous and make it difficult for the cameraperson to keep you in focus. For a studio interview, sit slightly forward on the chair and lean slightly toward the host.

Keep in mind that a sharp-looking tie or new dress will not guarantee a successful interview, but the visual aspect plays a role in delivering your message.

Remember Two Golden Rules

Always keep in mind two Golden Rules during an interview:

Never say, "No comment."

While there will be times when you can not and should not answer a question, stay away from the words, "No comment." They tend to deliver the perception that you are hiding something.

Rather, if there's a reason you can't comment such as on personnel issues, explain that. If you don't know the answer, promise to find it and get back to the reporter in a timely fashion.

Remember, the microphone is never off.

When the interview ends, the microphone and tape may still be running. In a TV interview, frequently the cameraperson will take a few shots over your shoulder to get the reporter's face. During a recess from a meeting, a reporter with a mic or notebook could follow you around the corner.

Your comments are still fair game. As a noted television reporter once said,

> If you don't want to be quoted saying something, don't say it.

Handling the Hostile Interview

Most interviews will be friendly, especially if you take the initiative to seek interview opportunities on positive stories. However, with the influx of cable news programming, a wide array of shows promote specific agendas. These can result in hostile interviews and require special attention.

Consider these strategies in preparing for a potentially hostile interview:

■ **Decide whether agreeing to the interview is in your best interest.** Does it meet your communication objectives? It can be easy to answer, "No" to this question, but keep in mind that if you don't participate, your position may not be communicated. The "other side's" story will be reported whether you participate or not.

■ **It's essential that everything you do for a normal interview, you do even better in a hostile interview.** Spend more time on preparation. Have your message points clearly in mind. Spend time anticipating questions and thinking about how you will handle each of them.

■ **Give the reporter important information on the subject in writing before the interview begins.** This is the best way to ensure that information is accurate. Before the interview begins, tell the reporter that you are making an audio tape of

it. This will let the reporter know you have a record of what you said and it will make him or her a little more cautious about getting your quotes right.

■ **Go over any areas that you consider "off-limits" with the producer, news director, or reporter.** A professional reporter will respect those agreements. If not, you have grounds to stop the interview.

■ **If you have a public relations professional on your staff, have her or him sit through the interview.** That's one more person who will hear what you say and make the reporter a little more cautious. Also, if you face another hostile interview later, the public relations person can suggest strengths and weakness from the first one.

It's essential to be prepared.

Managing the Hostile Talk Show

Today, there are more talk shows than ever. And since education is high on the public agenda, educators are invited to participate. Consider these guidelines if you are invited to appear on one of these talk shows:

■ **Know the shows that are heard in your community.** Some shows may be very good while others may promote specific agendas. Know the audiences, the host, whether calls come in from the audience, and the types of questions that are typically asked. Listen or watch the show before you appear.

▨ **Use this information to decide if you will accept the invitation.** Sometimes you will be "beaten up" on one of these shows. But remember that if you are not present, the "beating" may be considerably worse. It's much easier to attack an action or institution if no one is there to defend it.

▨ **Remember, if you agree to go on a show, you don't have to be on for the entire show.** For example, if the show lasts for one hour and you are invited to be on for the entire hour, you could suggest a shorter time.

Consider how long it will take you to deliver your message and what will happen for the remainder of that time. Will that time be filled by questions from callers who are waiting to attack you? After weighing all the possibilities, you may want to say that you'll be available for 30 to 40 minutes.

▨ **Do everything you would do for a standard interview, but do it better.** Just as with the hostile interview, it's essential to be prepared. Usually you will have a day or two before the show, so you'll have more preparation time. Take advantage of it.

▨ **Forget everything your parents taught you about being polite when you go on one of these shows.** Your job is to deliver your messages. You are likely to be interrupted, told you are uninformed, and subjected to other unpredictable things. Stay focused on your goal, and be ready to state your case emotionally and strongly — be aggressive.

▨ **Probably the best advice for anyone going onto a hostile call-in show is to have a lot of friends with telephones.** There's absolutely nothing wrong with encouraging people who support your view to listen to the show and call in.

While there's no guarantee of success in a hostile setting, these suggestions will help you better survive the ordeal.

When you make an accurate, early announcement, you'll develop trust.

Dealing with the Media in Difficult Situations

The first rule in successfully dealing with the news media when a crisis arises is to be the first to announce the problem. This practice may go against basic instincts and can be difficult gaining agreement from top management, but it's essential to effective communication.

Here are reasons a school district or school should be the first to announce any challenge or difficult situation:

■ **You develop credibility, not only with the news media, but also with other audiences when you make an early announcement.** The worst thing is for a reporter to think is that you are trying to hide something. If that perception develops, the media will likely be more suspicious of you in the future. However, when you make an accurate, early announcement, you'll develop trust.

■ **You are the first to communicate the "facts," which will establish an accurate communication agenda for the situation.** If naysayers in your community begin talking about your situation, calling the news media, or even writing letters to the editor before you have delivered your message, you are likely to find that considerable mis-information surrounds the situation. Now you have more problems; you will be bombarded with questions and complaints based on rumors. This will take away time from recovering from the situation and returning the educational program to normalcy.

■ **You are likely to have a 2- or 3-day "story" instead of a 2- or 3-week "story."** When information is communicated quickly and accurately, the media will not see a

need to "dig" into the situation to undercover facts and the public will soon tire of hearing information repeated over and over. The story will not last as long.

Collect all the facts before you ever start communicating.

Having urged quick communication, it's essential to remember to collect all the facts before you ever start communicating. Nothing is worse than communicating inaccurate information; if you do, you'll only create additional "difficult situations" for yourself.

It is important to be prepared so you can quickly communicate with the media during a crisis. You can gather the following information ahead of time:

■ Phone numbers directly into the TV or radio stations' newsrooms so you don't want to have to go through the switchboard

■ Newspaper reporters' direct dial phone numbers, cell numbers, pagers, e-mails, fax numbers, and perhaps home phone numbers (It's useful to have a conversation with the reporter now to determine whether he or she wants to be contacted at home after work hours if a major crisis develops.)

■ The same information as above for any television stations that have education reporters

■ Deadlines for all media

■ Names and contact information of city editors and news directors in case you can't reach the reporters with whom you normally deal

If you don't have a school public relations office, you may want to contact a neighboring district that does and has already collected this information.

If your crisis is large enough, the media will swarm into your district, and having people to handle all the additional communication needs will be a major issue. If your district has a public relations office, this office should lead this effort. However, if not, you should think now about where you might find volunteers who can do everything from answering phones to drafting message points. Possible volunteers include:

■ PR professionals in neighboring districts

■ Your county office of education, state department of education, or professional association

■ Retirees from your district

■ APR professionals from a business partner

■ Members from the state NSPRA chapter

Reaching the Media in Difficult Times

If a crisis hits, you aren't going to have time to prepare and disseminate a news release. That is the time to consider a news conference or briefing. This approach allows you to deliver information quickly to a large group of reporters. It's wise time management to deal with reporters all at the same time. Since many educators don't manage news conferences frequently, understand these important tips when you plan a news conference:

■ **The news conference should be in a place convenient for the news media, but away from the site of a major crisis.** With most TV stations having "traffic helicopters" now, it isn't as likely as in the past to have cameras stampede onto a school campus or to an accident site. However, having media at the site of a problem, especially during the first 24 hours, won't help the recovery. Plan your news conference site ahead of time.

■ **Have only a few people speak and keep "opening comments" brief.** The best person to speak is the district's primary media spokesperson, who probably is the chief communication professional. He or she can provide basic information and handle key questions. You can always make the superintendent, principal, attorney, or other people available at specific times, but their primary responsibility during a crisis is not speaking every hour with the media.

■ **Provide information in writing.** The best way to ensure that reporting is accurate is to put it in writing. Certainly there will be verbal communication, but have the key facts down on paper along with prepared statements.

■ **Set a time length for news conferences.** News conferences should not go on forever. The district will have specific information to deliver and should be willing to accept a few questions. When you feel the questions are repetitive or are going into areas where you don't have information yet, simply thank the reporters for coming, announce when the next briefing will be held, and end the news conference.

Media Training Makes All of This Easier

One of the most important yet overlooked activities in educational public relations is media training. School public relations professionals should provide media training for staff members who could be interviewed by the news media. If your district doesn't have a public relations person, consider hiring a consultant on this topic for a professional development day.

While the chief communication officer will likely be the district's primary spokesperson, at times it will be appropriate for the superintendent, business official, principals, or others to go before the cameras. Professional

development will be especially important in a crisis when time will not allow training.

The training should review the information in this chapter on handling a news interview, plus include ample opportunities to practice those skills. After reviewing such topics as writing message points for an interview, anticipating questions, bridging, and using other interviewing skills, give participants 2 exercises. You can divide your participants into 6- to 8-person groups, give them a scenario, ask them as a group to develop 2 key messages they would deliver during an interview, and have them put those messages into memorable language.

Then they can write questions they think the reporter might ask. After the entire group reviews this information, have volunteers role play an interview with the district's public relations professional or consultant acting as the reporter. Give as many of the participants as possible the opportunity to role play.

The Best Ways to Communicate with Reporters

You can deliver information to reporters in many ways. The strategic communicator asks which way is most effective for each reporter. It will be a good investment to communicate in the way that each reporter wants, if you want the best coverage.

Consider the following options for communicating with reporters and remember that the same method may not be best for all reporters:

News releases

Releases are likely to be more effective with small papers that have a small staff. Since they have fewer people to produce copy, they rely more on what is given to them. If you produce news releases, the following are important guidelines, many of which are useful for any writing:

■ **Keep the material as short as possible.** Use short words, short sentences, and short paragraphs. Put the most important information first. Journalists use what is known as the *inverted pyramid style*, where the essential information is always in the first paragraph (or lead). Important additional information comes in the second or third paragraphs, and less important information follows. That way, if a story has to be shortened, if can be cut from the bottom and the most important information is still there.

■ **Use active verbs.** Stay away from educational jargon and abbreviations.

■ **Use journalistic style.** Most public libraries have copies of *The Associated Press Stylebook*, which contains all the rules for usage.

■ **Always have a contact person's name and phone number on the release.** This is helpful in case the reporter has questions.

Tip sheets

Frequently schools or school systems describe a number of news events in one-paragraph summaries on a tipsheet. This enables a reporter to find information he or she likes without reading volumes. It also saves you work and time.

Make sure tip sheets include a contact name and phone number for each item. You can send the same tip sheet to both print and electronic media.

E-mail

More and more newsrooms are receiving information electronically. If media in your community do, this is another efficient option for sharing information.

News conferences

Hold a news conference only when you have extremely major news that will interest a large number of reporters. If you schedule news conferences for minor news, you will hurt your credibility with the media.

Lew Armistead, APR

Lew Armistead, APR, is a past president of NSPRA and has delivered education's message to the news media for more than 30 years, including 22 years working with the national press. Currently president of LA Communications, he has appeared on NBC *Nightly News* and prepared guests for *Good Morning America*, *The TODAY Show*, and CNN *Morning News*. He has worked with reporters at *The Associated Press*, *USA TODAY*, and *The New York Times*.

In the first month after the Columbine High School tragedy, Armistead served as a consultant to the Jefferson County Public Schools in dealing with the 700+ reporters from throughout the world covering the situation.

Armistead provides training for school systems and other organizations in media relations. Clients have included the National Teacher of the Year Program, National PTA, National State Boards of Education, and school systems throughout the United States and in Japan.

Armistead was director, public relations, for the National Association of Secondary School Principals for 16 years and spent four years as a school system public relations professional. He has also worked with two metropolitan dailies, four network-affiliated television stations, and other media.

Internal Communication

By Jim Cummings, APR

We all talk a good game about the importance of internal communication, but when it gets right to it, many of us become consumed with issues outside of our organization. Someone has to step up and be the voice for active internal communication, and it should be the school district's PR professional.

Why?

Because while internal communication has always been an important part of any effective public relations program, the advent of the 24-hour news cycle, the Internet, cell phones, text messaging, e-mail, blogs, podcasts, and hundreds of other communications tools in use (or about to come online), it's importance has never been higher.

Employees are our first-line ambassadors.

Employees are our first-line ambassadors and it is important that they be equipped with the necessary information to carry our organizational messages forward. Every year, the Gallup Poll survey on the most trusted people in our society consistently ranks teachers at or near the top. Research also tells us that school support workers — custodians, food service workers, bus drivers, and secretaries to name a few — are some of the most believed sources of information in our communities.

Let's face it, whether they work in the cafeteria or the classroom, school district employees are perceived by the public as being experts on schools, and as having "inside" information. And since perception is reality, it is in our best interest to make sure employees have accurate, reliable, and up-to-date information.

Few people like to read about what's going on in their organization in the morning newspaper. Good news or bad, employees should hear it from the district first. Armed with good, up-to-date information about their work place gives employees the ability to speak with authority to their network of neighbors and friends, and that makes them some of the strongest public relations ambassadors a school district can have.

Well-informed employees are not only happier; they're also in a strong position to stop rumors before they get started.

Ready, Plan, Communicate

Like all good communication, internal communication needs to be planned, systemic, and focused. Internal communication plans should include the following:

▓ **Be part of a written policy** that is distributed to all staff and that states the organization believes in open and timely communication.

▓ **Provide employees with accurate, reliable, and timely information.**

▓ **Listen to employees** because they know what works — and just as important, what doesn't — in terms of communication.

▓ **Be accessible to all employees,** with particular attention paid to groups that are not easily engaged, such as part-time employees, substitutes, and those without access to electronic communication (e-mail and the Internet).

▓ **Build team spirit, pride, and a sense of belonging.**

▓ **Promote open, two-way dialog** within your school district and ensure that rank and pay scale are not barriers for communication.

■ **Ensure that the entire staff is well informed of school district issues.**

■ **Educate employees on academic issues** facing their schools, such as No Child Left Behind and statewide educational standards legislation.

"School employees are more than just teachers, secretaries, or bus drivers," said Stephanie Bateman, director of communication and public relations for the Jefferson County Public Schools in Kentucky.

They need to know that they have a more important role than the responsibilities of their job descriptions. All school and district employees are vital to shaping the future of young people in their community.

Although it develops specific plans for each of its clients, Fleishman-Hillard International in London recommends a nine-step approach to developing an internal communication program:

1. Assess the situation through research.

2. Develop a core communication document or policy.

3. Align senior management.

4. Engage middle managers and supervisors through training and to better engage those who report to them.

5. Begin a dialogue, not a monologue, with employees.

6. Determine the right mix of communication channels.

7. Measure and report results to drive accountability.

8. Establish a system of reward and recognition.

9. Stay the course and sustain communication.

Finally, no internal communication plan should be made without consulting employees first. They know what works, what doesn't, and what has worked well in the past. Consulting with them before launching your program is time well-spent.

No matter how you establish your plan, it is important to remember that the end goal is to have well-informed employees. Keep all of your employees in the loop and you'll find that they will become the single biggest advocates for education in your community.

Training Counts

Now that you know what your internal communication policy should cover, you have a couple of other key questions that need to be answered:

■ Who is responsible?

■ How do you get it to work in action and not just on paper?

The quaint answer to the first question is that **internal communication is everyone's business**. In some ways the quaint is also true. But, from a practical standpoint not everyone is willing or in the position to play an active role in communicating messages on behalf of the district.

In larger school districts, at least one person from the public relations staff should be charged with internal communication. Most school districts, however, are relatively small and, in those instances, a team of top executives, led by the public relations director, should make sure the internal communication policy is carried out.

The answer to the second question is simple: **training**. Communication training is essential to all school district employees. The follow up question — "What kind of training?" — isn't as easy and will vary from school district to school district.

One place to start is through NSPRA's *Unlocking Sensational Service* training program, which offers a plethora of research-based methods for improving customer service and internal communication.

Consider these tips adapted from the program to encourage a stronger approach to internal communication:

- **Build in a component on "ambassadorship" at staff orientations.** Win veteran staff support by involving them in the program — ask veterans to share their best "ambassador" tips.

- **Ask staff to help define the positive district culture you want to create.**

- **Ask veteran staff to "mentor" new employees** and help them feel part of the team.

- **Stress the importance of relating accurate information and facts to the public.** Do some "myth busting" on employee and community perceptions of the district.

- **Give all employees opportunities to tour the district.** School staff rarely visit other sites, and unless they are administrators, central office staff almost never get out to the schools. Encourage them to see for themselves. Help them make the personal connection to the schools that will make them better ambassadors in the community.

- **Make sure all staff members receive copies of handbooks, newsletters, brochures, calendars, schedules, dress and discipline codes, menus, or other important information sent to parents.** If there are new state regulations, district guidelines for procedures, or other operational or program changes, make sure employees are fully informed.

- **Encourage administrators to give staff opportunities to meet with them and** talk about activities, changes, and issues that affect the school or district. Administrators are great at holding "administrative" meetings, but important information doesn't always make its way through the employee ranks in a reliable manner.

Training such as this introduces employees to their roles in the district's communication and public relations programs. It is an opportunity for them to see, usually for the first time, how what they do or say affects the way people feel about their schools.

Other training sessions can help participants learn the following:

■ Targeting messages to specific audiences

■ Getting the most out of parent-teacher conferences

■ Handling difficult people and conflict

■ Understanding customer service

■ Marketing the school and district

■ Connecting with community groups

Use every tool at your disposal.

Communications Tools

When it comes to internal communication, it is important to use every tool at your disposal. You can never do enough to get the word out to your employees and you can never have enough ways to communicate. Here is a series of tips and ideas designed to help you improve your internal communication program.

■ **Have an internal key contacts list.** Every organization has key employee leaders. You not only need to identify them, but you have to make sure they're getting the information they need.

■ **Start an internal newsletter.** Everyone says they want information, so give it to them. Whether it's an update on salary negotiations or news that the parking lot is going to be torn up and resurfaced, use an internal newsletter to spread the word. Like any good publication, an internal newsletter needs to provide a good balance of news and features. A sample electronic format of an internal newsletter is included at the end of the chapter.

The communication must be timely, clear, concise, informative, and interesting.

▓ **Use technology.** Design an e-newsletter or format an e-mail to send to your staff. For those few staff members who do not have access to e-mail (bus drivers or cafeteria workers) make sure you send reminders to their department heads to print out and post the newsletters. If your school district has a closed circuit television system, you may want to consider doing a weekly or bi-weekly district update on video.

▓ **More technology.** Newer technologies are making communicating easier. Podcasts, for example, allow your employees to listen to the latest news. Some organizations are also using blogs to communicate. Like podcasts, blogs allow for increased internal communication by increasing access to important information. If both are combined with an RSS (Really Simple Syndication) system, employees and others can receive updated information automatically.

▓ **In case of emergency.** Just like parents and community members, employees need to know where they can get information when a crisis occurs. Although e-mail is a great place to start, make sure you have backup plans if electricity and phone lines go out or if your internal network goes down.

▓ **Make sure it's two-way.** Communicating is great, but don't forget to make sure it's two-way. Always include a contact name, phone number, and e-mail address at the end so that people can reach you.

No matter what method you use to communicate, remember that the communication itself must be timely, clear, concise, informative, and interesting.

Your communication to staff must be:

▓ **Timely** means that employees hear the news from their own organization first.

▓ **Clear** means that the key message is obvious and easily understood.

▓ **Concise** means that you have considered that busy people must prioritize their time, so all communication should present the crux of the issue quickly.

▓ **Relevant** means that the key message needs to be important to the reader.

▓ **Interesting** means that materials are attractive and easy to read.

Engaging Employees

While communicating to employees is important, hearing back from them is equally so. A disgruntled group of employees can do more to damage your school district than a week's worth of bad publicity in the newspaper. Because of that, it is vital to your internal communication program to find ways to engage your employees.

The following are tips to help you foster two-way communication with employees:

■ **Meet with staff regularly.** Whether it's regular, town hall-type meetings or communication groups where each site provides representatives to meet with the superintendent and his cabinet, meetings with employees need to be held regularly. Employees are the eyes and ears of the school district; these meetings can provide critical insights and reality checks, not just for the school district, but for its individual schools as well. At the building and department levels, staff meetings that involve all staff remain one of the best ways for disseminating information, sharing concerns, and setting goals.

■ **Confront issues.** Critical issues can arise at these meetings, and when they do, make sure that you confront them head on, even if it means convening another dreaded meeting. Focus on solving the problem. Staff members who participate in these meetings will generally be more receptive to their role as public

relations ambassadors because they feel informed and a critical part of the school or district.

■ **Use technology.** Conducting surveys has become easier through the use of technology. The ability to conduct independent, anonymous employee surveys is as close as your web site. Easy-to-use survey software allows you to gather feedback from your employees on issues ranging from the school calendar to changes in the district's health care plan. Anonymity could generate some negative feedback, but, in general, employees will take advantage of these survey tools to give constructive and valuable advice.

■ **Report the results.** As important as surveys can be, it is just as important to report the results and tell employees how you plan to address issues that were raised in the survey. Whether that action means forming a committee to further study an issue or making an immediate change to a procedure, employees need to know that the time they took to respond to the survey was meaningful.

■ **Use focus groups.** Not every issue will need to be solved with input from all employees. Addressing issues that affect a small number of people can be done through focus groups. Bringing together 10 to 15 people who have similar jobs for an hour or two can produce far-reaching results.

It Starts at the Top

For any internal communication program to be effective, the commitment to it must start at the top. School board members, superintendents, and other administrators must be role models in practicing effective internal communication strategies.

In the end, a strong internal communication program benefits everyone in the school district. A tremendous side benefit that often occurs after organizations bulk up their internal communication is that it helps with your external communication as well.

Information that is first communicated with staff members can easily flow to external audiences. In addition, well-informed staff members can be ambassadors and carry messages to parents and community members.

A good internal communication program also will alert school districts to growing trends, not just among employees, but in the community as well. This is particularly true among support personnel, who more often than not live in the school district in which they work.

The

BRAG SHEET

Peoria Unified School District

March 2007

Peoria Educational Enrichment Foundation Grants Awarded

Twenty-six elementary and high school teachers across the Peoria Unified School District received grants from the Peoria Educational Enrichment Foundation (PEEF), totaling $34,982. Funding for 22 educational projects in 11 instructional categories was awarded, and individual site grant amounts range from $800 to $2,500.

Sunrise Mountain's Cheryl Andress accepts her PEEF grant from PEEF president Kris Murray.

Click here to read more

Two PUSD Schools Recognized for Excellence in Education by Arizona School Board Association

Heritage Elementary School and Centennial High School were both winners of a prestigious Golden Bell award from the Arizona School Board Association (ABSA) for programs that exemplify excellence and provide leadership in curriculum development. The awards were presented at the ASBA luncheon on Dec. 14.

Click here to read more

PUSD Governing Board Elects New Officers

At the first meeting in January, the Peoria Unified School District Governing Board selected Pat Galbraith as president and Diane Douglas as clerk for the year 2007. These officers will serve until December.

Click here to read more

Pat Galbraith   Diane Douglas

Students

Three PUSD Schools Excel in Future City Competition

Frontier, Marshall Ranch and Paseo Verde elementary students participated in the tenth annual National Engineer's Future City Competition at the Phoenix Preparatory Academy and brought home three society awards.

Click here to read more

Paseo Verde's Future City team won the Environmental Engineering Design award at this year's National Engineer's Future City Competition.

PUSD Board Meetings Now Available Through Podcast and Videocast

Meetings of the Peoria Unified School District Governing Board are now available to District patrons in both podcast and videocast formats.

Staff and community members can now subscribe to an RSS (Really Simple Syndication) feed and automatically download both the podcast and videocast directly to their computers. Those not wishing to take advantage of the RSS feed can still download either file directly from the District's website, www.peoriaud.k12.az.us

Click here to read more

Spelling Bee Champ

Oasis Elementary School eighth-grader Derrick Johnson took the top spot in this year's PUSD Spelling Bee after spelling "disciples" and "pillar" correctly in the 12th round.

Students

Ironwood Standout Named Gatorade's Arizona Volleyball Player of the Year

Ironwood High School's volleyball star senior Sarah Reaves was named the 2006-07 Gatorade Arizona Girls Volleyball Player of the Year.

Click here to read more

Canyon Elementary Students Jump Rope for the Heart on Valentine's Day

Canyon Elementary kindergarten through eighth-graders, as well as special needs students from the school's Sunflower Center, celebrated Valentine's Day by jumping rope for a healthy heart. The jump-a-thon took place during each grade level's regularly scheduled physical education period from Feb. 14 to Feb. 16 on the basketball courts.

Click here to read more

Alta Loma Keeps Homefires Burning with Artist-in-Residence Performance

When Zoe Seymour and Sara Yeager wrote the docu-drama, Homefires, the purpose was to help students develop poise and enrich their ability to speak in public. What they didn't expect was how the play would encourage junior high students to consider drama as an elective in high school. Nor did they realize how the script would open the eyes of the actors to the bigger social picture of homelessness.

Click here to read more

Staff

SRP Grant Awarded to Cactus Biology Teacher

Cactus High School students are exploring the deep, blue sea in the comfort of their classroom, thanks to a $5,000 grant from Salt River Project (SRP). The students in biology teacher David Serafin's class designed and created a solar-powered fish tank for saltwater sea creatures, plants, coral and a living rock.

Click here to read more

Ironwood and Peoria High Bands Participate in BCS National Championship Pre-game Show

Marching bands from Peoria and Ironwood High School participated in the Bowl Championship Series (BCS) national championship game pre-game show at the University of Phoenix Stadium. The band members held the 100 yard long American flag during the national anthem before the Ohio State/Florida game.

Arizonan to Present at Model School Conference

Shannon Ferguson

Shannon Ferguson, elementary mathematics specialist with Peoria Unified School District (PUSD), will share her passion for math at the 15th Annual Model Schools Conference in Washington, D.C. June 29 to July 3. Ferguson is the only Arizona educator invited to present at the International Center for Leadership in Education's signature event.

Click here to read more

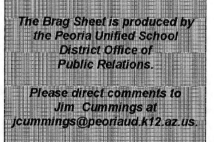

The Brag Sheet is produced by the Peoria Unified School District Office of Public Relations.

Please direct comments to Jim Cummings at jcummings@peoriaud.k12.az.us.

Jim Cummings, APR

Jim Cummings, APR, has more than 22 years' experience in school public relations. He currently serves as the director of public relations for the Peoria Unified School District in Arizona.

Before that, he worked as director of public relations for the Phoenix Union High School District in Arizona. As the sixth of seven children in a house with only one bathroom, Cummings learned early in life about the importance of internal communication and how to handle crisis and hostile people.

Cummings has presented to public relations organizations groups throughout the U.S. and is a regular presenter at the National School Public Relations Association annual Seminar.

He has served on a variety of NSPRA committees and is a past president of the Arizona School Public Relations Association. He is the winner of multiple public relations awards.

Web Pages and Electronic Communication

By Edward H. Moore, APR

The development of the World Wide Web has ushered in a new era for school communication and the people who manage school public relations programs.

Driven by rapid advances forged by commercial web sites, schools have quickly adopted online communication strategies in recent years. In an NSPRA survey of members, the majority (72%) reported recently that all of their schools maintained web sites. Only 13% said that none of their schools maintained web sites. Clearly, web sites and the online communication tactics they offer have quickly become a key communication vehicle for both school districts and individual schools.

It's little wonder. The use of the Internet to obtain information and communicate with others continues to grow among the general public. The expansion of lower cost, high-speed Internet access promises to make web communication even more important for schools. The growth of the

---

Internet to do everything from buying books to researching term papers is creating a new level of expectations that schools will have to manage. For example, people expect institutions to actively communicate online.

A survey by the Pew Internet and American Life Project, when asking about the Internet and information or services from government agencies, found that the majority of all Americans (65%) expect the Internet to offer such information. An even larger majority (82%) of actual Internet users say they expect the Internet to have such information.

Schools and the Web

So how are schools putting the web to good use? They're finding success in many different ways, often driven by the specific communication needs of the district itself. In fact, few consistencies are revealed when reviewing the web sites of school districts who've earned Awards of Excellence in NSPRA's publications and electronic media contest. The following are some recent award-winners to consider:

- Clear Creek Independent School District, League City, Texas, www.ccisd.net

- Carrollton-Farmer Branch (Texas) Independent School District, www.cfbisd.edu

- Fairfax County (Va.) Public Schools, www.fcps.edu

- Henrietta (N.Y.) Central School District, www.rhnet.org

- Hurst-Euless-Bedford (Texas) Independent School District, www.hebisd.edu

- Kingston City (N.Y.) Schools, www.kingstoncityschools.org

- Paradise Valley (Ariz.) School District, www.paradisevalleyschools.org

- Virginia Beach City (Va.) Public Schools, www.vbschools.com

- Montgomery County (Md.) Public Schools, www.montgomeryschoolsmd.org

These sites represent ways that school districts have expanded the use of the Internet and other forms of electronic communication. This chapter will provide more tips and ideas on creating an effective web site.

The Basics

While every school web site is unique, some basic components tend to be universal no matter the size of the district. The following are ideas that provide the basic content outline for a school district web site:

- **An entry portal or home page** including a brief description or statement about the district often accompanied by a brief welcoming statement and easy-to-follow links to all major content areas. Increasingly, school systems are adopting the use of audience-specific, entry portals that are designed to better target audience-specific links and information. Such audience-specific home pages might be designed, for example, for students, parents, staff, new residents, business partners, alumni, translated material for non-English speakers, and other audiences.

■ **Contact information**, including names, titles, e-mail addresses, and phone numbers for district administrative leaders, principals, board members, and other key staff

■ **Copies of recent district print and electronic publications**, including calendars, menus, key policies, and student handbooks. These can be downloaded or printed by users.

■ **Current news**, student and staff recognition items, and schedules of district events and activities

■ **Basic information and contacts for follow up on academic programs**, extracurricular activities, athletics, and other programs

■ **Key information and contacts for support services** with frequent public contact, including transportation, guidance, food services, and other areas

■ **Essential district and school information**, such as operating hours, main phone numbers, and addresses

■ **Job openings and application information**

■ **Boundary and registration information** and other information for new residents and businesses, such as real estate agencies that serve people moving into the district

■ **A site map** offering links to frequently used content

■ **Links to the sites of organizations or partners** working with the schools or district, which may include the school foundation, PTA or PTO, volunteer programs, alumni associations, and business partners

---

The Internet is becoming the platform for schools to offer a variety of communication tactics.

Your Online Options

Static web pages are just one part of how schools are using online tactics to communicate. Increasingly, the Internet is becoming the platform for schools to offer a variety of communication tactics.

The following are examples of other online tactics:

■ **E-newsletters and other electronic publications** — Schools use e-newsletters and other electronic publications to send out information regularly as well elicit feedback and drive traffic to school web pages. (See more on e-newsletters later in this chapter.) Related tactics that schools use include sending mass e-mails, posting information on listservs, and managing discussion groups.

■ **Really simple syndication** (RSS) — Some schools have begun offering RSS (See http://en.wikipedia.org/wiki/RSS for more.) feeds to send news and content to users who want it.

■ **Online video and audio on demand** allowing for instant access to school news or downloading for use later in cell phones, ipods, or other digital media players

■ **Blogs and other forums** for input and debate

■ **Blast text messaging or e-mails for rapid communication** of important information during crises or other breaking news events

■ **Wikis** — You can develop wikis (See http://en.wikipedia.org/wiki/Wikis for more.) to cover special topics or issues and to help outsiders better understand key points.

All of these tactics can also serve schools well during times of crisis or when rumors need to be squelched because they allow schools to communicate information and elicit feedback much more quickly than traditional print methods.

The web increasingly is used to deliver customer service by schools.

Online communication technology also is being used to accommodate special interest, online communities covering issues such bond initiatives and fundraising drives. These technologies can also be used to serve special audiences such as key communicators or alumni.

The web increasingly is used to deliver customer service by schools. For example, user-friendly online databases allow public users to instantly access information about things such as attendance boundaries, tax and budget data, and other information.

To help boost parent involvement and support the corresponding boosts in student achievement that usually follow, schools are finding ways to link classrooms and homes online. These secure databases, which offer parents and students real-time information, can be found as online grade books, lesson plans, course descriptions and requirements, and school policies.

Successful school web sites take advantage of the two-way nature of online communication.

But more than words and photos are being used by schools to communicate online. The explosion of MP3 players and the related advances in audio and video software now allow streaming audio and video to be made available at very low costs. Schools are finding ways to use video and audio to report on school issues and events including breaking news, athletic programs, student productions, and regular information updates.

Importantly, successful school web sites take advantage of the two-way nature of online communication and build in feedback devices to all of the web communication tactics. Click-and-send comment boxes, e-mail links, and more formal online surveys all offer school public relations practitioners an almost endless array of new tactics for collecting data and insights from audiences.

E-Newsletters and Other E-Publications

While web sites often wait for people to find them, school districts and even individual schools are going out to find readers by communicating with e-newsletters and other online e-publications.

When beginning, communication programs often are best served when things are kept simple. In that spirit, electronic newsletters, often called e-newsletters, should be formatted much like a standard e-mail.

Much like office and personal e-mail, e-publications are a way to get electronic messages to many people quickly and efficiently. They can be overwhelmingly complex or incredibly simple. But in the end, they are little more than e-mail.

Unlike traditional print newsletters, however, e-newsletters offer the following advantages:

- Recipients can quickly forward the e-newsletter to other interested people with whom they'd like to share your news.

- The e-newsletter can include links to more detailed information where other sites of interest help readers better understand the story.

- The e-newsletter can help schools evaluate their communication program and help them collect feedback from readers.

In short, unlike the stagnant presentation offered by print publications, e-publications offer school communicators many opportunities to be interactive with audiences and engage in conversations rather than simply deliver a one-way message.

All of the glitz in the world is worthless without strong content and dependable delivery.

Despite these advantages over traditional print publications, however, it's important to remember that you should still follow many of the rules used in developing successful print publications when you develop e-publications. Technology is great — but all of the glitz in the world is worthless without strong content and dependable delivery.

Along with content, design matters, too. Accommodating designs, which attract readers and ease reading, are the necessary ingredient for fostering strong readability and readership.

And finally, as with print publications, deliverability is key. How well e-publishing technology works in delivering school e-publications is crucial to e-publishing success.

After all, if even a few people don't get a school district's e-newsletters — or can't view them if they do get them — then the dividends from all of the effort and money invested have been diminished. Undelivered e-mails are the e-publishing equivalent of having boxes of print

newsletters end up in the dead-letter office.

Choosing the wrong technology or failing to foster good list management for e-publications are two key items too often overlooked in the rush to establish e-publishing programs. It's clear that the hurdles to adding e-publishing options to an established print program can be daunting. So if a school district has a successful print publishing program in place, why should it consider migrating to e-publishing?

Savings in costs and time are clear. The benefits can be quickly quantified. But often schools are reluctant to jump onto the e-publishing bandwagon despite the obvious advantages. The following are questions to consider when developing an e-newsletter:

■ Will our audiences have access to computers to receive our newsletters?

■ Do enough people in our community have high-speed Internet access, making easy access to our newsletters available?

■ Can we make our material unique enough to stand out from the avalanche of spam and other unwanted e-mail that clutters many e-mail boxes?

Obviously, school districts want to do some basic research in their schools and communities to try to answer these questions. However, it's important to note that personal computer usage and high-speed Internet access have been growing tremendously in most communities throughout North America.

Many early-adopting schools found initial acceptance of e-publishing by parents and others to be significantly higher than they anticipated.

In its work with school districts while conducting communication audits, the National School Public Relations Association (NSPRA) has interviewed a number of school superintendents and communication professionals who reported having been surprised to find a high level of acceptability for e-publications in their communities.

Often these districts tread slowly into e-publishing, fearing that a lack of personal computer or Internet access in homes throughout the community would create an appearance of exclusivity or a "have's-and-have-not's" environment for e-newsletter readership. School communication traditionally has been inclusive, and any move that might seem to exclude some of the population would appear to be undesirable.

But in fact, many early-adopting schools found initial acceptance of e-publishing by parents and others to be significantly higher than they anticipated. Often, school communicators were surprised — and delighted — to find that parents were more likely to read e-publications than some traditional print publications.

One key reason is that many in the community would access e-publications while at work where they have ready access to personal computers and high-speed Internet access.

While traditional print publications often are seen as "products" that parents would "use" in their homes, e-newsletters and other e-publications are more likely to be viewed as "resources" that audiences will "access" at home or work.

This opens up exciting new communication opportunities for school districts, giving schools the ability to reach parents at times when traditionally they could not be contacted.

The anecdotal observations made during NSPRA communication audits help to illustrate other data compiled by the Pew Internet and American Life Project. Pew found that only 30% of those surveyed access the Internet only from home. The rest access it from a combination of home, work, and other sites.

People expect schools to use the latest communication technology to reach them.

Ongoing tracking by Pew also supports the case of using e-mail in e-publishing programs. When tracking what people are doing when accessing the Internet, Pew found that the overwhelming majority (91%) are accessing e-mail.

Many other top Internet activities relate to finding facts or answering questions — clear indications that the medium has become a prime source for those seeking insights and information.

Growing evidence exists that people expect schools to use the latest communication technology to reach them. Increasingly, parents and others in the community are being conditioned by businesses and other organizations to expect prompt communication through e-mail and other sources.

As banks, credit card companies, online merchants and many branches of government go online with instant access to information, people naturally extend this expectation of rapid communication to their schools and school districts.

In other words, the day quickly appears to be coming when it won't be a question of whether or not schools should adopt e-publishing programs. Rather, lagging schools will find aggrieved audiences demanding greater access and quicker response through e-communication.

Design and copy on the web need to work together to guide visitors to quickly find and understand key messages.

Success: Good Design and Content

Clearly, success for online communication by schools depends on offering content that works, and this means creating both good online designs and copy. Similar to what makes good print publications work, design and copy on the web need to work together to guide visitors to quickly find and understand key messages. Design and copy also work together to help users quickly decide what content to read or skim, based on their personal information needs. Design and copy should work together to help build credibility for the site as a reliable source of good information.

The moral in this mix is that both design and copy are crucial. Great copy presented poorly or a great design filled with weak copy will undercut the site's ability to communicate well. The way in which the design presents its copy and illustrations helps create a directional "flow" for users.

So what's the difference between designing for print and designing for the screen?

While many design components (headlines, subheads, photographs, and color as examples) are used in both print and screen design, the guidelines for using such devices are not always the same. For example, the smaller "page" space offered by typical computer screens means online designs may need to be "shorter" than print designs for the same content. The act of scrolling by users on web sites and e-newsletters (moving a page both up and down and from side to side) creates a very different set of positioning needs than those faced when creating a static print page.

Web pages, e-newsletters, online publications, and other screen-based tactics do offer school communicators the chance to better divide information and messages into attractive, "bite-sized bits" of information. Using links well are key. Links give readers the option to access the information only if they feel they need to and only when they want to. Links can be created to open new pages on the screen by retrieving information stored on other pages.

Navigation — or helping users find their way through your labyrinth of online pages — is also an important part of good design. A successful web site should always incorporate design components that make it clear to users how they can return to a previous page or main starting point. The goal is to not allow users to get the feeling that they're lost within your site.

To judge how well your site helps users find information, consider using focus groups of typical web users. Let them tell you about their experiences when trying to locate information on your site. You may also ask participants to search for a specific point of information on your web site during the focus group. Watch as they do and look for clues as to how quickly they did — or did not — find what they were after.

Time-pressured parents and others will quickly delete your e-mail if it doesn't get to the point.

Writing Copy for Online Readers

Just as good copy builds readership of print publications, clear and to-the-point copy will ensure readership of online media.

Remember, it takes only a click of a mouse to instantly delete an e-newsletter or move on to a different web site. Time-pressured parents and others will quickly delete your e-mail if it doesn't get to the point.

Successful e-communication often results from:

■ Providing only information that parents want and need and, in the process, clearly indicating that the e-communication respects their time

■ Using words and creating copy structures that recipients will be comfortable with

Consider that the effort parents will make to open and read an e-communication is in direct proportion to the personal benefit they identify in it. As the writer of online copy, you must determine how to best drive this effort/benefit relationship. To increase readership of your e-newsletter, consider the following:

■ Boost the personal benefit that copy offers parents

■ Decrease the amount of effort it takes to open and read the copy in your e-publication

■ Ideally, find ways in which to do both

Smaller words in short sentences communicate better. Creating copy that people find interesting and comfortable to read relies on choosing the right words and putting them to work in an appropriate combination of short- and medium-length sentences.

Why?

Generally, ease of reading is determined by familiarity with most of the words being used and the structure in which they're presented.

It's a simple formula. But this doesn't mean that as a copywriter, you should shy away from all larger words and long sentences. But, it does mean that overall, you must monitor your word choice and sentence length to make sure you are consistently producing reader-friendly copy.

Long sentences and unfamiliar words lose readers and damage the effectiveness of any e-communication. No matter how impressive it may seem or sound, puffed-up copy that nobody reads is worthless. Keep it simple and short.

Editing for Effectiveness

Editing also is key to producing reader-friendly copy. Many writers focus too much on getting copy right on the first draft. That's tough to do. Generally, first drafts will get all the facts in, but the copy itself will be overloaded with poor word choices, including jargon. To boost the reading ease of your copy, look for the following things when you edit.

Limit passive voice

Passive voice verbs (any form of the verb "to be" + a verb's past participle) can add emphasis and variety to your copy. But passive voice is frequently overused in educational writing. Using the passive voice too much creates dull and dreary copy, resulting in longer sentences that actually make copy more difficult to read. For action-packed, readable copy, rewrite your sentences so that you make your verbs active, not passive. For example, rewrite *The Outstanding Teacher of the Year Scholarship was presented to Pat Jones yesterday* to *Pat Jones won the Outstanding Teacher of the Year Scholarship yesterday.*

The passive sentence takes 13 words to make its point and the activity in the sentence centers on the thing (*the scholarship*) and not on the person (*Pat*). The revision uses only 11 words — a significant 15% cut in the number of words and it focuses the action on the person.

Feeble verbs are another sign of weak copy. Good copy depends on strong, active verbs to create a sense or motion for readers, maintaining their interest and sense of accomplishment.

Short, punchy verbs communicate a clear, specific action.

Pick strong verbs

Verbs can lose impact when writers, often unknowingly, convert them and use them as nouns. Here are some examples:

Instead of:	The superintendent made a suggestion that we change boundaries.
Consider:	The superintendent suggested that we change boundaries.

Instead of:	The board's report gave an explanation for the test-score declines.
Consider:	The board's report explained the test-score declines.

Be explicit

Sometimes in the interest of political correctness or perhaps as the result of dealing with the language of bureaucracy, many writers often lose the ability to create clear, inspiring copy. The result is dense, fuzzy copy that fails to prompt a clear action from those who read it. Ask for specific actions whenever possible.

Remember, unlike print publications which may be kept for future reference, online communications are more prone to immediate deletion or are a click away from losing the reader. Ask for what you want and give readers a deadline for action. Here are some examples:

Instead of:	Parents should make it a high priority to read the new testing report which can be found on the school's web site.
Consider:	Parents can read highlights from this important new testing report now by clicking here. Read the full report now by clicking here.

Instead of:	Each student should schedule a meeting with his or her guidance counselor soon.
Consider:	For the best chances of getting the most college aid available, all juniors should schedule meetings with their guidance counselors before October 15. Stop by the guidance office, call us at 555-1234, or e-mail us at guide@yourschool.com.

Cut unnecessary words

Look for unnecessary words when editing. Most can easily be deleted or rewritten to shorten sentences and remove unusual words and phrases.

Check the beginning of sentences for the phrases "There is" or "There are" and delete them. Here are some examples:

Instead of:	There are 40 students who won scholarships.
Consider:	Forty students won scholarships.
Instead of:	There is a no person who is better at teaching than Mary.
Consider:	No one teaches better than Mary.

Look for extra words lurking in prepositional phrases. Here are some examples:

Instead of:	She is the conductor of the student choir.
Consider:	She conducts the student choir.
Instead of:	He is the winner of the state speech championship.
Consider:	He won the state speech championship.

Look for redundancies and multi-word combinations that simply repeat what one word could do. Here are some examples:

Instead of:	Cancel out
Consider:	Cancel
Instead of:	Revert back
Consider:	Revert
Instead of:	New innovation
Consider:	Innovation
Instead of:	Past history
Consider:	History
Instead of:	8 a.m. this morning
Consider:	8 a.m.

Content Guidelines

Guidelines on content — what can and can't be used on school web sites and other online products — remain an issue for many school districts. Just as web sites vary from district to district, rules about content also vary greatly.

One thing is common, however: a school district should have a guiding policy on what is and is not acceptable for online content. Because of privacy issues, such policies may prevent using any names on web sites unless the district has a signed release from a parent or guardian for students, or from a staff member or other individual for adults. Some school systems forbid listing student last names in many circumstances.

Identify best practices in your region to guide content development.

Contact information presents another dilemma. Many school web sites list employee e-mail addresses or phone numbers. It makes for good customer service, as parents and others can contact teachers and staff directly. But other school web sites list only general district or school e-mail addresses to protect staff from unwanted e-mail. Personal addresses and phone numbers and such generally aren't offered in any circumstances.

Photographs can present another predicament for school web sites. Some school systems suggest using no photos if any students can be identified. Others restrict photo use to only older children. In almost all cases, school systems secure a signed release before using anyone's image.

Check with neighboring districts to see the types of policies and releases being used for their online offerings. Since both privacy and freedom of information requirements can vary from state to state, it's best to identify best practices in your region to guide content development.

Evaluating Online Communication

So what does "successful" online communication look like?

Attracting visitors who quickly find what they want might be one description. Web sites have traditionally used traffic counts as a measure of success. But as sophistication in online communication assessment has grown, linking traffic to success in delivering information or sparking a behavior has become the more common measurement standard.

While such measurement might seem easier for businesses, widgets, or books, schools too have any number of metrics they can use to help evaluate web investments. Consider one such effort undertaken by the Montgomery County (Md.) Public Schools (MCPS), which earned an NSPRA Gold Medallion Award. Details of the MCPS Web Site Communication Project are included on the next page:

The MCPS Web Site Communication Project

Strategic Goal

Improve communication to school system core audiences.

Assessment

MCPS conducted a variety of assessments to define its approach to publishing web content and to benchmark best practices, measure customer satisfaction and expose obstacles to publishing. These assessments included the following:

■ **Home page content analysis.** The home page was deconstructed by content type to determine the percentage of page space dedicated to specific content types such as refreshed content, navigation, branding and promotion

■ **Comparative analysis.** A comparative analysis of school system web sites was conducted to assess how other systems use their home pages, how much content they publish and how often, how they structure their sites, and what information they make available.

■ **Site visitor survey.** Web site visitors were invited to grade the site for its content value, navigation, ease of use, and other aspects. At least 75% of the survey respondents were from three critical audiences (students, parents, and staff) and results were used as a benchmark against results of a post-new site survey.

■ **Site metrics.** Site traffic metrics were analyzed over time to determine the role web communication and publishing plays in system communication

■ **Webmaster survey.** The 750 webmasters/publishers in MCPS were asked to complete a survey to clarify their needs and to identify obstacles in their web communication

Assessments Revealed

The assessments revealed the following conclusions:

■ MCPS was not updating its home page often enough and had little room on its home page for refreshed content. Other systems were publishing more content, more often.

■ Content for the three critical target audiences (students, parents, and staff) was not easy to find and "tab" pages for those audiences were infrequently updated.

■ Site navigation and structure were confusing to visitors.

■ Both internal and external stakeholders increasingly relied on the web for information about MCPS.

■ Webmasters needed help with site and content structure and had little time for web work.

Tactical Goals

Using information from the assessments, the following tactical goals were developed:

■ Increase and more frequently update the content on the home page and "tab" pages for students, parents, staff, and community

■ Develop and implement a web page template for all non-school sites to improve site consistency and relieve webmasters from having to design their own site structure

■ Develop and implement communication, training, and support plans to assist MCPS webmasters in using the new template and improving their site content

■ Strengthen MCPS branding using the new template

■ Improve site accessibility by meeting Level 1 508 compliance requirements in the template

Performance Goals

The following performance goals were developed to measure progress:

■ Increase site traffic (at least 10%) in first year of template

■ Improve site visitor satisfaction (grade of B or better from 80% of visitors)

■ Migrate non-school sites/pages to template (20% in first year)

Planning

A three-year plan was developed to transition the site from a collection of more than 500 unstructured, non-standardized "mini-sites" (school and office web sites) to sites adhering to a consistent structure.

A year-one project plan was developed to upgrade the home page and create and deploy a site template for all non-school web sites and pages. A series of presentations about the current and desired state of the web site were made to key leadership and stakeholder groups to gather input and foster discussion. The department of communication and web services team created an editorial and production plan to support weekly updates to the home page and three "tab" pages for students, parents, staff, and community.

A training and communication plan was created and implemented to support webmasters and assist them in improving their site content and migrating their sites to the template over a 2-year period.

Communication

A communication plan was developed to explain the improvement plan to key leadership groups and customers such as webmasters. Webmasters could discuss the plan in an online forum called the "Webmasters' Conference" and the web services team used a targeted e-mail distribution list to alert them to developments.

A promotional campaign tied to the launch of the new home page and template included a press release, articles in system newsletters and a letter from the chief information officer on the web site. A new "marketing" web address — www.montgomeryschoolsmd.org — was launched later in the year.

To support webmasters, the web services team improved its web site to include documents about the new site, a sample site in the template, and worksheets webmasters can use to improve their web content and sites. Training sessions were held to teach webmasters to use the new template.

Evaluation

The new home page, "tab pages," and site template launched in March 2003 and post assessments were conducted throughout the year to gauge impact and effectiveness. Post assessments showed the following progress toward the tactical goals:

■ Home page content is updated at least once a week — frequently more often — and "tab"

■ pages for students, parents, staff and community are updated weekly. Deconstruction of the new home page showed a three-fold improvement in space for refreshed content.

■ The new site template has been deployed on all high level pages. Seven high-level "office sites" are in the template and four are in planning stages.

■ Webmasters rely on the webmasters' conference for communication and collaboration and receive targeted e-mails from web services about site developments.

■ Strong MCPS branding was built into the header banner of the new template, ensuring consistent system branding at the top of every MCPS web page in the template.

The post assessment also showed the progress on the performance goals:

■ Site traffic grew by at least 80% in critical metrics (views, visits and visitors) in the first year of the new home page and template

■ Grades from site visitors improved in all categories. The most dramatic improvements were in content value, content freshness and navigation

■ All high level pages have migrated to the new template, seven high-level office sites have migrated and four others are underway.

Edward H. Moore, APR

Edward H. Moore, APR, is an associate professor of public relations and advertising at Rowan University and a former associate director of NSPRA.

Moore started his career as a school public relations practitioner and has served more than 25 years as a communication executive and counselor, as well as a journalist and educator. He's worked with a wide variety of educational, corporate, and non-profit organizations in the U.S., Canada, Europe, and Asia.

Moore has taught public relations for more than 20 years, at the George Washington University and at Rowan University. He has written and presented extensively on communication issues and served six years as managing editor of *Communication Briefings*.

External Communication

By Tom Salter

While it may not be my fault that my school district has a bad reputation, it is my responsibility to try to change it. And while I may not be the reason my school district is revered and admired, I know that unless I work to keep the sterling polished, it will become dull and tarnished.

Schools are complicated microcosms of the communities we serve. The good and the bad of our society are reflected in the halls, teachers' lounges, and cafeterias of public schools.

While most practitioners recognize that internal communication is the first priority, external communication can be the most difficult. External audiences may or may not have a direct link to a school and, more than likely, do not regularly think about what is happening in your schools. The challenge in communicating with external audiences is to get and keep their attention.

Keep these few things to in mind when communicating with external publics:

■ There are more people in your community without school aged-children than there are with them. In most communities, 70% to 80% of residents don't have a child in the school district.

■ People with no direct link to your district usually must be given a reason to care about schools.

■ Often, what those without direct ties think about your schools is based on what they hear from your internal publics.

■ Technology is a great tool to reach external publics, but it has its limitations.

■ Test scores and student performance are important, but so is safety. It is critical for external publics to understand that your district cares about its students and the community as a whole.

Key Communicators

Human beings tell stories to help their world make sense. From the time Ugg the caveman first looked at the stars and wondered what they were, we have concocted explanations to questions that we can't answer. If no obvious rationale exists for something, we have a tendency to make up an explanation. For example,

if a district resident does not understand the reason for a school tax increase, the resident might offer his or her own explanation. Without a trusted source of information, it is easy for external publics to create explanations that fit their perspective, but may not be close to the truth. The district now has the challenge of countering inaccurate information and attempting to communicate the accurate message to a residents who has created their own message.

If you take care of your key communicators, they will take care of you when you need them.

Getting someone to adapt to a new belief system or perspective is not easy. In his *Theory of Cognitive Dissonance,* Leon Festinger tells us that human beings are uncomfortable when they are asked to behave in new ways. When pushed to change, people often resist the change and hang onto things that are familiar and comfortable.

People are more likely to change their minds when someone they know and trust provides the information. That means you need to be trusted by the opinion leaders in your community and they, in turn, must deliver your message to the people who trust them.

The hard part is identifying the opinion that leaders you need to reach, identifying (and cataloguing) the best ways to reach each of them, and setting up a system to deliver messages. Once those things are done, you simply have to craft the messages you want to send and listen for feedback.

Each of your publics is interested in public education for a different reason. The key to effective communication is to know which group cares about which issue and to use that issue to "push their button" and get them to act. You must then listen to their reactions and adjust your message to ensure your work is effective and efficient.

There are literally thousands of different external publics. Each one has a different structure and leadership. There are preferred and effective ways to communicate with each external public.

The first thing to consider is which external publics are the most important to your schools. The following are examples of major external audiences to consider:

- **Media.** The media are both an external public and communication tool. Information shared with the media usually gets transferred to another public. Nonetheless, it is critical to have solid relationships established with the reporters who cover your school district. Communicating through the media can be effective, but it should not be the only way to communicate with external publics.

- **Senior citizens.** Senior citizens today are more informed, more mobile and have more income than ever before and they vote. If you want to pass a tax increase in your area, you had

best spend some time courting this important group. If you want to improve your reputation, find ways to involve them in your schools.

- **Local business owners and workers.** Consider the number of people that a store clerk, cab driver, or hair stylist see and talk to every day. When the subject of public education comes up in community conversations, it is helpful to have local business owners and workers well informed about what is happening in your schools. Uninformed comments can seriously damage the reputation of your school district.

- **Religious leaders.** Religious leaders in your community have influence with people who attend their church, synagogue, or mosque. You must make sure these important stakeholders are "in the loop." Remember, some of them likely have their own schools and may be your competitors.

- **Real estate agents.** It's easier for a real estate agent to sell a house in a school district with a solid reputation. When real estate agents are informed about your school district, they are better able to answer their client's questions. Positive relationships with real estate agents can be a win-win situation — they will sell houses and you will have new residents with a better understanding of your district.

You can subdivide each of these groups into small sub-groups. For example, messages targeted at owners of small businesses may be different from those for corporate leaders. There may also be different ways to effectively reach each sub-group.

Using your list of key communicators

Identifying individuals from key external publics is the first step in establishing a key communicator network. Once you have collected contact information for your key communicators, the next step is to plan how to use this list. A key communicator network works best when members of the network are well informed with information they can use.

One often overlooked aspect of a key communicator network is the need to listen to them frequently. Make sure you give them a specially designated e-mail address that can be used to send questions and receive prompt answers. Other strategies to listen to key communicators include sending them occasional surveys to get their feedback on issues and inviting them to have lunch with the superintendent to share their perspective on issues.

Be careful not to overload your groups with too much work and information. If you overwork them, you may be added to their junk e-mail file. If you take care of your key communicators, they will take care of you when you need them.

For more information on implementing a key communicator network, see NSPRA's publication, *A Guidebook for Opinion Leader/Key Communicator Programs*.

Communicating with External Publics

There are a variety of ways to effectively communicate with external publics. The following are strategies to consider when communicating with external publics and establishing relationships with residents without children in the schools:

■ **Print or electronic newsletters.** A newsletter targeted at external publics is a way to regularly share information. It is an example of communicating directly to external publics rather than through the media.

■ **Conduct "See for Yourself" events and other activities to get residents into the schools.** Residents without children in school do not have reasons to visit schools regularly. These events allow residents to come into schools and see what is happening.

■ **Make communication an ongoing activity.** Communication with all publics — especially external publics — should be ongoing rather than done only when a school finance election occurs. Residents need an ongoing flow of information to build trust in the schools.

■ **Encourage participation in adult learning activities.** Most school districts conduct community education or other adult learning classes. Encourage participation in these classes as a way to get residents into the schools. In addition, encourage district teachers and other staff members to teach these classes to make further connections with residents.

■ **Distribute school and district publications in community locations.** Print a few extra newsletters and district publications and distribute them to local businesses and agencies. These publications can be a great source of information in the waiting areas for barber shops, car repair shops, and dentist and doctor offices.

■ **Place school and district information in community publications.** Seek permission from local churches, businesses, chambers of commerce, and other community organizations to place brief information items in their printed publications.

■ **Meet with existing community organizations.** Develop a schedule to make regular presentations to local organizations such as Rotary clubs, homeowner associations, and business organizations.

■ **Display school and district information at community festivals.** Schedule school board members and administrators to hand out information about the district at community festivals and activities. These events are great opportunities to connect with residents and have them meet key people in the district.

■ **Schedule conversations with district leaders at local restaurants.** Rather than waiting for residents to come to the schools, schedule small conversations with residents at local restaurants. The superintendent, school board members, or principals can make visits to cafes, coffee shops, and restaurants to connect with residents.

■ **Provide free or half-price passes for school events to senior citizens.** Distribute cards or tickets to senior citizens for free or half-price entrance into school events such as athletic events, theater productions, and concerts.

■ **Organize advisory groups of residents.** Residents without children in the schools still have a great deal to contribute to the operation of the schools. Organize advisory groups of senior citizens, business representatives, or empty-nester parents to get their input on district decisions and share information with them.

Dealing with Difficult People

Robert Kennedy once said that 20% of the people are against everything all the time. He may have been optimistic. Every district has a few parents that are continually complaining about something in the schools. These people may be well meaning, but are often disruptive to the overall process. Some are seeking media attention for their perspective and others are seeking to disrupt the process or meeting. In many cases, these people are seeking to make life more challenging for the district.

Dealing with difficult people is, well, difficult, and can lead to a great deal of bad publicity. Consider these strategies when dealing with difficult constituents:

■ When someone confronts you with a problem, **your first duty is to listen** and sometimes, that is easier said than done. It is critical to stay focused on what is being said and not jump to a conclusion or solution before you understand the full issue.

■ While listening, **remember that everyone is entitled to an opinion and respect for that opinion.** Try to keep an open mind. If you start with the perception this person is misguided, you may miss an important point that could have merit.

■ **Watch your body language and look at the person while he or she is speaking.** Take a note or two if needed, but give the person the respect of looking at them. Don't sit with your arms crossed; that usually indicates you are not interested in what they are saying. Use good posture; keep your shoulders square and your body relaxed.

■ **Make sure you state your own feelings and opinions frankly, but calmly.** Never raise your voice. The louder they yell, the softer you should respond.

■ **Don't try to win or engage the person in an argument.** Keep the discussion focused on solving the problem at hand. The goal is to solve this person's problem.

■ **Keep the discussion on a positive plane.** Don't bring up anything that is intended to hurt the other person's feelings or criticize him or her. If you do, you risk creating an enemy and causing irreparable harm.

■ As the discussion nears its end, **restate the important points the other person brought up.** This shows you were listening, and that you understand the problem. It also gives your complainer the opportunity to clear up any miscommunication.

■ **If there is something you can do to solve the problem, promise action, and then deliver.** If there is nothing you can do, be honest. The worst thing you can do is promise satisfaction and then do nothing.

It is important for anyone who has contact with the community to have some level of customer service and public relations training.

Many people are just mad and need someone to listen to their complaints. If you listen attentively and don't do anything to increase their anger, these people frequently will be satisfied that they told somebody their problem and that will be the end of it. However, if you take it personally and push back, you are likely to create a much greater problem.

There is a reason the squeaky wheel gets the grease. The sound is intensely annoying and that alone is motivation for those of us who must listen to it to fix it. Likewise, if a squeaky wheel isn't repaired, it eventually will cause additional problems. Don't back down from what you know is best for children, but listen to others politely and when possible, help them solve their problems.

Kennedy's perception may be accurate. There are some people who you will never satisfy, but do the best you can. Never attack them personally and always take the high road. Acknowledge their right to their opinion and explain calmly why you disagree. Always remember that your decisions should be based on what is right for children, not on what is politically expedient.

Preventing Complaints

One of the best ways to deal with difficult people and complaints is preventing them from occurring in the first place. When school employees understand the value and importance of treating others with respect, it is much easier to anticipate that complaints and difficult situations would be lessened. Preventing complaints and difficult situations can be achieved through training all employees in customer service.

Quality customer service has long been recognized as a necessity in the business world. Taco Bell estimates the average customer will spend $17,000 at its restaurants over the course of a lifetime. If you go to a manager of a Taco Bell with a complaint, how do you think the manager will respond? Will the manager suggest that the customer go to another restaurant? Not likely. The manager knows that keeping the customer happy means another $16,994 will be spent in Taco Bell restaurants. The manager will do what it takes to solve your problem.

It is important for anyone who has contact with the community to have some level of customer service and public relations training. That means everyone in your school system, from the part-time bus driver to the superintendent. All employees in a school district have a role as complaint managers and must strive to deliver quality customer service.

Use Common Sense

While training in customer service for all employees goes a long way in serving external publics, consider several common sense ideas:

■ Understand that your attitude and actions in handling the complaint can have a lasting effect on the reputation of the school district.

■ Offer an apology if appropriate, even if you didn't cause the problem.

■ Have a friendly attitude.

■ Solve the problem and explain why you can't solve the problem.

■ Follow-up to ensure the situation was resolved.

■ No matter how trivial the issue seems to you, it is a big deal to the person with the complaint.

■ Restate the problem in your own words.

■ Tell the person exactly what you plan to do to help them solve the problem.

■ Don't make promises you can't or don't intend to keep.

Good customer service is best summed up in a phrase that has been around for a very long time: **Do unto others as you would have them do unto you.**

It's that simple. How would you want to be treated if you had a complaint about your child's school?

It is up to you to make sure your employees offer good customer service. If they don't, your system will suffer and it will be almost impossible to accomplish the goals you have set. If you invest the resources in the necessary training, community support will grow. Parents and community members will find it a joy to visit your schools. And those with complaints will think your school system is caring and wonderful.

Final Thoughts

When you are communicating with external publics, remember you are not communicating with rocket scientists. You should always write on a 9th or 10th grade level when you are sending out information to external publics. When you are working with a specific group, like Realtors, you can use terms that are common to their area of expertise, but generally, keep things simple.

One of the problems we have in public schools today is that people get their news about schools second-hand. A very small percentage of your community members actually visit your schools. Look for ways to invite the community in so they can see that teaching and learning is going on and that children are learning.

Remember, the media is not an effective way to get your message out. It is unreliable, and the message it conveys is seldom the one you needed it to be. Find other ways to communicate your messages directly to your external publics.

◼ Tom Salter

Tom Salter discovered the joy of communicating at an early age, breaking all records for detentions given for talking in class at his elementary school. After graduation from college, a potentially brilliant career in professional theatre was cut short when Salter discovered the importance of little things, like paying for food and rent.

Salter exploited his oratorical skills for 14 years as a broadcaster, primarily in radio. For more than a decade he has worked for children as a public relations practitioner for schools in Mobile, Alabama, the Alabama Department of Education, and as a presenter and consultant for districts and associations around the country. He is a frequent presenter at NSPRA seminars and on NSPRA Power Hours.

Salter is the primary author of NSPRA's *Guidebook for Opinion Leader/Key Communicator Programs* and a past president of the Alabama School Communicators Association.

He currently serves as the senior communication manager for the Montgomery County (Alabama) School District.

Crisis Communication and Management

By Rick J. Kaufman, APR

Communities expect schools to be safe and secure for students and staff. Unfortunately, schools across the country may be touched by a crisis of some kind at any time. Crises and emergencies can happen suddenly and frequently without warning.

The threats facing schools in today's society are broader than ever before — from natural disasters to infectious diseases to terrorism to misguided students and adults who commit random acts of violence. While schools remain among the safest places for children, the tragic events of natural disasters and high-profile school shootings are horrific and chilling for communities and families.

Knowing what to do when faced with a crisis can be the difference between chaos and calm, or even life and death.

Other emergencies may affect a community and, thus inevitably, involve schools. In a crisis affecting a community, schools may be part of a network to assist in delivering public health services, such as serving as a shelter or providing buses to transport injured or evacuate endangered children and families. It may not seem like a school's responsibility, but schools are likely to be involved in the larger community's emergency response.

School emergency manuals and crisis plans once were typically limited to inclement weather, natural disasters, or the unfortunate accidental death of a student or staff member. Preparedness meant identifying shelters, understanding safety procedures, and conducting the required number of drills. That is no longer enough. While many schools today have developed and maintained emergency response plans, far too many are either outdated or fail to address emerging threats and contingencies.

Prepare for a Crisis

Knowing what to do when faced with a crisis can be the difference between chaos and calm, or even life and death. The first step in preparation is to accept that a wide range of emergencies can happen anywhere.

The second step is to complete a risk assessment to prioritize school response to various emergencies.

> **To be effective, a crisis management plan must include the best thinking and practices of all agencies that need to collaborate.**

Schools and district buildings need to plan for:

■ Intruders

■ Explosions

■ Weather-related issues

■ School bus accidents

■ Gas leaks

■ Exposure to hazardous materials

Additionally, critical incidents such as civil disobediences, epidemics, and biological and radiological attacks must also be a part of any plan, as well as updated steps for evacuating and relocating students and staff in a crisis.

To be effective, a crisis management plan must include the best thinking and practices of all agencies that need to collaborate — and cooperate — in an emerging situation. Establishing partnerships with public safety agencies, including law enforcement, fire, health, mental health, and specialized emergency services trained in biological, chemical and radiological events, is crucial in the development, oversight, and management of crisis plans.

Establishing personal relationships with key people in local response organizations is also very important. Police, fire, and emergency responders, among others, have very different operating cultures and vocabularies, and do not necessarily understand, trust or establish rapport easily with school personnel. Developing relationships in crisis preparation and planning — and not during a crisis — make it easier to act confidently and quickly when confronting an emergency.

To be effective, a crisis management plan must include the best thinking and practices of all agencies that need to collaborate — and cooperate — in an emerging situation.

Develop the Plan

There are too many potential scenarios to develop contingency plans for every known or as yet unknown scenario. The responses may be so detailed that school staff is unlikely to remember all that is expected of them in a crisis. Instead, a crisis management plan should focus on what schools must be ready to do in response to an emergency as opposed to identifying all of the sources of threat. In other words, the number of possible responses is much less than the number of potential disasters that would require response.

So how do schools prepare for a crisis?

The best preparation is to be ready to make decisions necessary to ensure that all students and staff are safe and protected. To do this, schools need to develop response systems, which are conceptual in nature, but address the following issues:

■ What is the "command" structure for responding to a crisis?

■ Who should lead the crisis response in a particular school or building?

■ How will school staff be organized for different crisis responsibilities?

■ What is the communication process during a crisis?

Any school district's crisis management plan has four critical components and should include the following:

■ **Prevention and intervention.** Addresses what schools and districts can do to reduce or eliminate risk to life and property

■ **Preparedness.** Focuses on the process of planning a rapid, coordinated, and effective response to a crisis

■ **Response.** Focuses on the steps to take during a crisis

■ **Recovery.** Deals with how to restore the learning and teaching environment after a crisis

It is also important to note that each school and district building must have a plan that reflects its special needs. One of the best resources available to schools and school districts in developing or updating their emergency preparedness plan is NSPRA's *The Complete Crisis Communication Management Manual for Schools.*

A crisis management plan must be efficiently organized so it is easy to use.

Organize Your Crisis Plan

A crisis management plan must be efficiently organized so it is easy to use. The following are three sections for organizing a crisis plan or manual:

■ **Approach to crisis management.** This section is designed to help school staff become familiar with the general crisis response structures used in the district, as well as give personnel general guidelines for district crisis preparation and response.

This section should detail the district's crisis response system, district and building crisis teams and responsibilities, alert procedures, how to identify and assess a crisis,

initial steps to managing a crisis, how to establish communication protocols, and crisis recovery.

■ **Guidelines for responding to specific crisis situations.** This section provides an overview of some specific crisis situations and has basic checklists of important actions. This section is usually a good reference for creating individual building response plans and may include situational overviews, response and recovery checklists, and other critical information on a variety of potential crises.

■ **Resources.** This section addresses information about crisis support, counseling, recovery, and other aspects of post-crisis intervention.

It should provide a general reference guide for dealing with the emotional trauma surrounding a crisis and templates for communication, training tools, handouts, forms, and other useful information for building crisis response teams and plans.

Any plan must be fluid. Plans must be living documents that are constantly updated, regularly trained and drilled, and communicated to students, staff, parents, and the community.

Communication is the foundation of any crisis planning, implementation, management, and recovery effort.

Understand the Role of Communication

Communication is the foundation of any crisis planning, implementation, management, and recovery effort. The best time to let students, staff, and families know what to do in an emergency is before it happens. But when a crisis hits, these same audiences and others expect the school and district to release accurate and timely information in a crisis. Emergency preparedness plans must account for multiple ways to disseminate information throughout the crisis. Parents need to know what their children's school emergency plan is and how to react to it.

Effective communication will instill confidence that the district is doing everything possible to address the situation and prevent a similar tragedy from occurring again. Leaders often lose the confidence of their communities — not because of the crisis — but because of how they responded to it. One misspoken phrase or uncorroborated piece of information about a crisis is often replayed over and over again by local and national media.

In any crisis, it is important to tell the truth, even if it may damage the district's reputation. Tell the truth and, in the same breath, tell what the district is doing to fix the problem. Once credibility is lost, there is little chance of bringing people together to resolve the problem. News media will find the truth — one way or another. They will talk to students, parents, staff, law enforcement, and others to get the story.

Structure Your Crisis Communication Plan

A good crisis communication and management plan contains a solid framework to direct school district decisions and response strategies. The organizational structure may vary depending on the type of crisis, but you should consider some essential roles. If possible, designate one person to be in charge of each area of responsibility.

Here are components of an effective crisis communication structure:

■ **Spokesperson and crisis communication team leader.** In a crisis or emergency, schools need a sympathetic and authoritative spokesperson to reassure the public that school and district leaders are handling the event in an aggressive and appropriate fashion. Designate one person as spokesperson for the district or school in a crisis. Ideally this is a person with strong communication and public relations experience who has a reputation for delivering accurate information and works well with the media. Determining where and when others besides the spokesperson will speak to the media and public is also a critical decision that must be made.

Designate one person to be in charge of each area of responsibility.

■ **Communication advisor and strategist.** The advisor or strategist assists in monitoring the effectiveness of ongoing communication; develops daily key messages and talking points; helps prepare speeches, letters, and statements; and counsels the leadership team on crisis response.

■ **Internal communication.** No audience is more important than teachers, support staff, and students. Internal communication about the crisis must be timely and ongoing to ensure that everyone speaks with "one clear voice."

■ **External communication.** Keeping parents, key communicators, and community leaders informed with timely information in a crisis can have a long-term impact on a school district's image and reputation.

NSPRA's resource, *The Complete Crisis Communication Management Manual for Schools* contains more in-depth information about other critical communication areas, such as telephone banks and hotlines, web sites, special event and memorial liaisons, donations, volunteers, media relations, and crisis counseling and intervention. Several other resources are included at the end of this chapter.

Crisis management is a team effort.

In Summary

To summarize, effective crisis management depends on sound and swift decision-making, and neither can happen without some kind of pre-planning. This includes periodically dusting off the crisis management plan and reviewing it. Practicing or rehearsing the kind of teamwork that will be needed during a crisis is a critical success factor in difficult situations.

Crisis management is not about researching and planning contingencies for every possible crisis that might occur, but rather about developing the capability within schools and school districts to react flexibly and to make the right decisions that are required when a crisis does happen.

In any crisis situation, the challenge is to make a decision quickly and accurately. A key component will be to balance "cardiac intuition" — acting without thinking what you believe is right in your heart and mind — with "analysis paralysis" — thinking instead of acting.

Crisis management is a team effort, and without a doubt, a team is more effective than individual decision-making if well organized and led. A key success factor for a good team decision is diversity in background and an ability to think and act under pressure. In the end, though, school leaders must be prepared to hope for the best and prepare for the worst.

Communication Command Structure for Crisis Response

Each position should be assigned to existing staff or volunteers from local, state, or national communication professional organizations or associations.

■ ■ Communication Director

Is responsible for overall management of crisis communication plan, including serving as spokesperson and ensuring that information is collected and disseminated to appropriate channels and audiences. Serves as communication counsel to superintendent and school board.

■ ■ Media Manager

Coordinates requests for media interviews, determines which interview requests will be honored, schedules interviews, and is responsible for press conferences and disseminating news releases.

■ ■ Internal and External Communication Officers

Coordinates all internal and external communication, including gathering information, writing key messages and speeches, and disseminating a daily fact sheet of information. Depending on the level of crisis, this position may be split between two people to ensure adequate communication is being disseminated to appropriate audiences. Also updates key messages on school and district Web pages.

■ ■ Research and Media Monitoring

Monitors media coverage of event and prepares daily assessment of key points addressed and "trends" in coverage for use in debriefing and preparing key messages.

■ ■ Communication Command Center Coordinator

Is responsible for day-to-day operation of volunteers and phone banks, updating crisis hotline messages, and assessing public perception based on feedback of callers.

■ ■ Crisis and Special Events Liaison

Coordinates and helps develop memorial events, parent and community meetings, funerals, and other events. Also works with affected site and staff affected by the crisis.

Tips for Working with the Media

Source: NSPRA's *The Complete Crisis Communication Management Manual for Schools*

Information to be communicated in a crisis

■ What happened? Avoid using sensational descriptions — stick to corroborated facts.

■ Omit information that can be used to encourage "copy cat" situations.

■ Who was involved? Use general terms unless names are public knowledge.

■ How individuals were involved may be reported in general terms.

■ Where did the incident happen and when did it occur? Be specific.

■ Include a prognosis of those involved once verified (work with families of victims).

■ Reinforce and stress the school and school district's concern for student and staff safety. If a student or staff member died, express condolences on behalf of the school district.

■ Avoid "No comment" responses; this suggests you have something to hide. It's okay to say, "I don't know." or "I don't have that answer right now. I'll have to get back to you."

■ Avoid "off the record" comments to reporters. Do not share anything unless you're willing to have it reported.

■ Consider whether a written statement would serve as the best approach to responding to media inquiries.

■ Focus on the positive actions taken by the school and school district in responding to crisis.

■ Be honest and show real emotion.

■ The interview is not over until the reporter leaves. Use caution in making any other comments before or after an interview — the microphone may still be on.

■ Avoid "what if" questions. Do not speculate or predict the future.

■ Understand all the facts, especially the technical information.

■ Staff members should refer reporters to the school or district spokesperson. Explain that this person will handle all information for the news media. If more than one spokesperson addresses the media, make sure all use the most current facts.

Suggestions for avoiding sensationalism

■ Clarify what interview is about. Don't agree if it is sensationalistic or takes you away from your message and focus.

■ Avoid playing the "blame game."

■ Avoid interviews that focus on perpetrators of violence.

■ Don't respond to negative questions by repeating words that inflame the situation.

■ Be wary of live call-in shows. You have very little control over the topic of conversation. Most callers will have a negative viewpoint that counters any attempts you make to "set the record straight."

■ Be alert to statements that begin with:

■ Isn't it true ...?

■ Aren't you really saying ...?

■ How do you respond to ...?

■ Are you aware that ...?

■ Focus on healing and moving forward as your overall goal.

Ten Steps to Proactive Crisis Planning

Source: NSPRA's *The Complete Crisis Communication Management Manual for Schools*

- Review existing policies on crisis communication and management.

- Review guidelines and procedures for implementing policies.

- Review any existing crisis plans.

- Establish crisis teams at the district level and building level. Have a safety task force.

- Build relationships with community agencies, volunteers, and opinion leaders.

- Have a dialogue with the community.

- Divide planning into manageable sections:
  - Identify crises most likely to occur
  - Outline action steps for each
  - Define roles
  - Identify possible issues and obstacles
  - Determine strategies

- Prepare tool kit and resource list ("go box").

- Determine format and prepare written plan.

- Train all staff and students.

Crisis Planning

Adapted from the U.S. Department of Education's *Practical Information on Crisis Planning: A Guide for Schools and Communities*

Mitigation and prevention

Goal: Decrease the need for response to a crisis

- Connect with community emergency responders to identify local hazards.

- Assess problem areas in buildings and on grounds.

- Assign official duties and responsibilities for safe and secure sites.

- Involve staff in crisis planning.

- Review data on critical incidents such as fires and floods.

- Determine major problems that are likely to reoccur.

- Develop a response protocol to safety problems.

- Assess district and building vulnerability to a variety of crises.

Preparedness

Goal: Facilitate a rapid, coordinated and effective response to a crisis

- Review crisis plans used in schools and surrounding community.

- Identify agencies and committees involved in crisis planning.

- Develop communication systems that include staff, students, families, and local media.

- Develop procedures to locate and account for every student during a crisis.

- Compile facility information, such as maps and locations of gas lines and shut-off valves.

- Assemble equipment needed to save lives and provide treatment during disasters.

Response

Goal: Follow a well-designed emergency plan

■ Determine the extent of danger and whether the danger amounts to a widespread crisis.

■ Identify the crisis and an appropriate response.

■ Activate an incident-management system.

■ Implement strategies such as evacuation, lockdown, or shelter-in-place.

■ Communicate with key staff positioned at pre-determined designated locations.

■ Oversee emergency responses such as first-aid and rescue services.

■ Call for more aid and assistance, if required.

Recovery

Goal: Return to a daily routine and restore order quickly

■ Allow adequate time for recovery, but draw up plans to resume classroom learning and restore damaged buildings.

■ Monitor signs of post-traumatic stress and other emotional disorders in students and staff.

■ Debrief with first responders and school staff; use suggestions to revise plans and conduct training and drills.

Crisis Management Assignments

Adapted from the *National Incident Management System* based on the Incident Command System

Note: Each of these positions should be assigned to building- or district-level personnel. A staff member should be assigned as a back-up for each of these critical assignments to ensure continuity in the event of absence.

■ ■ **Incident or emergency response commander**

Is responsible for overall management and control of operations of crisis response

■ ■ **Liaison officer**

Establishes a point of contact with responding agencies and serves as information resource to building emergency response team

■ ■ **Communication or public information officer**

Collects information about the event and the victims, coordinates all communication to the media and internal and external audiences, may serve as spokesperson, and facilitates information requests as needed

■ ■ **Operations chief**

Is responsible for all staff members who are not on the building emergency response or incident command team

■ ■ **Security coordinator**

Working with responding law enforcement agencies, this person is responsible for the immediate security of the scene and the protection of victims, witnesses, and emergency responders

■ ■ **Emergency response or first aid coordinator**

Provides initial first aid to victims, establishing triage area and assisting responding emergency personnel

■ ■ **Facilities and maintenance response coordinator**

Is responsible for emergency facility operations (e.g. power and gas shut off, alarm systems, etc.); coordinates with local and state agencies providing power, telephone service, etc.; assesses facility damage; and coordinates clean-up and facility restoration

■ ■ **Logistics and documentation personnel**

Procures necessary equipment and supplies and other support as required for response and recovery efforts, documents all emergency actions and responses

■ ■ **Crisis recovery coordinator**

Coordinates services for the emotional and psychological needs of victims

Rick J. Kaufman, APR

Rick J. Kaufman, APR, is a nationally respected presenter and consultant on crisis management and communication, media relations, and communication planning. Kaufman is the former executive director of public engagement and communication for Jefferson County Public Schools, Colorado's largest school system.

In April 1999, Kaufman led the crisis response team and became a familiar face and voice in national media coverage of the Columbine High School tragedy.

In 2005, Kaufman served a 30-day deployment as the PIO Field Coordinator for FEMA in Baton Rouge and New Orleans, Louisiana, as part of the national disaster response to Hurricanes Katrina and Rita.

He is a past president of the National School Public Relations Association and the recipient of the Public Relations Society of America's first-ever *Public Relations Professional of the Year* award in 2000. Kaufman has also won the prestigious *Silver Anvil Award* from PRSA and NSPRA's *Gold Medallion* in 2000 and 2005 for outstanding communication programs.

Kaufman holds a Bachelor of Science degree from the University of Wisconsin at Stevens Point, is accredited in public relations, and a member of the Future Council of Advisors in Vienna, VA. He is currently a public relations consultant and crisis management trainer.

Publications

By Harry Roberts, APR

Whether it's a community newsletter, a staff bulletin, or a program brochure — printed or electronic — a publication should be created by following the process used for any public relations project.

Before you put on the writer's or editor's hat, put on your counselor's hat and follow the four-step formula of research, assessment, communication, and evaluation. A publication is a product, but it is a product that should result from planning, and it should support a school district's or organization's public relations or marketing efforts.

The first step in creating a publication is research.

Research and Assessment: A Necessary Starting Point

While we recognize that effective communication requires listening as well as telling, we still have a need to write and "print" our messages on paper or electronically. Published documents, in hard copy or electronic file, convey important messages that our stakeholders need to know about our schools.

If we accept the notion that we still need to "publish," the questions we have to ask ourselves and education leaders are,

▓ Why?

▓ What?

▓ To Whom?

▓ How?

In other words, the first step in creating a publication is research — determining the need or the reason, the message, the audience, and delivery method.

Why?

We've heard the adage about publications, "Form follows function." Our publications should be useful and serve a purpose.

In addition to supporting the district's or organization's strategic mission, a publication can play a role in the organization's public relations plan, promote an educational program goal, or address an individual school's communication goals. There's a much better chance that a publication will be successful when it is the result of thorough planning.

If publications fail to capture the attention and interest of their intended audiences, they become a waste of time, money, and talent. Stated simply, when a publication is proposed by the superintendent, board president, principal, program director, or even the public relations professional, someone must ask, "Why?" We justify a publication by answering why we have to get this information out and why our audience needs it.

The best way to define our messages is to survey the audiences for our publications.

What?

The next step in our research and assessment is deciding what message we want the publication to convey. In part, we should consider, "What does the audience need to know?"

In the process of answering this question, we begin to differentiate between essential and unnecessary information. We separate facts and analysis from less significant items and identify the most important information and feature it more prominently.

Content also must be timely and worthwhile. While we typically think about informing people of the positive news and success stories from our schools or agencies, we shouldn't neglect more important issues of interest to key stakeholders. Most parents and community leaders may recognize that we have good schools, but they also realize we occasionally have problems. Our publics who care about education and schools are more likely to provide that support if we tell them when there are problems and what we're doing to address and fix them. Similarly, staff members are likely to be better "ambassadors" for our school districts or organizations when they feel as if they're "in the loop" and informed about issues.

Of course, the best way to define our messages is to survey the audiences for our publications. Evaluation should be built into the process for refining and updating any publication, but it can also be useful in determining what information our audience wants in a new publication.

Something else to consider is the kind of messages, in general, that we want our audience to receive about the district, agency, or school. Certainly we want people to get positive impressions about our work. We want our constituents to believe that we care about students, that achievement is a priority, that we have qualified and professional staff, and that we conduct business efficiently and economically. These are some of the priorities to always keep in mind as we develop publications.

To Whom?

Along with defining our messages, we have to identify our audiences. We get the greatest impact from our publications if they are targeted to specific audiences. No publication should be developed for the "general public." People who have experience in producing publications know that it is impossible to create one publication that effectively serves every audience identified in our public relations plan.

We consider audiences as we would for any public relations project. For example, parents, staff, students, community leaders, key communicators, non-parents, and senior citizens are some of the more common "publics" for whom we target publications. While some publications such as brochures or bulletins may be geared to one specific group, others such as newsletters may have to serve several of our targeted groups. For these, we can prioritize our groups and include something to interest each of the most important audiences we're trying to reach.

How?

Next, we select the method of producing the publication and the best way to disseminate it. Traditional "hard copy" publications are either printed on a press or photocopied. Typically, costs vary for both methods depending on the use of color and the number to be produced. To decide on the most cost-effective production method, the costs of various methods must be weighed against the significance of the publication, while also taking into account the quantity.

It is important to not overlook photocopying as an option. Many school districts produce attractive, eye-catching publications such as staff bulletins or informational brochures using this method.

Technology enables printers to provide a draft copy that mirrors the actual publication, and do it quickly and inexpensively.

If the publication is to be printed and you do not have access to an in-house print shop, it's wise to become familiar with the basics of printing and develop a good relationship with representatives from several commercial printing firms. An open, honest relationship with a printer should include conversations about how the cost of the job could be held to a minimum. Printers want to know if others are quoting or bidding for the job and usually offer more favorable quotes when competition exists.

Another factor to consider is a printing firm's ability to receive our work or the work of a consultant on a disk or through e-mail. Technology has not only given us the option of electronic publications, it has also facilitated the printing process with ever-improving desktop publishing software and ease of transmitting information. Coincidentally, this has become another means of reducing

printing costs and saving time. No longer must the printer produce complex and costly "mechanicals" or "boards" for the client to proofread. Technology enables printers to provide a draft copy that mirrors the actual publication, and do it quickly and inexpensively. This makes our job of proofreading much easier and reduces the chance of getting a printed product that is different from what we expect.

With paper publications, we also must determine how they should be distributed or disseminated. While mailing adds another expense, it is the most reliable practice. Other low-cost methods include sending publications home with students (if parents are the audience) or having copies available at athletic events, school programs, or community sites such as banks and doctor's offices.

Certainly one of the major reasons for the growth in electronic publications is the cost. Besides offering a timely way of disseminating information, electronic publications do not entail printing or mailing costs.

While many school districts and education agencies are becoming "paperless," we must weigh the pros and cons of electronic publications carefully before eliminating printed documents, especially if the publications are aimed at external audiences. While electronic publications unquestionably result in cost savings, we must gauge whether our audiences have the capability and the inclination to receive and read them.

Final step of planning

A final step in this planning process is deciding if the publication will represent a wise investment of funds. Once we're satisfied that the publication fills a communication or public relations need, that it will convey an important message, who the audience will be, and how it will be produced and disseminated, we must arrive at an estimated cost and determine if it will be worth that investment.

Typically, costs far exceed obvious expenses such as development (writing, editing, and layout), printing, and mailing. Even if it's an electronic publication, you will still have associated costs. During the production of any publication (printed or electronic), we incur costs for planning time, administrative meeting time, and in-house services that are often overlooked.

A helpful hint to determine real costs is to keep track of time for each job as if charging a client, as a public relations firm or consultant would.

Creating the Publication

When it's time to get started with the actual creation of a publication, work should focus on two main concerns — content and design. You should already have an idea of the kinds of messages you want to convey, as well as the audience. This will help immeasurably as you begin to write the copy.

Put yourself in the reader's place.

As a reminder, content has to be timely and worthwhile and should be what readers want to or need to know, not just what you want to tell them. In addition to any research to assess the audiences' wishes, the best advice is to put yourself in the reader's place. Make every effort to give the audience information that will make this publication valuable and useful to them as parents, staff, students, community leaders, business partners, or taxpayers.

Content

To quote NSPRA veteran Ken Weir, who wrote about publications for the previous edition of this book,

> Quality writing is the hallmark of any good publication.

While that fact should be obvious, we all have read school publications that suffer from weak writing. The most common problem educators have in composing text for publications is forgetting to "translate" the language so that it's understandable to the audience. A publication filled with "educationese," or jargon, usually creates a negative impression, or frustrates the reader.

Writing should be clear and concise. The copy should flow so that the reader can move easily through it. Good writing is typically conversational; it "sounds like" the way we would talk to our audience if we had the opportunity to interact with them face to face.

Be yourself and write as you speak.

Too often educators write copy for publications as they would write a thesis or scholarly paper for a graduate course. The result is predictable — the copy is too formal and reads like it was intended to impress a college professor, not to inform a parent or taxpayer. Again, the best advice for someone who is inexperienced in writing copy for publications: be yourself and write as you speak.

Suggestions for effective writing

The following are other content-related suggestions to keep in mind when producing printed or electronic publications:

■ **Write headlines, not titles,** even for brochures and bulletins. Use subjects and action verbs; for example, use "Lincoln students score high on assessments," rather than "State assessment results."

■ **Write "leads" for articles or stories that bring people into the copy.** Check out the first paragraphs of newspapers or magazine stories; typically, they're short and use some technique like analogy or contrast to spark interest.

■ If it's a newsletter story or a brochure, **follow journalistic style in arranging information.** The most important information should be included at the beginning followed by less important information

■ **Use a device such as the "Fog index" to measure readability.** This index counts multi-syllabic words and helps to keep writing free of jargon.

■ **Remember the "30-3-30 rule."** Write publications for all types of readers: those who spend 30 seconds looking only at headlines; others who spend three minutes, reading headlines, captions, pull-out quotes, and short items; and those who spend 30 minutes or as much time as it takes to read the entire publication.

■ **Keep articles short.** Research shows that 80% to 90% of people stop reading after the first 50 words. Especially with electronic publications, shorter is better. People seem to have shorter attention spans when reading on the screen than they do when reading hard copy. Plus, no one is likely to download and print an electronic publication that is too lengthy.

■ **Keep the copy in one "voice" as much as possible.** Choose either a first-, second-, or third-person writing voice throughout the entire publication. Likewise, try to use the same verb tense throughout the copy. Jumping from first to third person or from present to future tense breaks the flow for the reader.

■ **Vary sentence structure as much as possible.** Don't begin every sentence with a subject-verb pattern. Prepositional phrases, transitional words, and subordinate clauses are devices that can be used to start sentences and improve readability.

■ **When using a bulleted list, follow parallel construction.** Start each item in the list with the same type of word; verbs are usually the best choices because they engage the reader and show action.

■ **Testimonials can add impact to publications.** While positive comments from superintendents and board presidents may seem self-serving, quotes from parents, successful graduates and community leaders add credibility to publications.

Design

All excellent publications, from the simplest brochure to the most sophisticated newsletter, have a sense of style. Quoting Ken Weir again:

The best ideas can fall flat if they lack strong design to carry them.

Publications with "style" are pleasing to the eye, capturing people's interest before they read anything. Printed publications compete with various types of bulk mail and advertising that arrives at homes and offices. Electronic publications vie for interest with even more elaborate and eye-catching pieces of e-mail or web-based items. We must consider that many readers will never return to a publication after they first handle it or see it. Most publications, especially electronic ones, have only one chance to make a positive impression.

More than ever, school publications need strong design along with important messages to make them desired and valued. While you don't want publics to think you spent a fortune on publications, they have to look professional and be attractive.

Most publications have only one chance to make a positive impression.

School public relations professionals are well-trained and experienced writers, but may not have expertise in graphic arts. Many schools and districts seek the talents of graphics professionals to design publications. Many printing firms offer graphic design as part of their comprehensive services. Another option, especially with electronic publications, is a professionally designed template provided with desktop publishing software.

If you lay out and design publications without the assistance of a professional graphics designer, it would be wise to study design and layout in magazines and advertising brochures. In addition, copies of award-winning publications in the annual NSPRA Publications Contest can be excellent resources for ideas. A list of winning entries is posted on the NSPRA web site (www.nspra.org), and most members are willing to share copies of their work.

Guidelines for good design

The following are other design-related suggestions to consider when designing publications:

■ **Never use type smaller than 10 point for text copy**; 12 point is ideal.

■ **Avoid combining too many type fonts** in the same publication.

■ Many attractive, readable type fonts are available for use but **choose fonts carefully.** Readership surveys show that fonts with serifs, such as Times Roman are easier to read when used for text than sans-serif fonts. Strong, heavier type fonts, such as Helvetica Bold are often used for headlines.

■ Headlines and subheads should stand out from body copy, but **don't routinely put headlines in all caps**; it makes them harder to read.

■ **Use unusual type fonts, as well as italic and bold options, sparingly.**

■ **Avoid large blocks of italic type and large blocks of reverse type**; save these techniques for emphasis and "copy-breaking."

■ **Use copy-breaking devices** such as subheads or "pull-out" quotes to emphasize key points and separate blocks of copy. Avoid large blocks of type that look gray when glancing at a page.

■ **Use white space as another copy-breaking device.** Too many publications are jammed with headlines, copy blocks, photos, and clip art. The eye needs space to rest, whether looking at a piece of paper or the computer screen.

■ **Limit the width of type columns to 3½ inches.** Never run type all the way across a page because it is difficult to read.

■ **The use of color in printed publications is usually determined by the budget.** Traditionally, using black plus a second color was a cost-effective way to give publications more impact. However, advances in technology have made using four-color-process printing more affordable. Electronic publications can be developed with no limits on color.

■ **Use photos if possible,** but remember that photos do not reproduce well if the publication is photocopied. Many school publications are taking advantage of file photos available on the Internet. Some are public domain and others are available at a minimal cost. They offer high quality and typically are less costly than taking original photos

■ **Remember the "dime rule" when it comes to sizing photos.** The head of any person pictured in a photo should always be larger than a dime.

■ **"Head and shoulders" shots of administrators or board members should be professional portraits.**

■ **Use clip art sparingly.** A school newsletter that looks like a cartoon or comic book sends the wrong kind of message. Even though publications may be produced on tight budgets, they should still stress the same characteristics you want your schools to be known for — quality and excellence.

■ **Always consider how a printed publication will be mailed.** The look of a beautiful publication can be ruined if it has to be folded awkwardly to fit into a standard-sized envelope.

◼ Harry Roberts, APR

 Harry Roberts, APR, recently retired as public relations manager for the Central Susquehanna Intermediate Unit (CSIU), a regional education service agency based in Lewisburg, Pennsylvania. He now serves as a consultant for NSPRA and the Association of Education Service Agencies.

During his career, Roberts directed a comprehensive public relations and marketing program for the intermediate unit, including contracted services for local school districts. Through statewide initiatives coordinated by the CSIU, he had the opportunity to work with staff of rural, urban, and suburban schools, as well as state agencies. He earned accreditation from both NSPRA and the Public Relations Society of America, and he holds degrees in secondary education and journalism. Roberts began his career as a middle school teacher.

Active in the Pennsylvania School Public Relations Association (PenSPRA) since 1979, he was the group's president from 1987-89. Roberts' affiliation with NSPRA began in 1980. He served as Northeast Vice President from 1992-95, as chair of the accreditation committee for several years, and represented NSPRA on the Universal Accreditation Board from 1999-2002. In 2005, he received NSPRA's Lifetime Professional Achievement Award.

Roberts has made presentations at professional meetings of NSPRA; PenSPRA; Pennsylvania Department of Education (PDE); Pennsylvania School Boards Association (PSBA); Pennsylvania Association of School Administrators (PASA); and the New Jersey, New York, and Texas school public relations associations. In addition, he has served as chairperson of the Pennsylvania Association of Intermediate Units Public Relations Consortium, chair of the PASBO Communications Committee, and a member of public relations advisory committees for PDE, PSBA, and PASA.

Communicating with Diverse Populations

By Sylvia Link, APR

The future of school public relations is evolving and will include a greater emphasis on communicating with diverse populations.

Today, more than one-third of Americans are visible minorities. With the end of the "echo baby boom" of the 1990s, the birth rate in North America is on the decline. Net population growth — and therefore overall "real" enrollment growth in schools — will come from immigration.

The U.S. Census Bureau's midrange forecast is that the U.S. population will grow to about 400,000 million by 2050. Newcomers to North America will come from various parts of the world — mainly Asia and South America. By 2050, people of Caucasian racial background are no longer expected to be the majority in North America.

This newcomer population growth has already had an impact on public education and will continue to change the nature of communities. For example,

---

almost half of the 10 million people of Asian origin in the U.S. are newcomers within the past decade. Eighty percent of them speak a language other than English at home, and a quarter of them are school-age.

Diversity communication can provide your district with the competitive advantage it needs to attract new students and staff. But the word "diversity" is highly versatile. It tends to be used interchangeably with any or all of the following terms:

■ **Ethnicity.** Membership in a particular group with a common, distinctive racial, national, religious, linguistic, or cultural heritage

■ **Race.** A group of people distinguished by genetically transmitted physical characteristics

■ **Visible minority.** One who is readily recognizable as not being part of the majority

■ **Ancestry.** Ancestors (those from whom one has descended), as a group

■ **Nationality.** The status of belonging to a particular nation by origin, birth, or naturalization

■ **Country of origin.** Country from which a newcomer has arrived

■ **Culture.** Totality of socially transmitted patterns from a particular geographic place and time period

■ **Mother tongue.** The first language one learns to speak

■ **Religion.** A set of beliefs, values, and practices based on the teachings of a spiritual leader

■ **Faith.** A set of principles or beliefs

These concepts are all part of our understanding of diversity. They overlap and interact in the following complex ways:

■ Someone's country of origin (the country in which they lived before coming to North America) may be different from their nationality.

■ Two people with the same nationality may speak different languages, be of different races, and practice different religions.

■ Some members of a particular race may be visible minorities, while others are not. Many people do not descend from just one race, but claim mixed racial origin.

■ For generations after people have settled in a new country, they may continue to identify themselves with their ancestry.

■ Religion and culture are inextricably linked — it's virtually impossible to separate the cultural aspects from major religious celebrations.

These are just a few examples of ways in which diversity concepts interconnect and the perils of making broad generalizations about any "diverse" group.

> **Diversity communication should be integrated into every communication plan and initiative.**

In addition to these concepts, the term *diversity* is often also used to talk about people who differ from the majority in terms of socio-economic status, level of educational attainment, sexual orientation, or family type.

The interplay of the many dimensions of diversity requires a sophisticated and strategic approach to communication. Diversity communication can be effectively used to reach any target audiences who do not see themselves as part of the mainstream.

Diversity communication should not be an afterthought or an add-on. It should be integrated into every communication plan and initiative. The strategies and tactics should be highly tailored to the specific target audiences in your community.

Initially, it is best to get started by developing an overall diversity communication program for your district. As with all effective communication, this program should be based on the four-step public relations planning model.

Research the Needs of Your Diverse Communities

It is essential to understand the diversity that exists in your district. Start by developing an understanding of the community your district serves — what it looks like now and how it is expected to change in the next decade. Through census data and other local research, look at the following demographic characteristics of school-age children and their families in your community:

■ Language spoken most frequently at home

■ Preferred language for written material

■ Race and ancestry

■ Religion

■ If not born in the U.S., the country of origin and length of time they have lived here

■ Social risk factors such as family income, parental educational attainment, percentage of single-parent families, and mobility

If your district has a strong and well-developed diversity outreach program, it's most efficient to collect these data as a regular part of the school registration process for all children. If done well, this will give you the most complete and accurate picture of your school population and will provide information crucial not only for communication but also for program planning.

If your district is just starting a diversity communication plan, start with census data that are already available.

Due to sensitivities about this type of information, you should not attempt to collect it unless the district — from senior leadership to front-line staff — understands that this information is being gathered to better meet the needs of the diverse communities. Policies about the data collection should ensure that individual information is confidential and is reported only as aggregate data. It's essential that staff who are registering children for school be trained about how to collect this information accurately and with sensitivity.

If your district is just starting a diversity communication plan, start with census data that are already available and build an internal understanding of diversity before attempting to collect your own demographics.

Compare demographics for all district residents to those for families with school-age children, and identify key differences. At times when you are communicating with all residents — for example, during school finance campaigns — these differences will be important to your communication strategies.

Even if your district is collecting its own demographic information, use census data projections to form a picture about how your community is expected to change in the next decade. It's important to begin to plan now for those changes. For example, your community may have a very small Asian population today, but trend data may show that this will change over the next decade. Your district has time to prepare to welcome those new families, rather than struggling after the fact to meet the changing demands.

Ideally, you need the same demographic information for your staff as for your students and their families — to adequately plan internal communication programs. A staff census can provide a baseline, and then collect these demographics for new hires.

To avoid a staff backlash, you need to build strong understanding and support among employees, senior administration, and staff unions about how these data collection will help your district.

Demographic information can help you pinpoint distinct target audiences in your community. The next step in research is face to face. This strategy will not only provide rich information for communication planning, but will begin to build relationships.

Conduct interviews with community agencies that serve your target audience. Ask them to identify the main needs of the families they serve, as they relate to the school system. Talk about ways that your district can work with the agency to better meet these needs. Ask them to identify key leaders for the target community — and set up interviews with those individuals as well.

Conduct focus groups with parents from your target audiences. Each focus group should be 8 to 12 newcomer parents. Each group should be from a single language and cultural background. Arrange for an interpreter to be present, and keep in mind that questions and answers will take longer due to the need for interpretation.

Consider holding the focus group in the community at a location where the parents will feel comfortable (rather than a formal focus group facility) and using a trained facilitator from an agency that serves this community. In addition to audio or video recording of the focus group, have at least one person take notes.

Take the opportunity to include one or two senior leaders as observers, but limit observers so you don't intimidate the focus group participants. The following

are sample questions that can be used for focus groups with newcomer parents:

■ What were some of the challenges you faced when you first moved to our community?

■ When you registered your children for school, what kinds of things did the school do to make you feel welcome and help you understand the school?

■ What other things could the school have done to make you feel more welcome and to give you information about your child's schooling?

■ What do you feel is the most important information to receive when you are first registering your children for school?

■ Thinking of the information you receive from your child's school currently, what would you like "more of"? What would you like "less of"?

■ As a parent, what kinds of things would you like to be involved in at your child's school?

■ What could the school do to encourage you to become more involved at the school?

■ What agencies in the community do you go to for information?

■ What is the best way for you to get information about the school?

■ Do you have Internet access at home? How much time do you spend using the Internet, and what are the main things you use it for (for example: e-mail, shopping, research)?

■ Have you visited the district web site? If yes, how often? What pages do you visit most often?

■ Have you visited the web site for your child's school? If yes, how often? What information do you look for on the school's web site?

■ Would you visit these web sites more often if there were information in your own language?

■ What information would you like to see on these web sites that is not there now?

Assess Your Research Findings

Based on your assessment of the research findings, you will develop the components of your diversity communication plan including the goal, objectives, communication strategies and tactics, budget, and evaluation.

Your diversity communication goal is a broad statement of the preferred future that will exist as a result of your communication actions.

The following is an example of a diversity communication goal:

The goal is to have newcomer families have the most important initial information they need to help them

register their children for school in our community, become familiar with the school system, and support their children's learning.

The communication objectives to achieve this overall goal should be SMART— strategic and specific, measurable, ambitious but attainable, results-oriented and time-bound. For example:

By the end of this school year, 75% of newcomer families who registered their children in our district have the basic information in their first language about their children's schooling and perceive their child's school as welcoming.

By [6 months from now], 80% of employees are aware of new district policy to provide 3 paid faith days per year. By [18 months from now], 20% of employees have accessed at least 1 faith day.

Develop Communication Strategies for Diverse Audiences

Select communication strategies and tactics based on the objectives in your communication plan. The strategies and communication vehicles should reflect your research about the ways in which each of your target audiences prefers to receive information and about their information needs, as well as the objectives your district is aiming to achieve.

If your district is developing a diversity communication plan for the first time, the emphasis should be on beginning to build relationships with the diverse communities. Districts with well-established relationships will want to strengthen existing relationships and build on the communication strategies that have proved successful.

At all reception desks, have a poster with the most commonly spoken languages in your community.

The following are examples of strategies to consider in developing your own diversity communication plan:

- **Create a visible commitment to diversity in your district.** Ensure that all school and district offices and all classrooms display the word "welcome" in a wide variety of languages to make all families feel connected.

- **Provide multi-lingual services at all district and school offices.** This can be done by hiring multi-lingual receptionists and through telephone interpreter service such as Language Line (www.languageline.com, used by the federal government and many health care institutions, among many other clients). At all reception desks, have a poster with the most commonly spoken languages in your community. Visitors who do not speak English can point to their language, and the receptionist can access an interpreter in that language

to provide on-the-spot service. A list of tips for producing effective and reliable translations is included at the end of the chapter.

- **Make sure that your district web site and all publications depict staff, students, and families from a range of cultures, backgrounds, and abilities.** Every publication does not need to show individuals of every background, but when all the publications are put together, the visual message should clearly demonstrate that diversity is part of the culture of your district.

- **Reach out to build relationships with diverse communities.** Identify leaders, including faith leaders, in each of the diverse communities represented in the area your district serves. Ask parents, staff, and community agencies to help identify these leaders. Create a database with contact information about these leaders and use the database to track contacts between your district and the leaders.

- **Hold regular meetings with community leaders (at least three times a year).** Use these meetings to foster two-way communication. The district can share information about important news that will affect the diverse communities. Community leaders can also share information about issues and concerns they are hearing in the community. The meetings are also an opportunity for the district to consult about future plans. These meetings will work best if most of the agenda is devoted to hearing from the community leaders, rather than presenting extensive information to them.

■ **Take every opportunity to go out into the community.** Consider holding some school board meetings in community locations, rather than holding them all in the district office. If your district is planning public meetings, work with community leaders to co-host some of these meetings in locations frequented by members of the diverse communities. For districts that already have well-established relationships with diverse groups, include leaders of the diverse communities in the decision-making process of your district. Make sure to include representatives on any district task forces, standing committees, and other decision-making structures.

■ **Help schools create a welcoming environment for all families.** Provide schools in your district with resources to help them create a welcoming environment for new families such as a *Welcome to School* tool kit. The kit could be given to all new registrants and translated into several languages. The toolkit should include the following:

■ Welcome letter from the principal

■ Fact sheet with the most essential information parents need to know about schooling

■ School year calendar, including parent-teacher conference dates

■ If your district web site has multi-lingual information, web site flyer directing them to that section of the site

■ Tip sheet on how to help their children with homework

■ Tip sheet on how to use their first language to help their children succeed in school

■ Explanation on the English-as-a-second-language program

■ List of community resources that serve newcomer families

In addition, make sure that front-line staff members who are registering newcomer children for school are trained to provide consistent, welcoming service.

■ **Districts with large numbers of newcomer families may want to provide one or more reception centers in the community.** Staffed by community outreach workers who speak several key languages, these centers would provide one-stop service for newcomer families, allowing them to register children for school and receive an orientation to the school system at the same time they are connected to other services they need in the community. These reception centers can be operated in partnership between your district and other agencies that serve the newcomer communities.

Develop targeted campaigns for prospective staff of diverse backgrounds.

■ **Work with your human resources department to actively recruit and retain staff from diverse backgrounds.** Based on your district's current and future hiring needs, work with the human resources department to develop targeted campaigns for prospective staff of diverse backgrounds. These efforts may include the following:

   ■ Provide information sessions for diverse audiences to explain your district's recruitment, interviewing, and hiring practices.

   ■ Develop programs to help foreign-trained teachers and other professionals assess the gaps in their skills, experience, and knowledge and gain the experience they need to successfully land a job in your district. Such programs can be offered with community partners.

   ■ Provide all supervisory staff that interview applicants and make hiring decisions with guidelines and resources about equitable hiring practices.

Addressing Diversity in Faith

A person's faith is an integral part of who they are — it has an impact on their learning (if they are students) or work practices (if they are staff members). Consider the following ideas when you address the needs of students, families and staff members of diverse faiths:

■ **Compile a calendar of important holy days in each of the major world religions.** Make sure this calendar is used when planning district or school events for students, families, and staff. This will make sure that some of your audience is not excluded because an event is scheduled on a day when they will be unable to attend due to religious observance.

■ **Provide posters to all school sites to recognize major holy days in other religions.** Encourage schools to create their own displays for major holidays such as Chinese New Year or Diwali celebrated by students and staff at their school.

■ **Visit various places of worship.** To create greater understanding of other religions, arrange visits to various places of worship for your district's senior leaders, school administrators, and other interested district staff. Organize presentations by faith leaders to district staff to inform them about the basics of the religion.

■ **Examine policies and practices.** Work with senior administration to create policies and practices to accommodate the faith needs of students and staff from all religious backgrounds. Also, **check with legal counsel about the ramifications of ideas** like:

■ Provide, as we do in our Canadian district, a space in each school and work site in your district designated as a prayer room. Some religions require prayers at specific times of the day, but students and staff of all faiths can use the prayer room for individual prayers.

■ Arrange for students who are fasting (for example, Muslim students fast during the month of Ramadan) to be supervised in a different area than other students who eat their lunch.

■ Provide consistent guidelines for schools in your district to allow for religious clubs, if there is sufficient student interest. The purpose of such clubs is to promote understanding, not to indoctrinate or proselytize.

■ Make sure dietary restrictions of those from other faiths (such as kosher, halal, or vegetarianism) are considered when planning menus. For example, require operators of school cafeterias to provide menu options that meet the needs of all students and staff at that location. When planning menus for staff events, consider the same requirements.

Evaluate Your Plan's Impact

Focus your evaluation on measuring progress toward the measurable objectives for your diversity communication program. Through formal and informal assessment, you want to determine the impact that the program has had on the district and to identify the communication strategies and tactics that have been most successful.

It's important to look at diversity communication as a long-term commitment, not a one-time initiative. Because of this, effective evaluation is essential to help you refine your program and focus your diversity outreach efforts where they will have the greatest impact.

The evaluation of your existing diversity communication program becomes part of the research for the next phase, as your district becomes increasingly sophisticated in its communication with its diverse student, parent, and staff communities.

Look at diversity communication as a long-term commitment.

Tips for Producing Effective and Reliable Translations

Prepare your document for translation.

■ **Revise your document with translation in mind.** Remove any jargon. Increase the "shelf life" of the translation by removing content that will quickly become outdated.

■ For a large or high-stakes translation project, **hold a focus group with members of the various linguistic communities** who speak both English and the target language.

Select a translation company

■ **Interview a number of translation companies.** Ask about the qualifications of their translators and their verification process. Find out prices and any surcharges. Check their references.

■ If possible, **meet with or speak by phone with each translator working on your project,** after the translator has read your English document. Encourage the translator to call you with any questions about meaning and context as the translation progresses.

■ For a large project, such as a web site or large publication, **hold an initial**

meeting with the translators and other members of the project team. Decide on workflow, project management, quality control, and methods of communication within the project team.

■ As part of its standard service, **the translation company should provide a verification step** in which a second translator independently reviews and proofreads the translation. Consider establishing your own internal reviewers, preferably staff who read the specific language.

Put the translation into a finished product

■ Reformatting the translation into a finished product — brochure, web site or manual — can present challenges, such as text reflowing or becoming garbled. Special care needs to be taken with non-Roman fonts. **Send the finished product back to the translator** for review before printing or "going live." Use your internal verifiers again at this stage, before you go into production.

■ Not all languages read from left to right. Arabic, Bengali, Japanese, and Urdu are examples of languages that read from right to left. **You need to create a design template to accommodate these languages.** If you are creating a publication, it will read from "back to front."

Sylvia Link, APR

Sylvia Link, APR, is manager of communications for Peel District School Board in Mississauga, Ontario, Canada. With 150,000 students in 230 schools, the Peel school district is one of the largest and fastest growing in North America. It is also one of the most culturally diverse, with more than half of students identified as visible minorities and speaking a first language other than English.

Sylvia has more than 20 years of diversity communication experience. Her work has been recognized with the NSPRA Gold Medallion and the IABC Gold Quill Award of Excellence for multi-lingual communication.

Creating a Strategic Communication Program

Reputation Management

By Tom DeLapp

Public education is laboring under a dichotomy. In the 1960s, American education was the envy of the world. People used to look at public education and ask, "How good is my neighborhood school?"

Decades of reform proposals, education-bashing critics, voucher movements, choice programs, and No Child Left Behind have taken their toll on that reputation. As a result, people's frame of reference for evaluating their schools has

fundamentally changed. Today, the common perception of America education is that it is failing the nation. Today, people look at their local school system within the context of a "failing" industry and ask, "I wonder how bad my neighborhood school is."

Public opinion surveys, like the one done each fall by the Gallup Poll for *Kappan* magazine, have chronicled this shift in public perception. Most polls consistently show that people rate our nation's public schools as being mediocre at best.

Remarkably, though, the same respondents rate their neighborhood schools much higher. In fact, 7 out of 10 parents give an A or B grade to the school their oldest child attends. In other words, individual schools and school districts are being judged at a higher quality level than from an industry that has a reputation problem.

Reputations are pretty tricky things. They can take a long time to develop, but can be destroyed very quickly. It can be difficult for a district to live up to a positive reputation earned in an earlier era under circumstances that have fundamentally changed over time. Conversely, living down a negative reputation can feel like an insurmountable obstacle as new leaders attempt to change and improve their schools. Is your district trying to live up to or live down its reputation from the past?

> **Getting people to understand that they contribute to your organization's reputation is crucial to long-term success.**

What Is a Reputation?

Reputation is the perception of an organization's vision, programs, practices, and people by the world around it. We aren't being measured in the court of public opinion by what *we* feel. We're being measured by what *they* feel. Success has to be conferred on us by the public. In doing so, the public defines our public reputation.

A positive reputation can be an organization's most valuable asset. School districts and educational organizations depend on their reputations for everything from voter support in bond and tax elections to parent enrollment decisions.

When you think of an organization with a good reputation, what words come to mind? Usually they are words describing its actions or accomplishments. When you think of a person with a good reputation, you usually think about their personal traits and characteristics. The reputation of an organization is shaped by the reputations of its people that are passed on as a legacy from one generation to the next. The reputation of your school district today was defined in part by former employees, leaders, and parents of the past. Getting people to understand that they contribute to your organization's reputation is crucial to long-term success.

In the early 1990s, Apple Computer was in trouble. It was facing a revolving door of top leaders and losing its market share. Apple Computer was seen as an industry leader living off its laurels from past decades. Then Steve Jobs was re-hired as Apple's CEO. From the outset, Jobs knew that Apple Computer was facing a reputation crisis that could threaten the organization's very existence. Apple was on the brink of losing the positive reputation it had built over 20 years as an innovative industry leader. Jobs knew that Apple needed to manage its reputation or face extinction. He chose to go back to the number one customer of Apple Computer to re-establish the company's reputation. That customer was its own employees — the people who made, sold, and administered Apple products. Jobs knew that if they weren't sold on the company, they couldn't sell anybody else.

Every day employees make or break the image of a school district and shape its public reputation. In public education we need our teachers, support staff, and administrators to be sold on the public schools. Do they opt out by enrolling their own children in private schools? Do they fail to vote in bond elections and tax elections? Do they stand by and let publicly stated negative stereotypes or criticisms of public education go unchallenged?

Every time one of our own comes into contact with a community member it is a "teachable moment." Employees must be encouraged to see themselves as stewards for our reputation in that contact. Their personal experience becomes an example of our reputation at work.

Here's a case in point. A school has been struggling with a reputation for being unsafe. The school district releases a study showing that campus safety has dramatically improved over the last 2 years. The next day, a teacher from the school is on the sidelines of a soccer game with a group of parents talking about the study. The parents ask the teacher for her perceptions about the study and safety at the school. If the teacher uses only her own experience, she might tell them that she is afraid to go into the school parking lot at night. When that

happens, she not only failed to validate the statistics of the study, but she also sent a much more powerful message that schools aren't safe. She reinforced the negative stereotype about the school. That teacher either did not appreciate or particularly care that her personal opinion would degrade the school's overall reputation.

If a school district does not have a reputation for treating staff fairly, for being a listening organization, or for practicing shared decision-making, then its own employees will not portray that reputation to the public. We must walk our talk and communicate from the inside out through both our words and deeds that our purported reputation is well-deserved. In other words, like Apple Computer, we need to convince our own people first before they can convince anyone else.

Your Reputation Is an Appreciating Asset

Your role as a communication professional is to understand that reputation is a valuable asset. For a business, reputation means customer loyalty, repeat business, and profits. For a politician, it means re-election. For a public figure, it may mean fame and fortune. For a school district, it may be the closest thing we have to a profit margin because it is a combination of tangible measurements of accountability and the public perception that we are a valuable and successful organization.

Take stock of the school district or educational organization's reputation.

Because your reputation is an asset, you need to manage and nurture it. The first task of a school public relations professional is to take stock of the school district or educational organization's reputation. Assess your reputation among various stakeholder groups. Is that perception aligned with what the district or organization believes about itself? If the district doesn't have a clearly defined vision or goals, then you have a difficult time measuring your reputation because it may be based on yesterday's perceptions. How many districts are living off their laurels earned in the good old days?

Frequently in communication audits, focus group respondents will say that they believe their school district is good or even very good, but they cannot really tell you why or give concrete examples to back up that belief. In this case, the reputation is at risk because the district runs the chance of being measured by the one negative example that may pop up, the crisis that is mishandled, or the shadow of doubt raised by a single-issue critic.

Do people know what to expect from us and are we meeting or exceeding their expectations?

Former NSPRA executive director John Wherry was renowned for asking his audience if they knew the number one rule of school public relations and then loudly proclaiming, "Do a good job!" The first rule of reputation management is to do a good job because your credibility is at stake.

We need public support to accomplish our mission of educating students. If we do not have a strong reputation, then we disengage our publics. People lose faith in their schools when they perceive that we have tarnished reputations or aren't measuring up.

With the challenges of choice, we need to compete for students against a growing number of options including inter-district transfers, private schools, home schooling, charter schools, distance and online learning, and vouchers. Since funding is tied to enrollment, our financial health depends on whether people perceive that we have a good reputation and can deliver a quality education that meets their needs.

In school finance elections, people actually cast 2 votes when they mark the ballot.

■ The first is a vote of confidence in your reputation.

■ The second is actually a vote on the measure itself.

You can't have the latter if you don't have the former.

Creating a Reputation Management Program

It is critical for school districts to build and manage a desired reputation rather than allowing others to create a different reputation. Plan to manage your reputation by using sustained, pervasive, reinforcing efforts that nurture and enhance your reputation and image. Random acts of public relations or drive-by public relations stunts will not work.

People will support your organization if they value what you do, know about it, and see that they have a place in it. They will have confidence in your organization if they know that you know where you are going, how you intend to get there, and what it will look like when you arrive. The following are the elements of a positive reputation that you should include in a reputation management program:

Core values

Stakeholders are able to identify your basic beliefs, values, objectives, and vision as an organization. The way your people behave in carrying out these core values defines the character of your school system. Core values have to be ingrained in employees and extended to stakeholders.

Credibility

To be credible we must be believable. To be believable we must be accurate, open, reliable, and trustworthy. Trust and reliability are key components of a positive reputation.

Clarity

Bad reputations are frequently based on rumors and innuendo, misinformation, jumping to conclusions, or not having enough facts or information at your disposal to make sound judgments and choices. Organizations with strong reputations usually have a track record of transparency, accuracy, and accessibility to a common knowledge base.

Consistency

Reputations are validated at every entry point into the school system. Districts that manage their reputations well promote consistency and quality control in customer interactions. They have earned a proven track record over time. Districts with solid reputations provide service to customers at a consistently high level; it transcends the individual performance of any one employee.

Competence

Organizations with positive reputations are known for their adaptability to changing circumstances, responsiveness and flexibility, and shared accountability for results. They also showcase the caliber of their people in doing a good job.

A Systemic Approach to Reputation Management

Too often school communication professionals create communication plans that simply arrange and schedule a series of tasks. Those plans become a "to-do" list of activities, publications, and events set to a calendar and budget. This is certainly helpful in getting organized, but it doesn't advance the real needs of the district to enhance and extend its reputation.

Reputation management combines the following elements:

■ **Strategic communication** to target key messages to diverse audiences to raise awareness and understanding

■ **Quality customer relations** to reinforce and personalize the district's reputation at every point of contact

■ **Community engagement** that connects various publics to our reputation and build relationships of support

These three reputation management elements are supported by the following actions:

■ **Marketing and publicity** so that stakeholders know what to expect from their schools

■ **A decision-making system** that is based on integrity and ethics using responsive, two-way communication and strategic listening

■ **An evaluation and continuous improvement mechanism** to learn from mistakes, seize opportunities, and perfect the reputation management process

An effective communication plan ties all actions and systems back to a set of strategic goals and objectives that nurture and enhance the long-term reputation of the school district or organization. Every action plan should reference the strategic plan element it is trying to accomplish. Producing products without a purpose behind them is a random act of public relations.

Tips and Techniques for Managing a Positive Reputation

Managing a positive reputation for your district or organization is an ongoing process. It must be a key focus of your strategic communication plan. The following are tips and techniques to effectively manage your district's reputation:

■ **Attack stereotypes, myths, and embedded misperceptions.** Word-of-mouth communication can kill an organization. It can also be your most persuasive communication tool. You can't overcome a bad reputation if stereotypes remain embedded in the public mind. It takes a bold stroke or aggressive campaign to root out misperceptions; challenge them with facts and endorsements and refute them. Feed the rumor mills with accurate and positive information so they don't erode your base of support.

■ **Position the district on key issues.** Too often, school districts wait to react to public policy issues. A positive reputation comes from being perceived as either the leader on an issue area or a high visibility responder to an issue that affects public schools. The goal here is to be an organization of consequence, not just a victim of the latest trendy reform movement to sweep over public education.

■ **Reflect a positive reputation every day through good customer relations.** The reputation of a school district or educational organization is the collection of reputations of its employees. Internal communication systems that connect employees to the district's reputation for success and accomplishment can improve morale and convert employees into amplifiers of your reputation in their daily interactions with customers.

■ **Build a common body of knowledge that is easily accessible and understandable.** Use your district web page as a wire service. Make your web site user-friendly and organized so it is easy for visitors to use. Too often organizations create web sites that are like phone books, file cabinets, or organizational charts. The web site should not just tell people what you do and how you do it. The site should also show the effects, results, and outcomes of those efforts.

■ **Engage new generations of influential leaders and stakeholders to reinforce your reputation.** You are known by the company you keep. Engage new generations of leaders into the schools so they can reinforce your reputation as they gain visibility and currency within the community. The leaders of tomorrow can have a huge impact on expanding your reputation into newer audiences.

■ **Refresh the evidence, examples, and data that** support your positive reputation. Too often we used stale data to support our positions. To refresh your reputation, use current anecdotes, examples, endorsements, and examples to show how your reputation is growing and improving. Relevance is as important as accuracy when it comes to the information you use to define and shape your reputation.

■ **Orient new employees and infuse them with a sense of responsibility to be reputation stewards.** New employees need to be "inducted" into the school district or organization. Whether you like it or not, new employees have an impact on the culture of the organization. Employee orientations and support systems can stress the importance of positive public relations throughout the organization's table of organization.

■ **Neutralize or marginalize the critics, negativists, and change-resistors.** Frequently, the only voice that is heard is the loudest voice in the room. One strategy for managing your reputation is to make sure the critics, negativists, and change-resistors do not dominate discussions about your schools. Reputation management puts these negative voices in their place by insisting that they back up their complaints. In addition, implementing an ongoing community engagement process will bring other perspectives into discussions that will help balance negative voices.

■ **Watch for times when your reputation is on the chopping block.** Change is always a good indicator for when your reputation is at stake. Key times to watch when reputations are on the line include changes in administrative or school board leadership, shifts in policies or major district practices, closing schools or changing attendance boundaries, racial unrest and diversity challenges, labor relations conflicts or tension, or high-profile incidents or crises.

Final Thoughts

Establishing and then maintaining a positive reputation for your district or organization requires constant attention. As a part of the process, it is important to monitor your "reputation health" by gathering perspectives from key stakeholder groups. Evaluation methods such as surveys, focus groups, study circles, and town hall forums can help

you understand how stakeholders perceive the district's overall reputation.

If problems arise that could affect your reputation, it is essential to address these issues before they affect your district's reputation. Don't let your reputation just evolve without having influence over the direction it is taking. Be proactive to shape what you want people to think about your district or organization.

Tom DeLapp

Tom DeLapp is President of Communication Resources for Schools. For more than 12 years, his firm has provided communication counseling and support to more than 400 school systems in California and across the country.

He is a former president of CalSPRA and served as NSPRA Southwest Region Vice

President from 1998–2001. He was the recipient of NSPRA's 2006 Barry Gaskins Mentor Legacy Award.

Before creating his consulting practice, DeLapp served as assistant executive director for membership and communications with the Association of California School Administrators. He was responsible for all marketing, media relations, member communication, and publishing and reputation management for the 15,000-member statewide association.

Customer Service

By Buddy Price

The customer service train has left the station. "Customer service? This is a school district. Why are we talking about customer service?"

This is a sentiment commonly heard 10 years ago for anyone brave enough to stand before a room full of principals or other staff members to talk about customer service. We often heard statements such as,

> Everyone knows schools are built in a community, attendance lines are drawn,

and most everyone in town goes to the community school because there are no other choices. Where else would they send their children to be educated?

That is the way it used to be, but things have significantly changed. All around us the world moves faster, things change more quickly, and we have all become more impatient. It wasn't too many years ago we would order a burger and a shake and expect to wait 5 or 10 minutes —not today! Now we place the order and we expect our food to be delivered to us by the time we have picked up our napkin and straw. When we go to the checkout line in the grocery store and we see eight or nine lanes, we expect them all to be open so we can get out in a hurry. Most of us can read the handwriting on the wall — we just think it is addressed to someone else.

How can we expect the rest of the world to respond to us with customer-friendly service and not expect schools to be community friendly? If we go to a store or restaurant and do not receive good customer service, we don't go back and we tell all of our friends about the bad experience.

Schools are no different. In today's world, private schools, home schooling, choice schools, vouchers, and charter schools are all options for parents who become dissatisfied, and newcomers who may hear negative things about the neighborhood school.

In addition, tuition tax credits are being pushed as an alternative to public education in an effort to fund these other choices. Legislation such as No Child Left Behind makes it possible for parents to transfer their children from under-achieving schools to higher achieving schools.

As the world becomes more demanding and educational choices become more and more competitive, it is essential that schools and school districts focus on becoming community-friendly schools. In addition to everything else that has to happen to ensure a successful school, we have to focus on having a public relations plan that includes customer service. A

plan that identifies who our customers are, determines what their needs are, and does all it can to meet those needs.

Yes, the customer service train has left the station and it is critical for all public school districts to be on the train and focus on customer service.

Who Are Our Customers?

There are 2 major groups of customers: **internal** and **external** customers.

Internal customers are our co-workers. And just like internal communication, the quality of customer service for our internal publics — our co-workers — is critical.

Consider the following customer service quote:

> Attitudes are contagious. Is yours worth catching?

I heard this question posed years ago and it has stuck with me. How can good customer service to our co-workers possibly be delivered if we do not have a good attitude and good team spirit? Office politics, angry words, and a bad attitude can all get in the way of good internal customer service.

A strong spirit of cooperation must exist between people and departments. Building and departmental meetings should reinforce the need for internal customer service. One way to do this is to establish an internal recognition program that allows staff members to nominate fellow employees for going beyond the call of duty. At an appropriate meeting, you might give a small token such as a coffee mug, notepad, or mouse pad to the employee along with a brief description of why this person was nominated. Set aside a section of the employee newsletter or somewhere appropriate on your web site to spotlight the noted employees.

Schools that are community-friendly create an environment where people feel welcome and comfortable.

Improved team spirit and employee attitude go a long way toward improving internal public relations and can dramatically affect how well we serve our external customers. Our external customers include students, parents or guardians, grandparents, senior citizens, community leaders, legislators, businesses, and community residents.

For parents and students, schools can be very intimidating places. The environment of a school can and will affect parent involvement and student learning. Schools that are community-friendly create an environment where people feel welcome and comfortable. In addition, community-friendly schools are perceived as places where people's needs are being met and they are treated with respect.

In many communities, 70% of adults have no connection with our schools. More and more adults are either single or married without children, and people are living longer so our senior citizen population is growing. All of these community members are taxpayers whose support we need. It is very important that we engage them in our schools.

Volunteer and mentoring opportunities are examples of ways to encourage adults to connect with your schools. A warm and friendly staff and an inviting atmosphere will help make it easier to get these community members to be involved and stay involved.

Identifying Customer Needs

Paper or plastic? Remember when grocery stores began the conversion from paper bags to plastic? After you had negotiated the check-out line and the cashier began ringing up your purchases, you hear from the person bagging your groceries, "Paper or plastic?" The basic need was known. You wanted your groceries gathered in some fashion so that you could get them from the store to the car and from the car into your home. In a very plain and straightforward way, your specific need about how your groceries should be bagged was determined: you were asked.

When asked, community members nationwide have indicated that they all have several basic customer service needs in common, which include:

■ Schools as safe and warm environments

■ Compassion and understanding from school staff members

■ Fair treatment

■ A sense that people's opinions are welcomed and considered

■ Options and alternatives that address people's needs

■ Information to help make decisions about their child

Your customer service plan must incorporate strategies to meet these needs and others that may be specific to your community.

Building a Customer Service Plan

A school or district can only truly become focused on the customer if every member of the staff believes that customer service is critical to the success of the organization and is willing to invest the time, resources, and effort to make that focus a reality. When this commitment has been made, the next step is to begin implementing a strategy.

The following steps provide a foundation for developing a customer service plan for your school or district:

■ **Appoint a team to create and implement your overall customer service strategy.** It is important for staff members to have ownership in a plan and to understand the need for good customer service. The best way to begin this process is to appoint a team that represents all staff members. Everyone will feel they have input into the process.

■ **Include the importance of good customer service in your mission statement.** This is a simple step that states clearly your commitment to quality customer service and provides direction to everyone.

■ **Survey internal and external publics for customer service feedback.** Do this at the beginning of the plan development and periodically after the plan is in place. Getting feedback in the beginning will give you an idea of problem areas you need to focus on, and the follow-up feedback will tell you how well you are doing.

■ **Include customer service workshops in your staff development programs.** All staff members must be fully informed of the importance being placed on customer service and then they must be appropriately trained. This can be done during formal staff development activities and then followed-up with a "customer service minute" during staff meetings.

■ **Establish customer service standards and make a commitment to keep them.** Develop the standards with input from all staff members. Once they have been developed, everyone must make a commitment to meet them.

■ **Develop a recognition program to reward excellent customer service.** A recognition program similar to the one we discussed earlier for recognizing good internal customer service could be extended to include customer service to both internal and external publics. Nominations for people who go beyond the call of duty would earn staff members a small gift presented at staff meetings and a feature in the employee newsletter. Recognizing quality customer service demonstrates the value your district places on meeting customer needs.

Team spirit and a cooperative attitude are critical to good customer service.

Good Customer Service Habits

For a school or a district to provide good customer service, the staff must be well trained. A good place to start is to give information about how to develop good customer service habits to employees.

Here are customer service habits for employees to consider:

■ **Be on time.** I once had a great barber, but he was never in the shop when I needed him. He did me no good so I found another barber. We must be available to provide the service when it is needed.

■ **Follow up on your promises.** When you promise to do something for any of your customers, be sure to keep the promise. Following through on commitments will build trust and credibility.

■ **Go the extra mile.** Most members of our communities expect good customer service. However, when we go beyond what is expected, people notice and appreciate it.

■ **Offer your customer options.** Nothing is more frustrating than being told there are no options when dealing with a problem. If at all possible, seek to provide more than one solution to address a customer's problem.

■ **Express empathy.** Sometimes circumstances are such that there are few options for a customer who is seeking a solution. It is important in those situations to have a caring and compassionate attitude.

■ **Treat your customer as the most important part of your job.** "I am profit and you are overhead," is a favorite saying of one of my friends when he deals with someone who is not giving the service he feels he deserves. In a service industry such as education, it is hard to understand how anyone could forget that we are there to serve, but it happens.

■ **Treat your coworkers as customers.** Team spirit and a cooperative attitude are critical to good customer service. Think of ways to help co-workers make their work easier and more pleasant.

■ **Give the customer your name and telephone number.** By providing this information, you make it easier for your customers to call you back if they have additional questions. It will also give your service a personal touch.

■ **Smile when you are on the telephone.** It is really hard to come across with a bad attitude when you are smiling, even on the telephone. It will make your customer feel better and it will make you feel better.

Barriers to Good Customer Service

Even though delivering good customer service is not complicated, sometimes the atmosphere surrounding the situation can complicate things.

Here are a few common barriers that can get in the way of delivering quality customer service:

■ **Physical barriers such as office layout, telephone systems, lack of sufficient parking, and poorly marked entrances.** Many times the customers you are trying to serve become angry — justly or unjustly. They try to call your office and only get a busy signal or no answer. So they climb into the car and drive to the school, deal with all of the traffic, and can't find a parking place because there is not enough visitor parking. They were angry before — but now they are really angry.

To avoid making things worse, take a physical inventory of your school or office.

■ Is there ample parking that is clearly marked for visitors?

■ Are there enough signs in clearly visible places to direct visitors to the front desk or office?

■ Is your telephone system adequate to handle the volume of calls coming into your building?

■ Addressing these and other physical barriers will make it easier for your customers to connect with you.

■ **Difficult customers who fuss and cuss.** It can be a real challenge to deal with people who are just mad and want to stay that way. Make certain that all of your employees are trained to deal with the difficult customer. Many techniques can be used including "finding a lily pad to climb on." Frogs sometimes will struggle in the same pool of water to gain a foothold on a lily pad. This is common ground. When we are having difficulty with a customer, we need to look for that common ground — a lily pad. Climb onto that pad and work to create understanding with the customer. This being accomplished, it is amazing how quickly you can move forward.

■ **Inadequate customer service staff development.** After your customer service strategy has been developed, make sure everyone knows those strategies and everyone has a commitment to meet them. Good customer service training must follow to provide the tools necessary for all staff to be successful in providing the customer service expected. Integrate customer service workshops into staff meetings and staff development training. This is not only a convenient way to provide the training but it also demonstrates its importance.

■ **Indifferent attitudes by employees.** It may just be a bad attitude or a defense mechanism related to the lack of training. Whatever the reason, an indifferent attitude can undermine and destroy your customer service program. It takes just one staff member to poorly treat a customer before they leave a building to make a lasting impression, regardless of what other

staff members have done. This reinforces the need for quality customer service staff development.

Employees should understand the expectations, receive proper training, and then be held accountable. Indifference will derail sincere and thoughtful treatment of all customers.

■ **Bad telephone manners.** Even if you have a good telephone system, the telephone can be a barrier to good customer service if it is not used properly. Research shows that 90% of the message a customer gets over the telephone is from the tone of voice. To ensure that your telephones are answered properly, use the following tips:

■ **Smile** when you talk on the telephone and focus on what the caller is saying.

■ **Train staff** how to answer the telephone, to put callers on hold, and to transfer calls.

■ **Avoid the "telephone hand-off."** Train employees to answer questions asked by callers and be informed enough to know to whom to transfer callers for prompt answers without being passed around several times.

■ **Call in to the school or office regularly** to check how well calls are being handled.

> **Outstanding customer service attracts customers and also improves the chances of keeping them.**

Moving from Good to WOW

We have talked a great deal about good customer service and what to do to ensure that is what our customers are receiving, but is that good enough? As we talked about in the beginning of this chapter, the world is changing. Our customers expect good customer service and deserve it. But educators need to mirror what many businesses have learned in the competitive marketplace: outstanding customer service attracts customers and also improves the chances of keeping them.

Customer "WOW" is expecting good customer service and getting something beyond that which makes us say, "WOW!"

Many stories demonstrate WOW customer service. Just as I began writing this portion of this chapter, I was interrupted by the plumber I called earlier today. My hot water heater was leaking and I had been putting off calling the plumber for a couple of weeks. I was at home unexpectedly so I decided to give him a call on the chance that he may be able to work me into his schedule. I was impressed by his customer service when he agreed to be at my house around 2 p.m. and would bring a hot water heater

just in case mine needed to be replaced. He showed up at 2 p.m. just as promised and checked out my old hot water heater. After about 15 minutes, he determined that I had a slow drip at the bottom of the heater, tightened the connection, and corrected the problem, avoiding the cost of a new hot water heater.

When I asked how much I owed him for his time, he said, "Not a thing." I live 15 miles outside of town and he had invested his time and the price of gasoline into the trip and was not going to charge me at all. THAT is customer WOW. Of course, I paid him for his time, thanked him, will certainly tell all my friends about him and I will always call on him when I need a plumber.

So, how do you move from good to WOW? The process begins by following the guidelines we talked about earlier in this chapter to bring a focus by all staff members on customer service.

Steps to good customer service

■ Appoint a team to create and implement your overall customer service strategy.

■ Include the importance of customer service in your mission statement.

■ Survey internal and external publics for customer service feedback.

■ Include customer service workshops in your staff development program.

■ Make certain all staff understand the importance of customer service and that each makes a commitment to deliver it.

Once these basic steps are in place, you can begin moving to customer WOW by setting the following expectations for all employees:

■ All staff members understand that Customer WOW starts with everyone.

■ Customer WOW is not just what you say, but what you do.

■ Good customer service is for all customers — both internal and external.

■ All staff members will be held accountable for providing good customer service.

Part of achieving customer WOW includes eliminating distractions that could affect how customers perceive your level of service. The following strategies can help move from good customer service to customer WOW:

■ Entrances to the school or office are plainly marked.

■ Grounds are well kept and free of trash and litter.

■ Ample visitor spaces can be readily found near the main entrance.

■ The front entrance it is clean and appealing.

■ Welcome signs are everywhere directing visitors to the main office.

■ Colorful displays of student work are in the hallways.

■ The front office is neat and clean with a waiting area that has sufficient seats for visitors.

■ Warmth is added by having live plants and other special touches in the office.

■ Reading material about the school is available in the office.

■ Staff members are professionally dressed, greet visitors promptly, and offer assistance.

■ Visitor badges are readily available.

■ Everyone is smiling.

■ Telephones are professionally answered within three rings.

■ A friendly greeting is used, identifying the school and person who is answering the call.

■ The person answering the telephone is informed and can share basic and timely information.

■ Callers are connected to the appropriate party promptly.

■ Callers who are put "on hold" are checked on every 30 seconds or so with updates or a connection.

Evaluate Your Strategy

When you feel you have most of your customer service initiatives in place and your staff is comfortable with them, put your customer service program to the test. One way to evaluate your customer service program is by using secret shoppers. These are people who come to your school in varying roles — a parent, a community activist, someone new to the community, a grandparent — and give you feedback about how they are treated and how they felt the school, department, or office did in meeting the established customer service guidelines. This feedback, along with the feedback that can be obtained by surveying your various publics, is a great way to measure how well you are doing and what you need to do better.

Buddy Price

Buddy Price is a 32-year public relations veteran, with 23 years in school public relations. He is currently director of community services for School District Five of Lexington/Richland Counties, near Columbia, South Carolina.

Price has been a member of the South Carolina Chapter of the National School Public Relations Association (SC/NSPRA) and a member of NSPRA for the past 23 years. He has served in many leadership roles in both organizations, including Southeast Region Vice President for NSPRA from 2000–2003.

He has been a frequent presenter at state chapter conferences around the Southeast, the NSPRA Seminar, and many statewide education conferences in South Carolina. His workshops include all aspects of school public relations, including many on customer service.

His Community Friendly Schools Program in School District Five serves as the basis for the South Carolina Red Carpet Schools Program, a recognition program for schools who demonstrate exemplary customer service. All 19 schools in his district have been named Red Carpet Schools by the South Carolina Department of Education.

Price has written many articles for state and national publications on school public relations and has been a contributor to NSPRA's *Wit and Wisdom of School Public Relations*, *Scenario Collection*, and the *Principal Communicator*.

Marketing Your Schools

By Nora Carr, APR

Educators need to market their profession and their schools as if theirs lives and their livelihoods depend on it — because they do.

In general, today's consumers are more demanding and harder to convince than ever before, and education consumers are no different. They want it faster, better, cheaper, hassle-free, and tailor-made just for them.

Quality is no longer a differentiator in the marketplace — it's the ticket for entry into the game. Our customers expect quality: That's a "given."

High academic standards, good grounding in the "basics," caring teachers, solid discipline, and a safe, orderly environment aren't going to set a school or district apart. Parents, students, senior citizens, business leaders, and taxpayers expect this "minimum" level of

---

service. Schools that want to market themselves competitively in today's high-stakes environment are going to have to provide something more.

Today's consumers also are harder to reach. They work longer hours and they suffer from a collective case of information overload as technology increases both the pace of life and the amount of data that clogs our communication channels.

Added to that, distrust of traditional institutions and organizations, including local, state, and national government,; corporations; unions; the news media; and the public schools is at an all-time high.

As noted in NSPRA's publication, *Making/Marketing Your School the School of Choice*:

> ...the tenure of superintendents, board members, and in some cases, principals, has been greatly reduced. Reform movements abound, although most taxpayers and parents aren't likely to know much about their schools except that "improvement is needed." After all, that's what report after report tells them.

Is it any wonder that national research conducted by Gallup, Public Agenda, Phi Delta Kappa, and other organizations that track consumers' views toward education all show a growing gap between the public and the public schools?

Parents, students, taxpayers, the business community, and educators are seeking new alternatives, as witnessed by the

rapid growth in home schooling, private and non-profit schools, school choice plans, and the charter school movement. Support is gradually increasing in many areas of the country for tuition vouchers, for-profit alternatives, and other efforts at privatizing public education.

Public education — and the concept of the "common" school that is accessible to all — stands at a crossroads and the competition is only going to get greater. Only market-driven organizations will survive.

Why market?

Who can afford not to?

What Is Marketing?

Like public relations, marketing is a key management function that requires planning and a systematic approach that is tied to the mission and strategic objectives of the school or district.

Marketing means bringing the consumer or customer perspective into every aspect of a school or district and using that critical information to develop a high-quality product that meets the needs of students, parents, and the community in a unique and powerful way.

Marketing typically involves an exchange: Tax dollars for an educated citizenry, tuition for an educated child, for example. Marketing is much more than selling or promoting a product that has already been developed. Marketing means actually changing the school, district, program, or service when needed to improve both the product and the organizations' responsiveness to its customers.

In other words, marketing is a two-way street. It requires finding out what the customer wants and then designing high-quality programs and services to meet those needs at a mutually agreeable "price." For example, having a first-class image in the community is meaningless if the educational program and achievement data don't back it up. At the same time, having a strong curriculum, superb faculty, and high test scores won't help recruit students or secure business partnerships if the prevailing community perception is that a competitor is better.

Some educators resist the idea of marketing, as if responding to customers also means abdicating leadership and the special professional knowledge and expertise they've worked on so hard to develop. Nothing could be further from the truth. Designing effective schools that meet the needs of today's children and families and doing it in a way that garners the financial support and respect of taxpayers and the community requires more vision, leadership, and creativity than ever before.

A keen understanding of the customers that schools serve is essential because this is certain: Marketing schools successfully today and in the future is going to get more challenging and it's going to require change in how schools and districts function.

Bring the customer perspective into every aspect of the school day.

The Marketing Perspective

If schools want to be more market-driven, they must bring the customer perspective into every aspect of the school day. One practical way of doing this is to analyze the school in terms of the seven "P's" of marketing:

- Product
- Price
- Promotion and publicity
- Packaging
- People
- Place
- Position

Descriptions for each of the marketing "P's" are below.

Product

Students and their success or failure academically, socially, and on the job are the ultimate measures by which a school is going to be judged. In essence, they are the school's "product."

That's why an ongoing school improvement initiative that involves parents, students, faculty, support staff, and the community is at the heart of every successful marketing effort. Product improvement has to come first.

Schools that are keyed into today's education consumer are willing to customize their product to meet individual student needs. Enrichment classes, tutoring, childcare before and after school or during school vacations, summer and evening sessions, partnerships with area private schools or businesses, individualized instruction, distance learning, and flexible deadlines for completing required coursework are all examples of the new, tailor-made approach to education.

Developing a marketing perspective also means viewing the product in terms of customer service. The following are examples to consider regarding the customer service of your school or district:

■ How quickly are phone calls and e-mails from parents returned?

■ Are callers and school visitors always treated courteously?

■ Are parent-teacher conferences scheduled in the evenings, on weekends, or at work sites in the community?

■ Is information about the school or program mailed within 24 hours of the original request?

■ Do parents have frequent personal contact about positive aspects of their children and their progress from a member of the school staff? Or do they hear from the school only when a problem occurs?

■ Are concerns that are voiced by parents, students, or teachers researched and responded to promptly with a plan of action or information about why a course of action isn't going to be taken?

■ How difficult is it register a new child at the school or to sign up for adult learning classes?

Price

Price is becoming more and more an issue in marketing schools and must be considered from a variety of perspectives. Price can mean the average homeowner's tax bill, the school's average cost-per-pupil, the tuition charged to non-resident students, the tax contributions of local businesses, or the school or district's total budget.

For both parents and educators, the most important bottom line of all — the only acceptable price — is high student achievement for all learners. To many education consumers, price can also mean the costs of administration, operations, building programs, personnel, and insurance. Consumers want to see their hard-earned dollars poured into instructional resources for children in the classrooms.

In today's competitive market, wise educators know how their school's price compares to the tuition charged by nearby public, private, and parochial schools. Today's parents and taxpayers want to know why public schools' cost per pupil is significantly higher than the local parochial school's tuition, or why those same dollars can't purchase the same type of education available in a selective private school.

Packaging

For years, public school marketers shied away from producing materials viewed as "too slick" or "too corporate." In today's media-saturated world, however, school districts must take a more professional approach when it comes to producing web sites, brochures, posters, newsletters, and other collateral materials. Themes, messages, colors, artwork, typography, copywriting, photography, and other building blocks of a district's brand image require careful attention and are best handled by professionals who specialize in producing first-class creative work.

Without careful attention to such areas as visual identity, brand image, positioning, and other key aspects of packaging, brands quickly weaken. The packaging has to be consistent over a period of years, not months. This means that everything from e-mail signature lines, name tags, fax cover sheets, posters, podium signs, building signage, PowerPoint presentations, web sites, and every other aspect of district

communication needs to share a common look, theme, and message.

While department leaders and other managers (including the district's graphic artist) may complain that strict adherence to visual identity guidelines is restricting creativity, the reality is that consistency in packaging is absolutely essential.

Coca Cola's corporate color is red, not blue. Nike uses the "swoosh" and, "Just do it." Bank of America uses red, white, and blue, not green, black, or maroon. Personal preferences don't matter when it comes to building strong brands. The key determinant is whether creative work is on brand, on strategy, and on message.

If every department can create its own logo or if managers can choose colors, fonts, and visuals based on personal preference rather than on a set of defined standards and guidelines, the brand is going to suffer. In today's 24-7, over-communicated world, cutting through the clutter is tough enough without adding to it by using competing messages, images, logos, slogans, fonts, formats, colors, photos, and graphic elements.

That's why a great way to test brand consistency is to gather a random sample of web site printouts, business cards, and collateral materials from various schools or departments. Then, scatter the documents across a conference table. Does everything on the table coordinate or look like it belongs together or as part of the same family? Do the colors complement one another? Does one strong look emerge?

If the answer is, "No," to any of these questions, it's time to clean up the school or district brand. Once the new or preferred look is created, develop detailed guidelines for logo use, font use, colors, and complementary colors, and create brand-consistent templates for letterhead, business cards, brochures, posters, e-mail signature lines, fax cover sheets, lunch menus, web sites, PowerPoint presentations, and other commonly used communication tools.

Promotion, people and publicity

Promotion is probably the most recognized aspect of the marketing process and often is where public relations and marketing intersect. Promotion can include the following:

■ Traditional marketing tactics such as publicity/news coverage, word-of-mouth and referrals, and special events (the free message)

■ Print, broadcast, online and outdoor advertising, and "give-aways" such as bumper stickers, magnets, pencils and coffee mugs (the paid message)

■ Data base and direct mail (the targeted message)

■ Use of district and school web sites, cable television programs, videos, school publications, special events, and communication channels (the controlled message)

■ Interactive and two-way communication channels such as online surveys, telephone polls, public forums, advisory committees and other public engagement techniques

Strategic marketing is based on building relationships with the customer and the opinion leaders who influence them.

Promotions can also refer to special offers and incentives, such as discounted tuition for siblings of current students or free parenting workshops offered to area residents by the local public school.

Many schools get too caught up in the "stuff and things" frenzy of marketing. Promotional items can be a nice way of saying "thank you" or providing recognition, but people won't make their decisions based on a token gift with a logo on it. Strategic marketing, like effective public relations, is based on building relationships with the customer and the opinion leaders who influence them. Two-way communication and the "personal" touch are essential.

Many marketers view building ongoing relationships with people, both internally and externally, as the fifth "P" of marketing. Keep in mind that it is better to have a whole lot of people involved in the school's marketing program, with each person doing a small piece, than it is to have one person going it alone — no matter how perfectly he or she builds a web of customer involvement into every aspect of the school program.

In today's fast-paced, highly competitive environment, the quality of these relationships represents the school's most powerful avenue form differentiating itself in the marketplace. As NSPRA points out in *Making/Marketing Your School the School of Choice*,

> Satisfied customers — your current parents — who speak positively about your school and its attributes are probably the single most effective marketing tool that you possess.

Publicity is also a related part of promotion. While word of mouth and its "viral" component thanks to e-mail and the Internet remain one of the most effective forms of marketing, the promotional aspect of free publicity is a powerful marketing tool.

Positive news stories, especially on television, reach a wide audience and have an enormous impact on the public's perception of public education. Packaging and placing news is tougher today than ever before, given the sensational nature and entertainment focus of the local news media. A gun on campus, an employee arrest, and school bus accidents are guaranteed media coverage. Getting reporters interested in the so-called "soft" news of effective teachers, high-achieving students, and involved parents takes research, careful planning, creativity, and exceptional writing skills.

Yet good things are happening in public schools everyday. Rather than cede the airwaves to anti-public school activists,

school leaders need to reclaim their community's public forums and the public's agenda.

Place

The physical environment of the school is ripe with marketing opportunities. Up-to-date marquee boards, well-kept grounds and exteriors, walls and bulletin boards decorated with welcome signs, student art work, photos, academic achievement awards, the student honor roll or community service projects all communicate volumes about the school.

The following are potential "trouble spots" that could send the wrong message about your school district:

- Warning signs posted on the school house door

- Messy offices and secretarial desks

- Poorly marked directional signs

- Graffiti

- Trash in the hallways and cafeterias

- Trash or discarded materials on school grounds

- Overgrown foliage or inadequate landscaping

- Peeling paint on playgrounds or exterior facilities

- Poorly maintained grounds around playgrounds

■ Unsightly rest rooms

■ Poorly maintained teacher lounges

Many schools have created a special nook for parents and visitors, complete with coffee pot and browsing materials, to welcome guests or to provide a comfortable waiting spot. The key is to create a welcoming environment for students, staff, parents, and visitors.

As the technology revolution makes learning more portable, the school building will no longer be the primary distribution point for education. Market-driven schools are figuring out ways to harness these new learning opportunities for students and adult learners through videoconferencing, distance learning, Internet courses, cable television, and school-business-university partnerships.

Position

To compete in today's over-communicated marketplace, educators need to carefully think through the "position" they want to hold in the marketplace and in the mind of the consumer. This is why having a clearly defined mission and purpose, knowing what makes the school unique, and understanding what the customer values are so critical.

The position is the ground the school wants to stake out as its special territory. It means identifying the school's greatest strength in the eyes of consumers and then hanging the marketing program on that hook. For example, in a community that values hands-on learning technology, the position the school wants to drive home might be "high tech, high school." This school might also have a distinguished fine arts program or exemplary special education services and may participate actively in community service projects. The position, the marketing hook, however, is "high tech" because that's what sells or is of greatest interest to consumers. All the other fine aspects of the school program become additional selling points.

By focusing on this single message, the marketing effort has a better chance of breaking through the confusing array of commercial messages that bombard the typical consumer daily.

Specialists are inherently viewed as more credible than generalists. It's the difference between marketing Sears, a general department store that also happens to sell clothing, and Abercrombie and Fitch, a specialty shop with a clearly defined target market and product. Public school districts can respond to this phenomenon by finding a brand position that captures the vision, is aspirational in nature, and can serve as an umbrella for a variety of initiatives. For example, Norfolk Public Schools' brand position is *World Class by 2010*. An urban school system, Norfolk views its diverse and international student body as one of its key marketing differentiators.

Who Should Market?

Everyone connected with the school, including the principal, teachers, support staff, parents, volunteers, students (especially at the middle and secondary level), senior citizens, and community members has a stake and a role in marketing.

Marketing can't be done effectively in a vacuum. The power of marketing can be realized only to the extent that it helps the school build closer relationships with its customers. This effort takes shared vision, commitment, and teamwork because effective marketing — becoming the "school of choice" in the community — is hard work.

Marketing can't be done effectively in a vacuum.

Many schools find it helpful to establish a marketing planning team. In some schools, this is also the site-based management or school improvement team. This core group should include representatives from all of the school's key internal and external stakeholders. As the team goes through the marketing process (outlined below), each step becomes an opportunity to involve new people.

The Marketing Process

The marketing process is similar to public relations planning and generally includes the following steps:

■ Assessment

■ Mission

■ Markets, mediums, and messages

■ Goals and objectives

■ Strategies and tactics

■ Action plans

■ Budgets and timing

■ Execution and monitoring

■ Evaluation

Descriptions for each step in the marketing process follow.

Assessment

An honest self-appraisal is required, with a special emphasis on the school's analysis of its strengths, weaknesses, opportunities, and threats (SWOT). Any marketing plan that doesn't address these four areas is almost certainly doomed to fail.

The marketing planning team should also identify the school's unique mission and appraise its faculty, support staff, educational program, services, special learning opportunities, building climate, and results.

Mission

This step of the process should include discussion on one key question:

What business are we in?

Answering this isn't as easy as it seems; it requires a clear, focused sense of purpose and direction.

Capturing the heart of the school in a powerful mission statement can set it apart in the marketplace and provide a measuring stick for all programs and services. If the school's actual mission statement is unwieldy, try boiling it down into a pithy slogan or theme. Develop a theme or marketing position statement you can stick to for several years. Good marketing takes time to take root in the mind of prospective customers. Changing themes or slogans every month or every year is a prescription for disaster.

Charlotte-Mecklenburg Schools' brand position, for example, is focused on educating students to compete locally, nationally and internationally. The primary strategy is increasing students' access to academically rigorous courses. Its theme is *Reach further. Global competitiveness starts here.*

Markets, mediums, and messages

The age of one-size-fits-all schools and communication is over.

Clearly identify the school's target markets and learn everything possible about them. Find out what they perceive, what they value, what's important to them, and who they listen to — and then develop messages that fit each audience. Then enlist the support and help of the people and communication channels — the medium — that each target group views as most credible and use those sources to carry the school's messages.

For example, research consistently shows that employees prefer to learn about important news and information directly from their supervisors rather than from newsletters, web sites, or other tools. Similarly, despite the growing reliance on the Internet and other new media tools, many parents still count on their child's teacher or principal as their most important — and believable — source for accurate, up-to-date information.

Measurement is increasing in importance in both marketing and public relations.

Goals and objectives

Strive for goals that are SMART (Simple, Measurable, Achievable, Resources, Tasks). Goals are the desired behavior or being that is sought; objectives are the individual steps or action items needed to achieve the goal.

Measurement is increasing in importance in both marketing and public relations, and solid plans include a mix of:

■ **Process measures** (Were the e-mails sent to prospective parents on time, on message, and on brand?)

■ **Benchmarks** (How many families have enrolled in the new school 90 days from opening day, 60 days out, 30 days out, etc.)

■ **Results** (What is the total number of children enrolled in a new facility by the first day of school?)

Strategies and tactics

Strategies represent the major initiatives that are being planned to accomplish the goals. Often couched in military terms, strategies describe how a goal will be accomplished and what themes, messages, psychology, or appeals may be used.

For example, the goal might be to increase enrollment in grades K-3 by 30%. The strategy would be to start an early childhood program to connect pre-school parents to the school during a critical decision-making time.

The tactics are the activities or tools that will be developed to market the preschool, such as asking satisfied customers to speak to prospective parents about the school's *Parents as Teachers* program or distributing baby bibs with the school's mission and logo as part of the local hospital's gift pack to new parents.

Keep in mind that good marketing strategies tend to show results early. If it isn't working, adjust accordingly and try something new.

Action plan

A plan of action for each major goal is essential and should include the:

1. Steps needed to accomplish the goal

2. People responsible

3. Resources (including budget)

4. Time line for getting it done

Graphing the plan in a chart or calendar can help keep the school from trying to do too much at once and can help keep efforts on track.

Execution and monitoring

Assign a "keeper of the plan" to make sure that action plans are carried out as designed or to pull the planning team together to redirect efforts, if needed.

Put into place some type of ongoing monitoring system to track progress and to break each objective into small accomplishable steps. For example, if a goal is to recruit 30 new community volunteers by the end of the year, how many should be in place each month? How many contacts are needed to produce one recruit? Who is going to make the contacts? Who follows up? By when? How will volunteers be screened before being deployed into the schools? Who will conduct the volunteer training and how will the impact of the volunteer program be measured at the end of the year?

Evaluation

Evaluation, like marketing, is an ongoing process. The purpose is to gain insight and information that can be used to more closely align the school with its target markets and to identify areas that need improving.

As with assessment, evaluation comprises both formal and informal measures including conversations with a few key questions like:

■ What worked?

■ What didn't?

■ Why? Why not?

■ What do we want to do differently next time?

While such "common sense" approaches are useful, tracking data on an ongoing basis is critical for the school's long-term marketing success and will help the team identify trends and issues that need to be addressed.

Research Overview: Why Parents Choose Schools

While current research on the choice movement isn't definitive, several recent national opinion polls reveal strong consensus among parents and the community about what they are looking for in schools. These areas include:

■ Strong academic programs in traditional subject areas and high standardized test scores

■ High expectations of students for learning and behavior

■ Orderly, safe, disciplined, and caring school environment

■ Special programs offered to meet student's individual needs

■ Emphasis on common values such as honestly, caring, perseverance, respect and responsibility

The following are other reasons that parents frequently cite as key factors in choosing a school for their children:

■ Academic and athletic achievement

■ Accessible staff and open communication

■ Strong parental involvement in decision-making

■ Convenient location to either home or work

■ Alumni speak well of the school

■ Above-average expenditures for pupil instruction, teacher salaries, library, media and technology services

■ Small class sizes and individualized attention

Sample Marketing Action Chart

Goal	
Relation to mission, goal, or objective	
Strategy	

Action steps	Target market	Person responsible	When	Resources needed	Budget/Source

Method of evaluation: _____

Evaluation completed by: _____

Results: _____

_____

_____

Suggestions for improvements in the future:

Adapted from *Planning Your School PR Investment*, NSPRA, Derwood, Maryland.

The Case for Brand Marketing

In the private sector, branding — staking out a clear and definable position in the mind of the consumer — is considered an essential component of the marketing process. That's why corporations spend millions to identify, articulate, and share (in words, pictures, emotions, and experiences) the key ways their product, service, organization, or company is better than everyone else's.

For Tide, it means, "whiter whites." For Starbucks, it's the ultimate coffee experience. For Nordstrom, it's customer service. For Mercedes Benz, it's precision engineering. For MySpace.com, it's the hottest online gathering place for the under 30 crowd.

Strong brands like these are known for something specific, something unique, and something special in the marketplace. Like the Good Housekeeping Seal of Approval, strong brands deliver a promise of value that consumers can count on, time after time after time.

These brand promises are proprietary to certain companies, figuratively if not literally. For example, Southwest Airlines "owns" the marketplace position as the first "no frills but fun" way to fly. Other low-cost carriers may compete on price, but they don't have the same reputation for happy, humorous, and off-beat employees.

> **School officials will have to be much more intentional and aggressive in packaging and sharing their story.**

Sadly, when most public schools or districts are mentioned, the first words to pop immediately into people's minds aren't "great education," "academic rigor," "cornerstone of democracy" or "world's best." This isn't because public schools, school districts, and the people who lead them aren't doing great things. They are. However, while public school leaders have been raising the bar and closing the achievement gap, pundits, politicians, and anti-public school activists have been saturating the airwaves and setting the education agenda.

Overwhelmingly, these stories, sound bites, and reports are negative and one-sided. As Gary Gordon, global practice leader for Gallup Poll, said in 2004:

> It's disappointing that less than half of Americans are satisfied with the quality of public education in the nation, but it is not surprising. Our attitudes toward the nation's schools come principally from the news media, and most of this information is negative.

As a brand, public education is struggling. To turn this around, school officials will have to be much more intentional and aggressive in packaging and sharing their story with parents and the 70% of voters in most communities who do not have school-aged children.

Building a better brand

The most difficult and time-consuming component of brand-building is determining the unique selling proposition — or USP — for the school or district.

More than simply designing a new logo or coming up with a catchy theme or slogan, developing a USP that's credible and relevant to the target market requires being able to instantly answer the following questions:

■ What makes your school or district different or unique?

■ What can your school or district truly own in the marketplace?

■ What does your school or district do better or more than everyone else?

■ What one benefit or message is the most compelling?

■ What will connect emotionally the most with our targets?

■ What reasons can we develop to bolster or support our claim?

Built on emotion and designed to evoke a visceral reaction from consumers, strong brands are also inherently rational — they make sense to consumers. Using Tide to get clothes cleaner and brighter feels right to consumers. Choosing Tide as an environmentally sound chemical bath doesn't resonate quite as well.

As the image associated with a company, organization, product, or service, a brand needs to be relevant culturally as well. Nordstrom, Marriott, and Ritz Carlton are all known for superior customer service. Taking care of their customers is so embedded in their organizational cultures that many employees simply view it as "how we do business here." Cable companies, on the other hand, are typically viewed as customer service nightmares by many consumers, as are most public schools and school districts.

Just as cable companies won't be able to change their negative image overnight, public school officials aren't going to be able to change their bureaucratic, rule-bound images easily. Radical cultural change that places customers first will have to occur if any kind of image makeover campaign is going to work. Otherwise, cynicism may only increase.

While Starbucks and other hot brands may seem like overnight successes, the reality is that these consumer darlings took years to build. Pay careful attention to the tone, manner, look, and feel — the emotional and conceptual elements — of the brand. Ask what kind of image is going to resonate best with the people who matter most. Is the tone inclusive, warm, sophisticated, funny, inspiring, or caring? Color, font, and creative choices should flow from the tone and manner a brand is trying to create, not the preferences of the graphic designer or the superintendent.

Hallmarks of strong brands

Focus and consistency are the hallmarks of strong brands. Ironically, one of the greatest branding challenges school districts face is also one of public education's greatest strengths: the fact that it's public, free, and open to all.

Strong corporate brands are known for something special. Public education is the epitome of the "all things to all people" enterprise.

According to Laura Ries, co-author of *The 22 Immutable Laws of Branding*:

> The perception out there is that private is better than public, when in reality, many times the public schools are better.

> The perception is that anything run by the government is lousy, even though that may not be the way it is.

Ries suggests combating this inherent bias toward private education by applying some of the principles top schools have used successfully, such as choosing names that convey prestige rather than the generic or haphazard names typical of public education. "What can be more generic than north, south, east, and west?" asks Ries, noting that schools simply assigned a number, such as Public School 121 is even worse.

> While the names of private schools are not all terrific, many of them are infinitely more powerful.

> How people feel when talking about something is important, and when they're using a more powerful name, it sounds better.

School leaders are the visible symbol of public education in their communities.

Visible leadership

An often-overlooked aspect of public school branding is the importance of having highly visible leaders who spend significant time each day on community relations and public engagement. As the embodiment of the public school brand, school leaders are the visible symbol of public education in their communities.

Every superintendent and principal should have a "stump" speech that is shared routinely with business and community groups, parent leaders, non-profit organizations, Realtors, and other key publics. Regular media briefings, cable television shows, guest columns in local newspapers, web site blogs, and other tools can also help maintain a time-stretched leader's visibility.

Ries says:

> Public school leaders need to be going out, doing speeches, giving interviews and promoting public education at multiple levels — including the local, state, and national level, Everyone should know their name.

While face-to-face communication remains the best relationship-building tool, savvy school leaders are backing outreach efforts with sophisticated relationship data bases that can be used

---

to track contact information, e-mails, phone calls, and mailings.

The power of brand

Creating a powerful and memorable brand can make a significant marketing difference for school districts. A strong brand can accomplish the following for your district:

■ Capture the imagination and helps consumers make an emotional connection with the product, service, or organization

■ Represent a unique position that is long-term, future-oriented and sustainable over time

■ Own a thought or a key position in the mind of the consumer, and markets aggressively from that focused position

■ Reflect the organization's culture and values; good brands know who they are and remain true to their position

■ Build credibility by being relevant, realistic and attainable

■ Communicate simply and effectively through design consistency and integrity

The checklist on the following pages will help you determine the progress toward creating a brand or assessing your existing brand.

Brand Marketing Checklist

Adherence to visual identity guidelines	Yes	No
Correct use of logo (size, proportion, placement, color, type)	❑	❑

Notes:

Recommendations:

Brand image/positioning		
Purpose of communications	❑	❑
Target audience	❑	❑
Attitudes/behavior trying to change/influence	❑	❑
Call to action	❑	❑
Key benefit	❑	❑
Reasons to believe	❑	❑
Tone and manner	❑	❑
Look and feel	❑	❑
Positioning of organization clear	❑	❑

Notes:

Recommendations:

Content		
Has clear, compelling, creative, and concise copy	❑	❑
Has interesting leads, hooks, angles	❑	❑
Uses active voice; is action-oriented	❑	❑
Has practical news, tips, information the reader can use	❑	❑
Uses educational jargon or acronyms	❑	❑
Uses executive/expert positioning	❑	❑
Follows AP or establishes style clearly and consistently throughout	❑	❑
Clearly identifies target audience	❑	❑
Provides resources or sources for additional information; is easy to access	❑	❑
Uses subheads, bullets, other graphic organizers to help pull readers and skimmers through copy	❑	❑
Appropriately uses headlines, cutlines, grabbers	❑	❑
Answers, "Why should I care?"	❑	❑

Notes:

Other Recommendations:

Creative (art, layout, design)	Yes	No
Overall creative concept (Fresh? Inviting? On brand? Pleasing aesthetic? Does the style fit the audience?	❏	❏
Photography (composition, quality, cropping, placement). Is the photography active and interesting (not just head shots and status poses)?	❏	❏
Proper resolution used for graphics, illustrations, photos?	❏	❏
Copywriting	❏	❏
Typography (all type treatments, color, graphic organizers)	❏	❏
Graphics/Illustration (minimal use of clip art)	❏	❏
Layout/Design (clean, not cluttered; active use of white space)	❏	❏
Paper selection (Is paper good enough quality to hold the ink? Are type letters bleeding together?)	❏	❏
Pre-press production quality (screens, lines, bitmaps, alignment)	❏	❏

Production/Printing		
Printing quality (Printer using high enough line screen to produce clean looking type and images? Color coverage and match? Proper registration on color separations?	❏	❏

Overall Effectiveness		
Meets needs of target audiences	❏	❏
Is consistent; reinforces brand image	❏	❏
Compels reader to action	❏	❏
Positions product/service clearly in mind of consumer	❏	❏

Overall rating (On 1–7 scale; 1 = lowest and 7 = highest)	

Other comments/recommendations:

■ Nora Carr, APR

Nora Carr, APR, is the chief communications officer for Charlotte-Mecklenburg Schools, North Carolina. Carr is a nationally known and respected authority on strategic public relations, marketing, and crisis communication. A sought-after speaker, Carr is a frequent presenter at local, state, and national conferences for education and business audiences.

She has won more than 85 local, state, and national awards for excellence in public relations. Her work has been published in a variety of news outlets and professional trade publications.

Carr leads and directs communication strategy and public relations for the Charlotte-Mecklenburg Schools (CMS) which serves more than 126,000 students and ranks among the nation's most-respected metropolitan-wide school systems. Carr also fields more than 2,500 media inquiries a year, serves as the district's official spokesperson, and oversees the operation of CMS-TV, volunteers and partnerships, employee communications, database marketing, community relations, special events, and web, print and electronic communications.

Before CMS, Carr served as senior vice president and director of public relations for Luquire George Andrews (LGA), one of the Carolina's leading marketing firms.

Before joining LGA, Carr guided communication efforts for the reopening of Charlotte's landmark desegregation case, designed and implemented the successful marketing campaign for the Charlotte-Mecklenburg School's new, district-wide choice plan, attracting more than 4,000 private school families and gaining an unprecedented 96% participation rate among the district's 109,000 students.

A former journalist, Carr has also worked as director of marketing and development for Cooperating School Districts of Greater St. Louis and as public relations director for The Network for Educational Development and the Normandy School District. She has also served as a writer and public relations specialist for Barnes Hospital and the Washington University Medical Center in St. Louis, Missouri.

In 1999, Carr was one of four national experts asked to provide onsite assistance to the Jefferson County Public Schools in Golden, Colorado. Carr coordinated media relations in the aftermath of the Columbine High School tragedy. While there, she dealt with more than 750 news outlets and more than 1,000 reporters daily.

Public Engagement

By Karen H. Kleinz, APR

Whether or not we are actively involved in our local schools, we all have opinions about how they ought to be run. After all, most of us have spent at least 12 years of our lives in school, which we believe makes us experts (based on our own experience).

Because of this connection and relationship we all have with schools, we each carry perceptions and emotional baggage related to our experience. This has an impact on how we relate to schools as parents, taxpayers, elected officials, and employees, even though today's schools offer a very different learning environment from those we attended. As a result, it is simply not enough to tell people about our schools and expect their support without also offering them an opportunity to become actively engaged in the education process.

In the competitive education environment of the 21st century, where charter schools and alternative educational programs abound, public schools must build solid relationships with the community as well as parents in order to succeed.

Generating news stories and information is not enough because people are not persuaded to engage by facts alone. What moves them to care about something beyond their personal context is when they can make an emotional connection to their own experience, beliefs, and values.

Educators have long understood the value of involving parents and community in the schools, but involvement alone is not enough.

What Is Public Engagement?

There are as many definitions and names for *public engagement* as there are process models for engaging people. The definition of public engagement that NSPRA likes to use was developed by the Annenberg Institute for School Reform:

> **Public engagement:** A purposeful effort, starting in either the school system or the community, to build a collaborative constituency for change and improvement in the schools.

No matter how it's defined, the key components of public engagement include:

■ Active listening

■ Dialogue and deliberation

■ Collaboration

■ Shared responsibility for outcomes

True engagement is focused not so much on the "how to," but on getting at the values that should drive decision-making. Public engagement is more than just bringing people together to share their thoughts and ideas. At its core, it is about connection and collaboration and the relationships we build with others who live and work in our community.

If we want the public to feel ownership in their schools as well as a sense of responsibility for student success, we must:

■ Make a commitment to expand the relationship

■ Determine the expectations we each hold for the relationship

■ Explore shared community values and beliefs

■ Create opportunities for shared decision-making

■ Find common ground for taking action that leads to improved education and student achievement

---

Public engagement is not for the faint of heart or for those wishing to maintain the status quo.

Creating a Positive Framework for Engagement

In his groundbreaking book, *Is There A Public For Public Schools?*, Dr. David Mathews, president and CEO of the Charles F. Kettering Foundation, argued that real school reform is impossible unless citizens feel they "own" their schools and take active responsibility for making improvements. He noted that,

> It's not simply that the schools need to be improved: the *relationship* between the schools and the community needs repair. Our research [Kettering Foundation] suggests that Americans are looking for a different way of working with educators; they want a relationship among equals.

This struck a chord with many educators who read Mathews' book and immediately sought out ways to "engage" the public in their schools.

Educators have long understood the value of involving parents and community in the schools, but involvement alone is not enough. If we are to realize the improvements we desire in education, we need to engage the public in reclaiming and taking responsibility for "their" schools.

Today's public is demanding improved student achievement and increased accountability from educators, as well as a voice in decision-making about schools and the education of their children.

Unfortunately, the public often finds it easy to criticize education because many people feel little or no ownership in the schools. Educators must reach out to the public, encourage people to reconnect, rebuild their sense of ownership, and rekindle their interest by setting school missions within the context of public objectives.

Public engagement is not for the faint of heart or for those wishing to maintain the status quo. While public engagement can be immensely rewarding, it can also cause problems if not approached intentionally. It can be time-consuming, challenging, and from a traditional education mind-set, risky in terms of outcomes.

Moving from Persuasion to Engagement

"Telling and selling" techniques for convincing the public that educators know what is best for students don't work anymore, as evidenced by the way today's parents "shop" for schools that best match their values and expectations.

If we are to realize the improvements and successes we desire in our schools, we need to do more than persuade the public that we have a problem and then ask them to support our solution. Instead, we must engage our stakeholders — both internal and external — in helping us think through the challenges we face and in making the tough decisions on how to address them in the best interests of students, families, and the community.

This means that long before a decision is made and action taken on an issue or concern, our stakeholders must be given an opportunity to explore what they believe and how they feel about it. They need time to work through their views, exchange ideas, and have a voice in possible outcomes.

This doesn't mean our publics want to control day-to-day school operations, but it does mean they want to feel connected to what happens.

Not only does "tell and sell" not work anymore, it might also work against you. Research conducted by the Kettering Foundation has found that when officials make a decision without public input and then announce it through a "tell and sell" effort, people are left with only two options — either to ratify the decision or to reject it. And if they want a voice and feel left out, guess which option they are likely to choose?

In his most recent book, *Reclaiming Public Education by Reclaiming Our Democracy*, Mathews points out that public engagement work requires considerable energy and notes that:

> Political participation begins on a very personal level.

> **Instead of inviting stakeholders to the table after the fact, we must bring them in at the beginning so that they can take part in setting the agenda.**

It's simply not enough to tell people how a problem is going to affect them and insist that they get involved. People have to find a personal connection between a problem and what is most valuable to them before they will engage. People connect when they feel that a possibility for change exists, and when they feel there is something they can do personally, however small, to make a difference.

They become engaged when they have a chance to interact, offer input, participate in problem solving, and take ownership of ideas. As a result, says Mathews, "New insights are sparked when people hear about different experiences that allow them to see familiar problems from unfamiliar vantage points," thus creating a source of political energy.

If we truly want to engage our publics and have them take responsibility for decision-making, we must begin to develop an authentic dialogue with them. Instead of inviting stakeholders to the table after the fact, we must bring them in at the beginning so that they can take part in setting the agenda.

What Is Deliberative Dialogue?

The objective in deliberative dialogue is to make sound decisions. It is exploratory, open to all options, and reflective. It is a process for finding common ground and determining what actions are in the best interests of the public as a whole as well as what the community will support after weighing the costs and consequences.

The National Issues Forum (NIF), a nonpartisan, nationwide network of forums and study circles for the discussion of public policy, has identified the following questions asked in the deliberative process:

▓   What is valuable to us in this issue?

▓   What are the costs or consequences associated with the various options?

▓   Where are the conflicts in this issue that we have to work through?

▓   Can we detect any shared sense of direction or common ground for action?

The nature of such "choice work" means that there is tension between the options being discussed because there is no right or wrong, no easily defined position that is the clear choice. It forces us to consider core values and the tradeoffs we are willing to accept in order to serve the common good of the community.

Context Matters

The good news is that more districts than ever are incorporating public engagement into their communication and strategic planning processes. Forums, town halls, and study circles are being used to initiate dialogue and gather public input. While this is positive, a closer look reveals some pitfalls.

One of the points Mathews emphasizes is that getting citizens engaged requires reframing school issues in the context of community concerns. However, in our work at NSPRA conducting communication audits and counseling members in public engagement, we find that this critical reframing component is often overlooked. This is not to say that the public is completely unhappy with the public education system in this country — research such as the PDK Gallup Poll proves just the opposite year after year. But as we talk with education stakeholders in focus groups around the U.S. and Canada, we find they are increasingly frustrated with issues being framed solely from education's side.

Given the parameters and mandates under which schools operate, educators often approach and name issues from perspective that is different from the publics they serve. As a result, some districts that implemented what they thought was public engagement on important decisions have ended up dealing with public disillusionment and even "enragement" as a result of their efforts.

Their mistake?

Not engaging stakeholders in the conversation until too late in the process for any major changes to be made, thereby negating their voice on the issue at stake. Though well-intentioned, unless we know what our stakeholders value most about education and our schools and frame the problem from their perspective, we won't be successful in creating the "relationship among equals" they desire.

Learning to Listen

One of the things NSPRA has learned through our work is that educators don't do a very good job of "listening." Participants of communication audit focus groups tell us consistently that their school systems offer plenty of opportunities for stakeholders to provide input and be "heard." The problem from their perspective is that no one is actually "listening."

We need to change the way we frame education issues so that they resonate with the communities we serve. The following are some things to consider:

■ **Be proactive in opening the dialogue on future issues.** If enrollment projections indicate a school may need to be closed in the next 3 years, start talking about it now. Don't try to force deliberative dialogue into a short timeline when you've known about an issue for a long time. Engage your stakeholders from the start so that they can own the outcome.

■ **Create a steering committee of parents, staff, and community members to help frame tough issues from a public perspective.** You may be surprised at how differently your stakeholders see an issue, which can also open the door to creative solutions. Don't forget to involve representatives who reflect the ethnic, religious, economic, and cultural diversity of your schools and community.

■ **Present specific parameters, such as budget guidelines or mandates at the outset of the dialogue process.** Don't engage people in a "blue sky" discussion when options are limited. Make sure they have access to all the information and background studies that will drive the final decision. Nothing causes people to disengage faster than feeling that their time and efforts have been wasted.

■ **Close the communication loop.** Whenever you ask the public for input, be sure to "close the loop" by reporting back what you heard and what actions will be taken as a result. Share the success by recognizing those who actively participated in the decision-making process. We all want to feel our opinions are valued and that we can make a positive contribution when we are asked to get "involved" in something. This will help build relationships and a culture of engagement for the future.

Foundations for Success

There are several keys to successfully introducing public engagement as a process that is integral to the life of our schools and districts. These foundations for success include the following:

■ **Realize that there is no one, correct way to engage the public.** This is both the challenge and the beauty of public engagement. Each community is different and the process for engaging your stakeholders should be developed based on the structure and needs of your community. Considerations should include the demographics of the community. It is important to engage people on their terms by paying attention to language, culture, socio-economic factors, meeting locations, and other factors, in order to create entry points for people to engage and a comfort zone for dialogue.

■ **Recognize that it takes time to develop real dialogue.** You cannot engage the public overnight. It is important to know going into it that this is a lengthy process. The goal is to create a culture in the schools and community that supports a deliberative process for involving stakeholders in determining what is valuable to them in their schools as well as involving them in decision-making.

One way to begin is to offer a series of study circles on a non-controversial topic, such as, "What do students need to know to be successful adults in today's world?" Once the process is established and people are comfortable, you can move on to more difficult topics affecting the schools such as closing the achievement gap or funding facility needs. As the community begins to accept responsibility for ensuring the success of its schools, it will be difficult to return to the old way of doing business.

■ **Accept the fact that public engagement is labor-intensive.** Public engagement requires a major time and energy commitment on the part of those responsible for coordinating the engagement process. It works best when a variety of people, including parents, staff, and community members, are involved in planning and developing the process. Working through discussion and deliberation to reach a decision may take more or less time depending on the issue, the makeup of the school and community, and the history and politics involved.

■ **Appreciate that public engagement requires skilled facilitation.** It is critical that those guiding the process remain neutral and open to the input and outcomes generated. Remember that a public engagement process is not intended to persuade and manipulate the public toward a particular point of view or action. Rather, the goal is find common ground and shared values around an issue or concern that lead to collaborative solutions. Facilitator training is an important component in preparing to engage the public. Along with staff members, schools should consider training parents and community members to be facilitators as well.

■ **Don't forget to engage employees.** Even the most extensive and effective external engagement processes will ultimately flounder if employees are not included as well. Staff members who feel left out and treated like second-class citizens can undermine the most well-intentioned efforts of the board and administration. They have a vested interest in successful schools from multiple perspectives — as parents, employees and taxpayers — and constitute an important group of stakeholders.

■ **Understand that public engagement requires a strong commitment from the school board and administration.** Once the process is set in motion, district leadership must be prepared to listen and act on the outcomes, knowing they may not always like what they hear. Communication throughout the process is critical. Keeping stakeholders apprised of progress being made as well as the rationale behind decisions will build confidence and credibility in the process. If that trust is violated, it is difficult to recover.

What Are Study Circles?

Study circles are facilitated groups of 5–20 stakeholders who meet in one or more sessions to explore an issue or concern, share ideas, and learn together as a group. The process is voluntary and highly participatory. Participants often begin their dialogue after reading and studying materials and information related to the issue. Unlike most public meetings and forums, the discussion does not begin with outcomes in mind and is not driven by a need for consensus. Rather, the goal is to understand issues from a community perspective and explore possible options for addressing concerns. This frequently leads to collaboration and action as participants begin to understand how they can make a difference and become motivated to take on new roles in the community.

Community-wide study circle programs are much larger in scale and often involve dozens of study circles convened collaboratively by various community organizations (i.e., school districts, city/county government, civic groups, and business leaders). These programs seek to involve a broad cross-section of citizens to address important community issues such as race relations, violence, health and welfare, and education.

Study circles provide an excellent opportunity for citizens to connect with one another and come to understand the important role they play in the life of their community. They provide a venue for people to hear points of view that differ from their own and a comfort zone to develop mutual understanding and explore common beliefs and values.

Getting Engaged

Public engagement is not just bringing people together at a town hall, public hearing, or focus group to share their thoughts and feelings on an issue. It's about creating a shared sense of direction and finding a way to work together even when we don't agree. It's about the idea that, "I can't get what I want unless you also get what you want," and collaborating as a "village."

In *Is There A Public for Public Schools?*, Mathews maintains that school issues (like student achievement and funding) cannot be treated in isolation from other community issues, and unless schools are reframed to embrace the larger context of community concerns, they will not be resolved because all the stakeholders are not at the table.

According to Mathews,

> What a school does makes little sense unless we know how its mission relates to the community's educational goals and public purposes.

He makes the case that we must first work to create healthy, functioning communities before we can focus on school reform. For example, the school board can change graduation requirements to demonstrate a commitment to academics, but the board alone cannot overcome the myriad forces in the community that put students at risk and interfere with their education, whether it's drugs, gangs, teenage pregnancy, or a dying economy and lack of jobs.

The interests of the schools and community are inextricably linked. We can't have good schools without a supportive, engaged community, and we cannot have a vital, healthy community without good schools. As with any successful relationship, there must be give and take and a mutual benefit for both parties.

The following are steps to begin rebuilding the public's sense of ownership in schools and creating a vision of a community where all students can succeed:

■ **Map community assets and assess the capacity for public engagement in your community.** Who needs to be at the table and what resources exist to support your efforts? By taking a closer look at your community infrastructure, you may discover potential support systems that have not been tapped in the past, as well as gain insight into how local issues are discussed and resolved, and which opinion leaders get things done.

■ **Educate all staff about public engagement.** Explain what it is, why it's important, and what their role is in the process. Staff support is crucial to the success of any public engagement project. Everyone needs to be a cheerleader for its value and importance.

■ **Regularly communicate.** You must share good information about the process and what you hope to learn and accomplish with stakeholders. Keep the process open and transparent.

■ **Provide time and a safe environment to explore concerns and find common ground.** The facilitated structure of discussion models such as study circles are designed to create and support a comfortable environment for dialogue. Consider venues outside of school facilities to convene your groups. This can be particularly important in engaging minority and immigrant communities.

■ **Develop a plan of action that involves the entire community in working collaboratively to find solutions and strategies that benefit children.** People get invested in an issue or concern when they feel they can do something to make a difference, and children connect us all to the future.

The public is ready to be "engaged" and asking to be heard. Community members want to be involved in determining the values that drive education, not just asked their opinions on how best to accomplish a goal already determined by the administration and school board. As school systems and communities search for ways to address the challenges facing them, the process of public engagement continues to evolve. Just as every community is unique, with needs specific to those who live there, the process for engaging the public will vary in response to those needs. In whatever form it takes, public engagement is now a critical component of any effective communication/public relations strategic plan.

Resources

National School Public Relations Association
19548 Derwood Road
Rockville, MD 20855
(301) 519-0496
Fax: (301) 519-0494
www.nspra.org

The Kettering Foundation
200 Commons Road
Dayton, OH 45459
1-800-600-4060
Fax: 1-937-435-7367
www.kettering.org

Study Circles Resource Center
P.O. Box 203
Pomfret, CT 06258
(860) 928-2616
Fax: (860) 928-3713
www.studycircles.org

National Issues Forum Institute
P.O. Box 75306
Washington, D.C. 20013-5306
www.nifi.org

Deliberative Democracy Consortium
1050 17th Street NW, Suite 701
Washington, D.C. 20036
(905) 972-0550
www.deliberative-democracy.net

Public Agenda
6 East 39th Street
New York, NY 10016
(212) 686-6610
Fax: (212) 889-3461
www.publicagenda.org

Annenberg Institute for School Reform
Brown University, Box 1985
Providence, RI 02912
(401) 863-7990
Fax: (401) 863-1290
www.aisr.brown.edu

References

Is There a Public for Public Schools?
David Mathews
Kettering Foundation Press, 1996

Organizing Your First Forum/Study Circle
National Issues Forum

Planning Community-Wide Study Circle Programs
Martha McCoy, Phyllis Emigh,
Matt Leighninger, Molly Barrett
1996 Topsfield Foundation, Inc.

Reasons for Hope, Voices for Change
A report of the Annenberg Institute on
Public Engagement in Education
Annenberg Institute for School Reform,
Brown University, 1998

Reclaiming Public Education by Reclaiming Our Democracy
David Mathews
Kettering Foundation Press, 2006

National School Public Relations Association
Resource materials and counseling
www.NSPRA.org

Karen H. Kleinz, APR

Karen H. Kleinz, APR, associate director of the National School Public Relations Association (NSPRA), has 30 years' experience in public relations, working in the private sector as well as public education.

As a school public relations professional, Kleinz developed and managed communication programs for diverse school districts in Arizona, from small, semi-rural districts with large, non-English speaking, minority populations to the largest elementary district in the state, serving suburban Phoenix.

Since joining NSPRA in 1998, Kleinz has led the association's public engagement efforts and has represented NSPRA in collaborative partnerships with the Annenberg Institute for School Reform, the Study Circles Resource Center, and the Kettering Foundation.

She also directed NSPRA's joint project with the Kettering Foundation to develop a community audit process designed to help school systems and communities assess their ability to successfully engage each other in supporting student achievement and building public ownership of schools.

Issue Management

By Ron Koehler, APR

Quite simply, issue management is the ability to anticipate and prepare for a problem before it happens. We do this all the time in education. For example, a large portion of the work of school district business managers is to anticipate future needs and budget for them. Will we need a new boiler in the high school within the next five years? If so, we need to set money aside for repairs for the next couple of years and create a capital expenditure account that will be sufficient to manage the cost of replacement.

Teachers are expected to anticipate the capacity of students to grasp difficult concepts and be prepared to differentiate instruction to meet the needs of those who have trouble with their studies. It is essential that we apply these same anticipation skills to issues that may affect schools.

Issue management as a public relations discipline was defined in the mid-1970s by W. Howard Chase as

> The capacity to understand, mobilize, coordinate, and direct all strategic and policy planning functions, and all public affairs/public relations skills, toward achievement of one objective: meaningful participation in creation of public policy that affects personal and institutional destiny.

One example of a corporation responding to external issues in the manner described by Chase during that era was Mobil Oil. Operating in an environment growing increasingly critical of corporate profits and production practices, Mobil Oil famously began a series of paid editorial advertisements to counter what it believed to be unfair and uninformed criticism of big business in general and the oil industry in specific. This innovative communication campaign by Mobil Oil marked the growth of issue management by major corporations and continues to this day.

How Issue Management Can Help School Leaders

Most school boards and superintendents operate on the theme espoused in the old, but still applicable, advertising campaign employed by the Holiday Inn hotel chain, "No surprises."

An effective issue management program can help school leaders in precisely the

same way the business manager's efficient management of the school operations budget. We anticipated the effective life of the high school boiler; we provided the resources for repairs and, ultimately, replaced it before it failed. There was no crisis; students and staff were not sent home because the boiler failed in February. Board members were not faced with an unexpected expenditure that forced them to dip deep into district reserves. There was no need to go to voters and ask for additional operating revenues.

The ability to effectively anticipate issues and adjust school policy in response, before a crisis occurs, is issue management. Continuing with the school budgeting analogy, I like to say a school district has two types of fund balance. One is the physical, fiscal fund balance of reserve revenues used to operate the district. The other fund balance is the reservoir of good will held by the district. It is the public trust engendered in the districts' administrators and board to make good decisions.

A district's goodwill fund balance is no less tangible than its fiscal fund balance. Once it is gone, it is gone. When the public no longer trusts the district's ability to make good decisions, the leaders will soon be gone. One board member will be defeated, and then another, and soon the superintendent will be out the door. This happens far more often with external issues than with concerns about teaching and learning. And it almost always happens because our administrators did a poor job of listening to their community and responding to their priorities.

It is well to remember the following formula for effectively managing a school district's image:

■ 90% of maintaining a positive image is doing an excellent job.

■ 7% is listening to stakeholders.

■ 3% is communicating to stakeholders.

Issue management is the listening part of the equation, combined with a process to feed into strategic planning that drives the 90 %. If you do those functions well, communication is a natural exercise of engaging your public in district activities. If not, it is trying to explain what you're doing. As NSPRA veteran Bill Banach says, the default excuse for many issues is "a communications problem." But communication cannot fix a structural problem. The inability to effectively listen and respond to community priorities is a structural problem.

How to Implement an Issue Management Program

First and foremost, issue management is an administrative function. The school public relations professional must be a trusted part of the district administrative team to play a role in the issue management program.

If the superintendent and the district's administrative team consider the school communicator a technician to implement the tactics of a communication strategy, they will pay little attention to warnings about the future implications of a long-term trend. That said, there is more to issue management for the trusted advisor and strategic thinker than going into the boss's office, closing the door, and pointing out the implications of an issue.

To effectively analyze and respond to an issue, a district needs a clear understanding of its values and vision. Without clearly defined and articulated values and vision shared by administrators and staff, it is impossible to examine an issue or societal trend, put it into context, and develop an appropriate response.

With a well-defined set of values and vision shared with stakeholders, an issue management program will prove invaluable to a district's reputation management, its overall communication, and crisis management.

The four steps of an effective issue management program

■ Environmental scanning

■ Strategic planning

■ Communication

■ Evaluation

Environmental Scanning

Organized environmental scanning is a process that should involve a team of staff across the district. The team reviews media coverage and shares information that is important to their stakeholder group with the purpose of defining how that data relate to the values and vision of the school district. The following are examples of issues that might be identified through an environmental scanning team:

■ Board of Education members in another state attempted to insert intelligent design into the state curriculum

■ News reports indicate our state will lose an estimated 20% of its manufacturing jobs in the next decade

■ Local church groups are active in providing aid and relief to victims of the genocide in Africa

■ The local newspaper reports the mayor of the region's largest city has challenged the mayors of several smaller communities to walk more than 10,000 steps each day

■ The Chamber of Commerce reports a major pharmaceutical company plans to locate a research facility that is expected to create 1,800 new jobs within the next decade

What do these things mean to your school district?

Once issues have been identified, the next step is to determine what, if any, impact each issue has on your school district. Some issues could have a direct impact on your district, some could have an indirect impact, and others could have no impact. The following are examples of how the above issues could affect a school district:

■ The local chapter of a parent curriculum organization appears at a school curriculum meeting, and later at a school board meeting, to advocate for intelligent design and evolution to be treated equally in science classes.

■ Business leaders advocate for a more rigorous state curriculum, proclaiming the era of middle-class employment for high school graduates (or even dropouts) has come to an end.

■ Church groups combine to provide refuge for Africa exiles and their children, who suddenly represent a substantial population in two district elementary schools.

■ Local politicians criticize the school district for accepting money from carbonated beverage bottlers and offering soft drinks and "junk" food in school vending machines.

■ A new population of highly educated scientists is attracted to the community and with them come extremely high expectations for the local school district.

A key part of environmental scanning is understanding the context of emerging issues. To put these issues into context, the environmental scanning team needs a tool to measure the potential impact on the school district. Futurist and former school communicator Gary Marx, president of the Center for Public Outreach, applies a simple grid to the process of evaluating an issue and its effect on a district. Here is a sample of the grid.

Identifying the Issues

| Critical | Ongoing | Emerging | Priority 1, 2, or 3 | | Impact | | | |
					Probability %	High	Medium	Low

Source: Gary Marx, Center for Public Outreach

In Marx's issue anticipation tool, the issue is entered and evaluated as being critical, ongoing, or emerging. It is assigned a priority and a probability of impact. Using the issues above, knowledge of the active community group should have prompted the environmental scanning team to assign a high priority and probability of impact to the intelligent design issue. This could well have been considered a critical issue.

The team may have also placed a high probability of impact on the location of a new research facility, but set the priority as low because the demand associated with a new population of scientists won't occur for several years. This would be an emerging issue instead of a critical issue. The loss of manufacturing jobs could make this a more critical issue, particularly if it is so acute as to occupy the attention of policymakers in the state legislature. Then, even though the loss of jobs may not be an issue for your particular district, it could be an issue statewide, which would prompt concern about the abilities of high school graduates among your business community.

Establishing a context for identified issues will help your district determine how to respond to an issue.

An organized strategic planning process accepts the issues identified through environmental scanning and identifies how the district will respond.

Strategic Planning

There must be an organized strategic planning process to accept the issues identified through environmental scanning and identify how the district will respond. This planning process is essential because it provides an opportunity to bring pertinent issues to a broad cross-section of district staff, put the issues into context for them, and give them an opportunity to collaboratively develop a response.

This brings several key components of effective response. The benefits of bringing the results of a high-priority issue to a well-organized strategic planning process include:

■ Provides an opportunity for communication to all internal stakeholders

■ Gives different departments of the organization an opportunity to assimilate the information

■ Creates a reasoned, systemic solution that all recognize as a comfortable fit with the district's values and vision

In response to the intelligent design environmental scanning issue, the district's strategic planning team may have developed two study groups — one among teachers and curriculum experts, and another among community stakeholders — to explore options. These groups may have come to a conclusion about what constituted good scientific instruction, how theories are presented to students, and what might be the appropriate environment for a discussion of intelligent design. All segments of the community might not be totally happy with the result, but engaging them in a process is more productive than waiting for the activist group to attack. In this type of process, the district manages the issue before it emerges as a challenge.

All good planning processes must include evaluation and adjustment.

Communication

Once a response has been developed, it must be communicated to internal and external stakeholders. This communication naturally follows the accepted formula of research, planning, implementation, and evaluation. The research was conducted during the environmental scanning process, where secondary research information was gathered through the media and primary research — usually qualitative — was gathered through evaluation among internal and external stakeholders within the school community. Implementation occurred as a result of action through the strategic plan. All good planning processes must include evaluation and adjustment.

Sharing the response to the issue with internal and external stakeholders will limit questions and concerns of how an issue is being addressed.

Evaluation

Evaluation may be formal, using surveys or focus groups to measure response to the changes implemented. However, informal evaluation methods may also be helpful. Some possible informal evaluation methods include:

■ How many people attended the board meeting to address the issue?

■ How many letters to the editor were sent?

■ How many phone calls did the district receive?

Sometimes, effective issue management is best measured by informal measures. The district anticipated community concern about juvenile obesity, the district announced the introduction of healthier fare at lunchtime, new lifelong fitness instruction in physical education classes, and a new policy to turn off pop machines during the school day. As a result, no angry parents appeared at board meetings, no complaints arose about the district's making money from vendors at the expense of children, and no activist groups formed to demand change. These informal measures helped to gauge the response to the issue.

Sometimes, effective issue management is best measured by informal measures.

Summary

Issue management is an integral part of any well-planned public relations program. It helps districts avoid crises and builds goodwill among the community because it demonstrates the district's willingness to listen and respond to stakeholder priorities.

The communicator who uses an issue management program must be a trusted strategic advisor who is an active participant in the district's administrative team. The entire administrative team should be engaged in the process, as it involves cross-functional involvement and engagement through the strategic planning process.

Ron Koehler, APR

Ron Koehler, APR, is assistant superintendent for organizational and community initiatives at Kent ISD, an educational service agency located in Grand Rapids, Michigan. He is also a former Mideast Vice President for the National School Public Relations Association.

Koehler brings a wide range of experience to education communication, with career ventures that include wire service editor and reporter, newspaper and magazine editor, media advisor, and speechwriter for former Michigan Governor James J. Blanchard, advertising and public relations agency principal and, finally, the creator of a communication department for Kent ISD.

As assistant superintendent for Kent ISD, Koehler works to engage the business, government, and philanthropic communities in productive partnerships with 20 public school districts, 17 charter academies, and private/parochial schools educating more than 130,000 students throughout the greater Grand Rapids metropolitan area.

Communicating Test Scores and Accountability Data

By Jim Dunn, APR

Accountability and the proper reporting of test scores are key components in a strategic public relations program. Parents, school patrons, and politicians expect schools to accurately and consistently report student progress, school board actions, business decisions, and safety concerns and procedures. Communicating clearly how students and the school district, as a whole, are doing is a fundamental public relations function.

Accountability builds understanding and support for education by focusing on the many specific ways good communication creates real success for students and schools. An effective school public relations program will help educators, parents, and patrons better understand and appreciate the connection between sound educational communication and student and school achievement.

Accountability and transparency are fostered by strong communication between schools and their communities.

As a result, long-term benefits accrue to students and their schools when parental involvement is high, community support is strong, and commitments to excellence are celebrated.

Students perform better when families and communities work together with schools.

Building the Case for Accountability and Communication

The National School Public Relations Association (NSPRA) is conducting an ongoing national project, the Communication Accountability Project (CAP), to improve public education by facilitating research and understanding into the important role communication and accountability plays in creating successful schools. The following are some of the initial findings from the CAP research that help build the case for accountability and communication.

▓ **Educational communication makes a difference.** A growing body of surveys and studies document that supporting, practicing, and modeling successful communication activities are essential to student, educator, and organizational success.

▓ **Students perform better when families and communities work together with schools.** Two-way communication, networking, staff and family training, partnership approaches and administrative support have been identified as the key components to increasing student achievement.

▓ **Accountability pays for itself.** Actively demonstrating accountability and transparency leads to greater support from parents and patrons.

▓ **"Honest communication" develops trust between parents and schools.** Parents and teachers who work together will most likely be less inclined to blame one another for lack of student motivation, poor performance, or misconduct. Studies advise teachers to establish partnerships with parents and keep them informed.

▓ **Cultural and diversity sensitivity work.** Understanding and responding to language and cultural differences help parents feel comfortable participating in their child's education both at home and at school.

▓ **Engage parents often and early.** Schools enjoy greater success in engaging parents in partnerships when they are responsive to the needs of parents and are perceived as friendly and welcoming to parents.

■ **Students with involved parents display more academic motivation than peers with less-involved parents.** Studies have found that rates of remediation, repeating a grade, and suspension and expulsion are much lower when parents monitor the academic performance of their children.

■ **Give parents clear information.** Parents want schools to give them information, but they want information that is free of technical jargon, comes from a credible source, and focuses on their concerns and questions.

■ **Poor attendance also predicts higher dropout rates and lower performance on achievement tests.** Data show that many schools can increase student attendance by implementing specific family and community involvement activities.

■ **Accountability and communication create goodwill.** Open, honest, consistent communication creates good feelings about schools that will sustain them in times of hardship or crisis. A prevalent sense of commitment and cohesion are essential for the long-term success of any school.

Schools must learn to tell their story in compelling and meaningful ways.

Accountability and Communication Play Important Roles in Education's Future

Almost 80% of the populations of many communities no longer have a direct link to public education because the majority of taxpayers no longer have children in school. As a result, school public relations must become much more sophisticated than a message home in a backpack or a press release to the local paper.

Accountability now means systematic research and an effective mix of communication that is both factual and results-oriented. Schools must learn to tell their story in compelling and meaningful ways. The daily bombardment of negative information about schools by sophisticated, well-financed, and emotion-driven ad campaigns creates the impression that public schools are failing. This steady drumbeat — much of it political in nature — threatens a fundamental building block of our democracy, education for all.

Communication leaders must learn to use a comprehensive range of public relations skills and assets to both counter attacks on public education and advocate for the important place public education holds in our system of government. Accountability and communication will play important roles in sustaining support for our democracy and public education.

Creating Accountability in School Communication

Communication accountability is based on tried-and-true basic public relations principles. Contrary to a common public misconception, effective school public relations practices do not include "spin," manipulation of facts, cover-ups, or misinformation. A truly accountable and strategic public relations program is planned, transparent, two-way, based on research, honest, and ethical.

In the modern era of 24-hour news cycles, instant digital information via the web, and an increasingly "report the story and check facts later" news mentality, it is almost inconceivable that a school district would think there was any way to control the media or a news story. It is standard practice to assume a story will get out and hiding it from the public will not work. The public relations management function is now focused on influencing how and when a story breaks, damage control, and reputation management. In this public relations paradigm, trust and accountability are almost synonymous.

Transparency, two-way communication, and honesty are the critical components of any school public relations program. Parents and students need to believe school officials will tell them information they need to know. School officials must develop trusting relationships with the news media and staff. School patrons expect to be told honestly and directly how tax money is being spent, what is being taught, and how well students are learning.

However, communication accountability is more than simply telling the truth and building trusting relationships. Communication accountability depends on using a wide range of tactics and strategies to ensure the varied publics and stakeholders in a school district are connected in meaningful ways to their school system, its teachers, and students. A community must understand a school system's mission and goals to know if students are succeeding at meeting them. Critical to any public relations management function is the development of a communication model that is collaborative and based on research.

A truly accountable and strategic public relations program is planned, transparent, two-way, based on research, honest, and ethical.

In a comprehensive communication plan, test scores are accurately reported and explained. Stories are communicated to a variety of different audiences in a number of different forms. Results from public relations programs are quantifiable and behavioral. Communication accountability, as a school district management function, ensures district goals and objectives are understood and being met, the public is informed and engaged, and, most important, teaching, and learning are occurring as prescribed. These results are ultimately measured by sustainable and continued student success.

Test Scores Offer Promise and Problems

Testing is an extremely valuable part of educational assessment. It allows educators to measure progress, evaluate both individual learning as well as program effectiveness, and perform diagnostic assessments.

Testing can also be used to ensure that all students are learning. Broken into the aggregate, educators can pinpoint cultural, ethnic, and developmental concerns and develop remediation strategies. Schools can learn what programs are working so they can duplicate that same success in other schools. Instructors and administrators can discover what teaching techniques work best for individual students and develop alternative learning opportunities designed especially for an individual student, class, or even an entire school. When the assessment is authentic, parents can have a clear picture of their child's strengths and challenges as well as clear suggestions on how to help at home.

Theoretically, testing can make everything better. Students will know exactly what they need to work on to improve. Teachers will have a clear picture of the needs and abilities of each student and parents will have the information they need to understand both their child's current level of achievement and their progress through a clearly articulated curriculum. It is a wonderful promise that testing offers education. However, like most things that offer so much hope, testing also has a dark side.

When testing stops being an aid to learning and is not used as a diagnostic tool to help students, it becomes destructive to the education process. When tests are used strictly to categorize and label students, they actually do harm. Unintended consequences, misinterpretation or misuse of results, and poor scoring make testing a nightmare in some districts.

Now that we know students have many different kinds of intelligence and learn and mature at different rates, it is clear there is no "one-size-fits-all test" given on a single day that can completely measure as student's learning. No single test offers a picture that is wide or deep enough to know how a student or a class is performing.

When this fundamental flaw in testing is misinterpreted or misrepresented, it is a communication challenge to counter these inaccuracies with facts. As a result, the media often reports test scores as if they are a horse race focusing on who wins and who loses instead of the more critical question,

> Are children learning and making progress, and are schools improving?

The first responsibility of a school public relations professional is to be the conscience of the school district and insist that testing is done right and for the right reasons.

Both the media and some politicians will sometimes use the word *failure* to describe an entire school or school district because one subgroup did not meet an arbitrary goal. This is an example of when test score reporting actually becomes destructive to learning. In truth, some schools and some children are failing, but it takes a battery of test results, over a period of time, to diagnose and offer a prescription for improvement on a large scale.

In relation to communicating testing and accountability, the first responsibility of a school public relations professional is to be the conscience of the school district and insist that testing is done right and for the right reasons.

Done properly, testing and test reporting can be a central piece of a school district's accountability program. A few simple guidelines will help create an effective communication plan for releasing test scores.

Interpreting and Presenting Test Scores

One successful model for reporting test scores is to create a district report that contains an executive report, disaggregated data, celebrations and challenges, and vital facts. The following are basic guidelines for creating an accountability report on test scores:

■ **Report a wide range of results.** Make sure your school district reports a wide range of test scores including nationally normed test scores, state scores, and local benchmark scores. This will help parents, staff, and residents better understand the overall accountability perspective.

■ **Use technology.** By posting test scores and related information on your web site, it will be easier to show more detail to help explain the results.

■ **Explain what the numbers mean.** Any reporting of test scores begins with a thorough review of the test scores. The numbers themselves are meaningless unless they are put in context and interpreted. A thorough review and analysis is the first step in creating meaningful messages about what the scores mean.

■ **Begin the report with an executive summary.** Beginning with an executive summary allows you to bullet important information about the results, any changes in the test, and guidelines for interpretation. This is where you can define terms and set the tone and focus for reporting the test results.

■ **Highlight good news first.** In the analysis, point out the positive aspects of the results and then explain any challenges or plans to improve.

■ **Report significant achievements and celebrations.** The accountability report does not need to just be a data report. Use the report to share stories about what students are learning and achieving.

■ **Interpret scores honestly.** When analyzing test results, provide an honest and straightforward explanation of the results. If there is bad news, share it and describe the plan for improvement.

■ **Share with all audiences.** Parents and residents are interested in the academic performance of your residents, but don't forget to share information with staff members. Staff members — especially teachers — can use the results to make improvements, but can also help to interpret results to parents and residents.

■ **Share plans to improve scores.** The accountability report is an opportunity to share "what's next" steps and to set the stage for next year's report. Plans for improvements will help explain what will be done to move forward.

> Educators should build bridges and connections with parents that involve them in the education process.

Be Proactive About Test Scores

The main things people want to know about their schools center on what is being taught and who is doing the teaching. Education, in the hearts and minds of patrons, is like politics, both personal and local.

Communities need a two-way, consistent flow of strategic information in many different forms and for targeted audiences to ensure messages are heard and understood. School public relations professionals should develop communication plans that continually highlight achievement and effective teaching to provide a background for reporting test scores.

Test scores become less important when parents are deciding for themselves that their children are getting a good education, teachers care about student learning, and school is a safe place for students. Educators should build bridges and connections with parents that involve them in the education process.

Most important, actual student learning and continuous student and parent assessment are more important than any single test. Testing only has value for what it does to enhance student learning. Regular communication about student learning and achievement will help build support for your schools and provide a context for reporting test scores and accountability data.

Jim Dunn, APR

Jim Dunn, APR, was the 2005 president of the National School Public Relations Association (NSPRA). He currently serves as the director of communication services for Liberty Public Schools, Liberty, Missouri, and teaches communication courses at William Jewell College.

In April 2003, Dunn was named the Missouri Professional of the Year by the Missouri School Public Relations Association (MOSPRA). Jim served as president of the Missouri School Public Relations Association in 1990–91 and twice as western vice-president. Dunn also served as NSPRA South Central Vice-President from 1996–99 and chaired the NSPRA accreditation committee in 2001. He has been a presenter at NSPRA annual Seminars and the National School Boards Association conference and has served on numerous national committees. He holds a Bachelor's degree from William Jewell College and a Master's Degree in humanities from Southern Methodist/Baker University.

Dunn has won five major writing awards for his weekly newspaper column, has written a tribute selected for inscription on a memorial to teacher/astronaut Christa McAuliffe, and twice served on the National Teacher of the Year Selection Committee. Dunn currently serves on the Board of Governors for William Jewell College and Liberty's Sister City Commission.

Dunn worked eight years as a youth minister for the Liberty Presbyterian Church. He was selected Liberty High School Teacher of the Year in 1983 and won the district's Honoring Excellence Award during his 26-year tenure as a public school teacher.

5

Special Topics

Legislative Communication and Governmental Relations

By Larry Wiget, Ed.D., APR

Government relations is a public relations function that builds and maintains mutually beneficial communication and advocacy relations with the local, state, and federal governments and agencies that determine the laws and regulations that affect public schools.

Effective government relations practitioners build networks and coalitions among the internal and external publics of a school district to provide the essential programs, services, and facilities to fulfill the district's educational mission.

To be most effective, government relations must be an ongoing communication effort to share the perspective of a school district with elected officials.

Take the Lead

To be effective advocates for children, school public relations practitioners must take on new leadership roles in the government relations arena. A way to look at this notion is through the acronym LEAD:

Learn the political process

Educate the publics

Advocate for funding, policy, and regulatory needs

Defend the role of pubic education

The following are a few ideas to consider when learning about the political process:

■ **Learn the names of legislators and their staffs, key government agency officials, and the state school board.** Which legislators represent your school district? What are their political affiliations? How do you contact them?

■ **Learn how to access the system.** When does the legislative session begin? How often does it meet? How does one find out about the status of legislation?

■ **Learn how the legislative process works.** What are the steps for introducing legislation? What committees must the legislation pass through before it becomes law?

> **Defending the public schools is essential.**

One part of advocating for children is emphasizing programs, services, and regulations that affect student learning. It is not enough merely to educate the legislature about the education system.

It is important to advocate for the solutions that promise to provide the resources and services that will ensure an adequate and equitable education.

In addition to educating the public and the government entities and advocating for public education, defending the public schools is essential. School public relations practitioners need to counter the half-truths and rumors that permeate the public's perceptions about education.

Engage in Government Relations Planning

Effective leadership in the government relations can be translated into a substantive plan by using the following four-step process:

■ Identify legislative priorities

■ Develop an action plan

■ Execute the strategies

■ Access the outcomes

Once priorities and an action plan have been developed, it is time to implement the strategies.

The responsibility for establishing the district's legislative priorities rests with the school board. The school board is the policy-setting branch of the district. Board members should elicit input from the district's key internal and external publics, either directly or through the district's administration.

Once the priorities are determined, the board should formally adopt them. In this manner, the priorities become official board policy, which members of the board as a whole have agreed to support.

The next step in government relations planning is to develop an action plan. The legislative action plan provides a framework for the legislative strategies, activities, and programs to be undertaken by the school district before, during, and after the legislative session.

The legislative action plan should:

■ Identify goals and objectives for the legislative program based on the stated priorities

■ Specify strategies, actions, tools, and tentative time frames

■ Outline responsibilities of the school board members, administrators, and other staff, and, if applicable, lobbyists to implement the plan

Once priorities and an action plan have been developed, it is time to implement the strategies. Meet with local legislators before the start of the legislative session to help achieve the district's goals.

The purpose of action plan strategies is to build networks and coalitions to help shape opinion and influence decision makers.

The final step in the process is to access the outcomes. Government relations is a dynamic field. Assessing the outcomes enables the school district to adapt to changes in circumstances and improve the strategic government relations process.

On a continuing basis, use informal assessment to evaluate the success of a particular strategy. Include informal interviews with selected members of the internal and external publics, as well as reflective self-assessments.

You should conduct a formal assessment of the legislative program annually.

Practice "CPR"

How do busy school public relations practitioners begin to get a handle on working with their state legislators? It is as simple as applying "CPR." The following are the three components of "CPR":

Communication. Ongoing, two-way, mutually beneficial communication with lawmakers and regulators is at the heart of an effective government relations program.

Perseverance. It is essential to demonstrate perseverance in accomplishing almost any worthwhile goal and objective. It takes time to educate lawmakers and to build the public support necessary to obtain funding or to enact new laws and regulations.

Relationship building. Creating and maintaining relationships is key for establishing and maintaining access and credibility with legislators. As public employees, our access to legislators is built on trust and knowledge rather than financial contributions to a campaign or political party.

Here are a number of strategies you can use to implement a "CPR" philosophy for a successful government relations program:

■ **Networks and coalitions.** Networking with internal and external publics means that information is exchanged, understanding is enhanced, and lines of communication are opened for dialogue to clarify issues or help shape opinions. Networks are webs of communication and not all members of the network will agree on every issue. Coalitions move beyond the network of communication to advocacy roles for supporting, opposing, or modifying funding and legislative issues important to the school district. However, coalitions extend only to issues with which the various publics agree.

■ **Community involvement.** Positive community involvement helps shape the community's opinion of the school district, but it also helps in understanding the community's concerns. Involvement opens channels of communication so that when it is necessary for the school district to go to the community for support, community members are willing to listen because the school district has listened to them.

■ **Community engagement.** Engaging the community through two-way communication in the form of town meetings, task forces, school board work sessions, and other strategies also helps build the district's understanding of the community's issues and concerns. In addition, active community engagement builds community support for district legislative goals and objectives.

■ **Timed actions.** You should take specific actions at specific times. For example, important times are before and after an election and during a legislative session. Some actions should be taken every year.

Timed actions	
Before an election	Identify the school district's legislative priorities
	Obtain a list of legislative candidates from your state's elections office
	Send an information packet on your district to all legislative candidates
	Invite legislative candidates to visit schools and to discuss the school's programs and needs with the building principal, staff, and community
	Send follow-up thank-you notes to all candidates who visited schools
After an election	Send a congratulatory note to all successful candidates for office
	Invite newly elected officials to visit schools in their legislative districts
	Invite newly elected officials to meet with the district superintendent, representatives of the school board, and appropriate district personnel to discuss the school district's legislative priorities and concerns
	Provide newly elected officials with background information on your district and an overview of issues facing the district
During the legislative session	Maintain an ongoing presence with the legislature, governor's office, and the department of education during the legislative session through implementation of the district's lobbying strategies; dissemination of information concerning district needs, legislative priorities, and concerns; committee testimony; and responses to requests for information
	Meet with local civic and community groups on an ongoing basis to provide information, discuss issues, and seek support for the school district's legislative priorities
	Meet with presidents, boards, and general membership of school parent organizations to keep them updated on legislative activities
	Share information with employees on legislative activity and the district's legislative priorities
	Meet with statewide education advocacy groups to garner support for district legislative priorities and to develop statewide strategies for achieving the legislative priorities that all groups can support

Use the Tools of Communication

Each school district must establish and maintain communication with legislators and the school district's internal and external publics to effectively educate the public, and advocate, oppose, or defend legislation, laws, or policies.

To this end, school district personnel must be able to communicate clearly. They must know the issues and be able to explain the district's position in simple, direct terms. They must be considerate and polite even in confrontations. And they must be able to state the district's case clearly and concisely.

The following are some specific tools and techniques to help internal publics communicate with legislators:

■ **Telephone calls.** While not as personal as a face-to-face visit with a legislator, a call can be just as effective. Begin by introducing yourself and explaining the reason you are calling. If you are calling about a specific piece of legislation, identify the legislation by bill number. Do not be surprised if the legislator is not available and an aide handles the call. Legislators count on aides for information about specific issues and often advise the legislator as to what stance should be taken on a particular issue or piece of legislation.

■ **Office visits to legislators.** Arrange office visits in advance rather than arriving unannounced. Plan initial visits early in the session when the legislation is being formed. Schedule other visits around the time when the legislature normally takes up annual issues such as school funding.

■ **Testimony before the legislature.** Prior to going before a legislative committee, learn the names of the members of the committee. At the hearing, introduce yourself and state whether you are representing yourself, your district, or a coalition of people or organizations. Identify the issue and whether you are for or against it. If it is a specific piece of legislation, identify the bill by its number and date.

■ **Letters, faxes, and emails.** Keep any written communication with legislators as short as possible. Limit letters and faxes to 1 or 2 pages and emails to 1 or 2 paragraphs. Identify the issue and the bill number, if appropriate, and state your position clearly. Thank the legislator for the time taken to read the document.

■ **Special events.** Open houses, luncheons, and ribbon-cutting ceremonies all provide opportunities for school personnel to mingle with legislators and for legislators to learn more about the school district, its programs, and its facilities.

■ **Handbooks for legislators.** A simple district handbook or notebook provided to legislators before the start of the session should give them important information. The content of the handbook may include:

■ Contact information for school board members

■ Contact information for the superintendent, central administration, schools, and departments

■ School-day schedules

■ Physical locations of schools and legislative boundaries

■ Background information about the district

■ **Legislative directory.** Similar to the handbook, the legislative directory is prepared for internal use by school board members, administrators, and other key staff members. An effective directory should contain:

■ Names and contact information for legislators and their staff members

■ Board-approved legislative priorities

■ Names and contact information for key governmental agencies

■ Names and contact information for state board of education members

■ Names and contact information for local officials and key legislative committee members

■ **Fact sheets.** Prepare fact sheets on the district to provide background information to legislators. Keep fact sheets simple. Use 1 sheet of paper if possible and limit the text to 1 issue. A fact sheet can be used to inform the public, specific interest groups, or legislators or to advocate a particular course of action or to defend a district position on an issue.

Good laws often take a long time to get through the legislative process.

Abide by the Principles of Effective Government Relations

Several principles of government relations help school public relations professionals and educators maximize their effectiveness when communicating with legislators. Consider these principles when implementing a government relations program:

■ **Remember who votes.** Taxpayers vote. Business owners vote, and parents and non-parents vote on education issues. School public relations practitioners must communicate with voters — as well as with legislators — because many individuals and organizations are affected by and affect the funding, legislation, or regulations of public school education.

■ **Education speaks with many voices.** Individuals and groups supporting public education do not speak with a single voice. On any given issue, many points of view and competing interests may exist within the education community. For example, the school board, the parent organization, and teacher and administrative groups all may have differing positions on a proposed piece of legislation. Because of this, building coalitions among the various education groups is an essential component of an effective government relations program.

■ **Education must compete for resources.** Providing for public education is a state responsibility and often the largest item in a state's operating budget. However, many in the legislature view public education as merely another special interest group, one vying for attention and public funds.

■ **Legislators are elected.** Legislators respond to the will of their constituents, to the needs of special interest groups, and to pressure from the media. Many decisions legislators make are politically motivated. Part of being successful as a legislator is staying in office in order to influence legislation.

■ **All decisions are political.** Every decision affecting public education is a political decision. Understanding the political climate of your state will help you more successfully navigate the political scene.

Success must be measured by the quality of legislation passed or the goals accomplished.

■ **Good laws take time to make.** Good laws often take a long time to get through the legislative process. In fact, it often takes longer than a single legislative session to pass a piece of important legislation. Sometimes it is necessary to put forth an idea over several sessions and let it gather support gradually.

■ **It is easier to kill a bill than to pass one.** Hundreds of bills are introduced during a legislative session, and only a few make it through to become law. Reaching agreement on the specifics of a bill means that a critical number of legislator's interests must converge. In working with legislators, school public relations practitioners and educators need to consider the following goals of legislative work:

■ To prevail by motivating a majority of legislators to pass a needed bill

- To urge compromise if it will ensure passage of key components of a positive bill

- To work for a bill's defeat if it is contrary to the legislative goals of your district

■ **Today's foe is tomorrow's friend.** The legislator who worked against the school district's interests last year or against the last piece of legislation the district supported may be the person whose support you need to pass the next bill. It is important not to alienate legislators you may need as allies in the future.

■ **Quantity does not equal quality.** Success must be measured by the quality of legislation passed or the goals accomplished, not by the quantity of bills introduced or passed. It is critical to focus on a few key issues important to the district.

■ **Work to solve problems and provide solutions.** School public relations practitioners and educators need to be prepared to offer suggestions and possible solutions to issues brought before legislators. If you are requesting funds, for example, be prepared to demonstrate why those funds are needed and how they will be used.

Follow Legislative Protocol

Following established legislative protocol will help you avoid costly mistakes that could damage your district's reputation. Commonly accepted legislative protocols are:

■ **Respect the institution.** The legislature or legislative process may not be perfect, but belittling the institution rather than working to change it will not make it more effective.

■ **Respect the position, if not the person.** Voters elect legislators. They may not all meet your personal standards for being a legislator, nor will they necessarily hold the "right" view on the vital issues, but treat each legislator with respect.

■ **Know and use legislator's proper titles such as senator, representative, or governor.** When speaking to a legislator, let the situation dictate the form or address. While one may be on a first-name basis in an informal setting, in public, address a legislator with his or her formal title.

■ **Dress appropriately when meeting with elected officials.** Formal meetings call for professional (business) attire, as do appearances before legislative committees.

■ **Know the issues, the pros and cons.**
Legislators are busy people, and few
have time for long-winded
explanations. Be able to explain the
issues concisely and clearly, and
know the arguments on both sides.

■ **When dealing with the sponsor of a
bill of interest, be clear in expressing
concerns.** Know the sponsor's
positions in order to respond directly
to them. Know the points on which
compromise will be acceptable.

■ **When testifying, politeness matters.**
Always thank the committee chair
and the committee for the
opportunity to present your position,
even if they disagree with your
position.

■ **Attack the issue, never the person.**
You may often disagree with
legislators, but it is critical to keep
the disagreement focused on the issue
and not become a personal conflict.
Remember, you may need a
particular legislator to assist you in
the future.

Larry Wiget, Ed.D., APR

Larry Wiget, Ed.D.,
APR, is the owner of
Baywind
Communications in
Anchorage, Alaska. He
is the former executive
director of public and
government relations
for the Anchorage
School District.

Wiget served as the NSPRA Northwest Region
Vice President from 2003–2006. He is a
frequent presenter at state and national
conferences.

Bond Issue and Levy Elections

By Gay Campbell, APR

A finance election is one of the most critical communication programs carried out by a school public relations professional. Unlike many other communication programs, the price for failure in a finance election has broad implications. Losing a referendum for operating funds can mean staff layoffs, larger classes, inability to adopt needed curriculum or buy learning materials, and other conditions that deprive students of the kind of education they need. Losing a bond measure can mean that students have poor facilities and much less opportunity to learn than students in a neighboring district.

Expertise in interpreting district finances and guiding finance election information efforts makes school public relations professionals worth their salary many times over. If you know how to communicate about finances, the funding needs of the district, and the learning needs of students, you make a significant difference in the education of students. A finance election gives you an opportunity to show how your expertise contributes to the bottom line of the district and enables it to carry out its mission.

In many districts, the communication director works outside of office hours with the advocacy committee and also lends expertise to that group. The ability and willingness to do this makes that staff member doubly valuable to the district. In many cases, the work of communication staff in finance elections demonstrates to a school district that the communication office is indispensable and is providing a sizeable return on the district's investment in that office.

Winning a finance election often requires sophisticated marketing strategies based on solid, definitive research.

Hone Your Marketing Skills

Like other communication programs, a finance election requires sophisticated strategy based on research. This is increasingly true as more communities find the traditional methods — sharing a lot of information and encouraging all residents to vote — no longer work. This author is called by many school districts and advocacy committees who are shocked because their traditionally supportive community has overwhelmingly turned down a measure for schools. In almost every case,

campaign tactics that had always worked for them didn't work this time. The sad truth is that they may never work again.

Winning a finance election often requires sophisticated marketing strategies based on solid, definitive research. This chapter describes some of those techniques. It is a very brief summary of some of the information and strategies found in the book, *Win at the Polls*, published by the National School Public Relations Association. In that publication, you can find detailed information about how to win a school district election.

Elections Are Not a One-time Event

Winning a school finance election is not a one-time, isolated event. Getting voter approval for a finance measure is often determined by the relationship the district already has with its voters. If voters believe their schools are doing a good job of providing the best possible education for the community's children and approve of how the district manages money, they are much more likely to trust the school district with their tax money. If the district has not built a long-term relationship, voters are less likely to approve a finance measure.

Building trust is an ongoing, year-round effort. It cannot be accomplished during a six-month referendum or bond campaign. Open communication about district finances and transparency of all operations are essential to building trust with a community.

When it comes to a finance measure, having a year-round communication program in place pays big dividends. This author has gathered data from seven states showing that school districts with an intentional, year-round communication/community involvement program in place have a better chance of passing a finance measure than districts without such a program.

An effective finance election effort is like any other communication program. To be successful, it requires research, analysis, effective communication strategies, and evaluation. Of course, it is more intensive than many other communication programs and there is no room for procrastination.

Unlike many other communication projects, everything must be done on schedule. The election date is set and the election will occur whether you are ready or not.

Carrying out each research-based element in your election plan is necessary. We have seen an election fail because the school district failed to write and mail one important piece of information to one group of voters. An evaluation of the results of that election showed that failure to act had cost the district millions of dollars.

In some states, school election dates are set by law and there is no second chance to get the funds your district needs. The future of students in your district may depend on doing it right the first time.

Know the Election Laws of Your State

Every state has laws that govern the activities of school districts and other public agencies during finance elections. These laws usually spell out what the school district can and cannot do. Laws vary from state to state, so it is important to learn what they are in your state.

Most states encourage, and some states even require, school districts to provide information about the measure. At the same time, most states do not allow district staff members to be involved in advocacy activities of any kind during regular work hours or use district resources to promote a measure. These resources include phones, e-mail, copying machines, inter-district mail, and other resources. In other words, district staff members — during work hours — can share information about the finance measure, but cannot advocate or encourage residents to vote for or against the measure.

The wise school public relations practitioner will want to know the election laws and plan the district's campaign to conform. Triggering an investigation by state watchdogs and having that on the front page of the local newspaper quickly erodes trust and gives voters a reason to oppose your measure.

The laws governing advocacy committees are entirely different. In most states, there are few limits on what a citizens' support group, operating separately from the district as a political action committee, can do to convince voters to support the school district measure. That's why most school districts need an advocacy committee working hard to "sell" the measure. Much of this chapter is devoted to advice about advocacy committee work, since the school district usually cannot do the type of selective campaigning required for winning a finance election.

will ultimately be decided by the great silent majority of voters: those who won't show up at a hearing or send a message to a committee member. They are watching and waiting and making up their minds. For your measure to be successful, you need to know what they are thinking before you decide what you will place on the ballot.

Start Early and Involve Your Community

Listening to and involving community members in the decision about what to place on the ballot needs to take place many months before the election date.

In many cases, it is wise to have a diverse committee of community members study the need for the measure and recommend to the superintendent what should be placed on the ballot. This committee should represent many groups in the community, and the district should communicate extensively about committee membership, what they are considering, how they are making decisions, opportunities for community input, and how a final recommendation will be made.

This committee should report its initial findings to the community in public meetings and listen to comments and, if necessary, refine its recommendation after listening to the community.

However, a committee to study the issue and make a recommendation is, all too often, not enough. The fate of the issue

What Your Voters Want and What They Will Pay For

It is increasingly difficult to gain voter approval for finance measures without conducting a valid survey of community members to learn their priorities for their schools and whether they are willing to pay for it. The only way to do this with some certainty is a well-designed random sample survey of voters. In some states, this survey can be paid for by the school district before the school board makes a final decision about what to place on the ballot. In some states, this type of survey must be paid for by the citizens' committee advocating the passage of the measure.

It is recommended that this survey be conducted by a professional survey firm. Voters are often reluctant to admit to someone from the school district that they will not support a measure for their community's children. They are much more apt to be honest when questioned by a professional survey firm that assures them their answers will remain anonymous.

In most communities, a properly chosen representative sample of 400 voters will give you an accuracy rate within 5% of the results you would obtain if you asked these questions of every voter in the community during the time frame of conducting the survey.

A well-designed survey will tell you the priorities of your voters, what they are likely to support, and what they are willing to pay. It names the specific items and the cost of each item. Voters are asked about the total impact on their taxes and whether they will support the measure at that cost. They are asked to prioritize projects identified for a bond issue. This is especially helpful if the school district must trim the measure. The survey also identifies the public's perceptions about some proposed projects and the condition of district facilities. It can measure trust and give an indication of the most believable and credible spokesperson for this issue.

Give Them What They Want

School districts whose operating referendums or facilities bonds have failed often call consultants for help. Invariably, these districts either did not conduct a voter survey or did not pay attention to the findings of the survey. Most of those elections have been turned into wins when the district did conduct and respond properly to a survey that listened to their community.

For example, a community desperately needed more high school space to relieve overcrowding. The measure to build new schools had failed three times to obtain voter approval. A random-sample survey of its voters clearly showed what the community would support and how to deliver the messages to receive that support. The district's board listened to its community and placed a trimmed-down version of the measure on the ballot. The revised measure included what the voters would support that would still meet the most basic needs for space. The citizens' support group used the survey findings to design a campaign that delivered messages that motivated specific groups of voters to approve the measure. Voters approved the measure.

Another example is a school district whose bond measure had failed in a community with a long history of supporting school bond measures. A well-designed survey showed that the community would support the added space needed at some schools and renovation of other schools, but a large majority would not vote for the measure if it included sports fields. Although this was a political issue with parents of athletes and they were reluctant to give up this feature of the bond measure, the data were clear: the measure would fail if the sports fields were included, and the measure was likely to pass if they were removed. District administrators explained the situation to the sports boosters and agreed that classroom needs were more important than the sports fields. The board removed the sports fields and information about the measure was clearly communicated. Again, voters approved the measure.

Work the Numbers, Know Your History

Your election may be your only communication program that can be extensively measured in concrete ways for total community response. An election has some people who vote, some who don't vote, a certain percent who vote for schools and a certain percentage who vote against schools. You can get that information on a precinct-by-precinct basis.

If your goal is to get parents registered to vote, you can analyze election data to measure your success. If you are trying to build positive relationships in one part of the district, you can look at precinct data from that area and see if you are getting the support you desire from that area.

Gathering data on a precinct-by-precinct basis for multiple elections can give you valuable insights into the success or deficiencies all of your communication programs. Looking at election results in a given precinct or adjoining precincts over several elections gives you a picture of how support is growing or waning in that area. That, coupled with other things you know about that area and how it is changing, can help you make decisions about your year-round communication programs as well as giving you good information about support for the measure you have on the ballot.

One of the first steps in preparing for an election is to analyze what happened in past elections in each precinct in your district and to look at how those

precincts have changed since the last election. In many states, if you are doing this only in an effort to strategize how to win your election, you are not allowed to conduct this type of analysis on district time or using district resources. If, however, your state expects you to work to register people to vote and to encourage people to vote in all elections, it probably is legal for you to spend work time looking at how well you are doing in that effort. In this, as with all other election activities, be sure to comply with the relevant statutes.

Recruit a Winning Team

Finding the right people for your advocacy committee is critical to winning. You must have a chairperson or co-chairs willing to work intensely to lead the effort for three to six months. Advocacy committee structures vary, but the following are four essential committees to consider when organizing an advocacy committee:

- **Fundraising.** Solicit the funds needed to run the campaign.

- **Volunteer recruitment.** Find the many volunteers who will be needed for the campaign.

- **Publicity.** Write and design materials on advocating for the finance measure.

- **Data.** Track and manage election data.

One of the most important members of your winning team is someone who knows how to manage and manipulate election data. Successful election campaigns are increasingly requiring management of voter data for phone calling, mailings, and other contacts with voters. Your best strategy for winning a campaign may require knowing where to get voter data and how to download it and to sort voters by age or areas of the district or frequency of voting or other demographic groupings. Having the right person for this job and all other work required to carry out an election can make the whole difference between a win and loss.

Tailor Your Advocacy Campaign to Your Community

In examining dozens of winning campaigns, it is clear to see that every community is unique, and the strategy that wins in one community does not necessarily win in another community. Each campaign must fit that community, its voters, its needs, and its circumstances.

In planning and carrying out dozens of campaigns, this author has never planned any two winning campaigns that are exactly alike. No hard-and-fast rules exist about support by age, parents or non-parents, or any other factor. Voters over age 65 can be depended on to support a school measure in one community, while in a neighboring community promoting extensive voting in all voters over the age

of 65 spells certain defeat. Some finance campaign committees can turn out the whole town to win, but for other committees, a massive effort to turn out all voters is a sure way to lose.

Winning campaigns have these things in common:

■ Strategy based on hard data about voters and their attitudes

■ A measure that is responsive to voters' needs

■ Adequate funding for the campaign effort

■ Dedicated volunteers who carry out a definite timeline

Successful campaigns also have a strategy based on community attitudes and data along with targeted messages to selected groups, but the message that works in one community may "turn off" another community.

The advocacy committee needs to concentrate its efforts on finding the "Yes" voters and getting them to vote.

About "No" Voters

People who oppose a finance measure usually do it to protect their pocketbooks. They simply don't want to pay the money. In a few instances, they are angry at someone in the district or about something the district has done, and they may give reasons like, "the district needs to do a better job of managing its money."

No matter what the reason, a well-designed survey invariably shows that the majority of these "No" voters don't want to pay the taxes that will be required to support the measure. They will not change their minds, so it is futile to spend time trying to convince them to change. The advocacy committee needs to concentrate its efforts on finding the "Yes" voters and getting them to vote. Unless the "No" voters become very vocal, the advocacy committee should ignore the "No" voters.

A district that has conducted a survey and has had appropriate community involvement in deciding what to place on the ballot has done a great deal to short-circuit the usual mantra of "No" voters who try to gather others into their camp. If the survey showed that the majority of citizens favor the measure and the survey results have been well publicized, the "No" voters have lost some of their favorite arguments. They can hardly say, "The district just isn't listening to the community," or "They are putting the wrong items on the ballot."

If the district has conducted a survey and had a citizen committee study the needs and make a recommendation, many of the usual claims of "No" voters hold little weight with voters. In most cases, using the right process results in the "No" voters remaining fairly silent. Even if those who are negative have a past history of forming a group to oppose school measures, an extensive process such as the one described in this chapter,

usually short-circuits that kind of activity. The "No" voters know they are in the minority. They know the measure the school district has placed on the ballot is carrying out the mandate of its citizens. They know most of their usual arguments won't work. They are likely to remain silent.

Concentrate on Positive Voters

Winning school finance elections today usually requires that the advocacy committee find the "Yes" voters and make sure they vote. To ensure a win, the advocacy group needs to identify one-fourth to one-half more "Yes" votes than they actually will need to win.

They may be able to do this through analyzing how many "Yes" voters they can count on in certain precincts and then working to get those voters to vote. They may also be able to use the survey results to look at the profile of those who said they would vote for the measure and then find those voters and get them to vote.

In some cases, finding the "Yes" voters requires actually calling voter households and asking voters if they favor or oppose the measure. Those identified as "Yes" voters then receive targeted messages through mailings and personal contacts to reassure them that the things they value most are included in the measure. Identified "Yes" voters are also encouraged to vote.

Use Messages that Work

Informational messages published by the school district must remain factual and, in most states, cannot in any way advocate passage of the measure. District-produced materials should be very clear, thorough, easy to understand, and designed to give voters the information they want and need.

Parents want to know what is in the measure for their child. Staff members may want to know what is in it to help them with their jobs. Non-parent school neighbors may want to know what the measure means for their neighborhood school. And most voters will want to know what it will cost them.

Materials that an advocacy committee produces should be brief while appealing on an emotional level of the voter. Very few voters want a lot of information and may actually start to feel negative about the measure if they are faced with a publication that tells them more than they wanted to know. In close elections, the advocacy committee will want to use survey results to send specific messages to specific demographic groups.

Too many campaigns have been defeated because the advocacy committee failed to carry out the last step: getting the voters identified as "Yes" voters to actually cast their votes. When you are involved in an election, having someone say they support you isn't enough. Their support doesn't mean a thing unless they cast a supporting vote. It can be difficult to get voters to actually go to the polls and vote or to return their absentee ballots. Advocacy committees often find they have to take unusual steps to obtain the votes they need. This may include repeated phoning of "Yes" voters to be sure they go to the polls or turn in their ballots.

Evaluate Your Results

Once an election is over, it is critical to evaluate the effectiveness of each campaign and communication strategy. The results of the district's informational campaign should be thoroughly evaluated to see if it met the needs of the voters. The advocacy committee should evaluate each action, each committee's activities, and the results.

A precinct-by-precinct analysis should be completed and compared with past elections to detect trends and possible insights into year-round communication activities in certain areas of the district.

The evaluation of election activities often provides information that helps guide other communication efforts and sets the stage for future finance campaigns.

The NSPRA publication, *Win at the Polls*, includes a complete guide for planning and implementing a finance or bond election.

Gay Campbell, APR

Gay Campbell, APR, is the original author of NSPRA's *Win at the Polls*, a complete guide to successful school finance elections. The book, which has guided hundreds of schools districts and other tax-supported bodies to success in finance elections, features research-based strategies that have resulted in winning school district finance elections throughout the nation. It is now in its third edition.

Campbell has strategized and carried out many effective communication plans for obtaining community engagement in schools and has guided dozens of school districts to success in their finance campaigns. She specializes in building grassroots support for schools and mobilizing communities for support of their schools.

She has wide experience in public relations and education, having been a teacher, a school district administrator, filling administrative positions in social service agencies, a private public relations agency, and public school public relations.

She was 2005–06 president of the National School Public Relations Association and received the 2003 NSPRA Presidents' Award, the highest award given to a member of her profession.

Campbell has won nine Gold Medallions, the highest award of the National School Public Relations Association for outstanding public relations programs, and numerous other awards, including the Washington State Learning and Liberty Award from the Washington School Public Relations Association and the Award of Merit from the Washington Association of School Administrators.

School Foundations, Partnerships, and Fundraising

By Mark Havens, APR

Since the 1980s, schools and school districts in every state have joined the world of professional philanthropy by creating education foundations. A foundation is an independent, nonprofit corporation (or, in Canada, a *society*) established under the laws of one's state or province and granted nonprofit status by the federal government.

Foundations are either public (accepting funds from the general public) or private (such as corporate or family foundations). They can be large or small, addressing many needs and interests or just a few. While many foundations are stand-alone enterprises, numerous others exist to benefit the needs of another organization. This other organization is often another nonprofit or governmental entity — like a school.

While colleges, universities, and many private schools have had education foundations to assist them for decades, public schools have started foundations only relatively recently. Some of these foundations serve the needs of a single school, while others benefit a regional consortium of school districts or an entire state. But the most common form is an education foundation established to benefit a single school district. Such foundations come in all sizes and types and engage in a variety of activities. Even so, they all have certain things in common.

Every school district in North America can benefit from having an education foundation dedicated to its support, if it is set up appropriately and if everyone understands its role.

How a Foundation Can Benefit Your School System

There are numerous benefits of having a school foundation as a legally incorporated, affiliated nonprofit organization many of which pertain to financial matters. The following are the financial benefits of a foundation to a school district:

■ A foundation can invest funds in higher yielding investment vehicles than public school districts.

■ A foundation may be better able to create and administer perpetual endowment funds.

■ As an IRS 501(c)3 organization, your foundation may be able to attract and

qualify for some grant and matching funds that your public school district may not qualify.

■ A foundation could recruit and manage large gifts from benefactors sheltered from the politics of the school district.

■ As an independent organization, your foundation may be able to raise money in ways your school district cannot such as with events involving alcohol or gambling activities, and could hold and disburse money for purposes your school district might wish to avoid such as for gender-based or racial-based scholarships.

■ Through its disbursements, a foundation can help even out the economic and funding disparities among different schools and communities in your school district.

However, the primary benefit of your school foundation will be to engage people and groups in the educational progress of your students. Many of these people or groups may not otherwise be involved in the school district. These people and groups may include the following:

■ Non-parents

■ Empty nesters

■ Senior citizens

■ Retired employees of your school district

■ High school alumni

■ Neighbors of your school campuses

- Business leaders
- Politicians
- Local celebrities
- Youth groups
- Civic groups
- Faith communities
- Other nonprofit organizations and charities

In most school districts in North America, fewer than one-third of households have children attending public schools, the lowest figure in a century. The implications of this statistic are dire. Your foundation can become the vital link building bridges between your school system and these important sectors in your community.

Your school district can reap benefits through an education foundation that will help you achieve your organizational goals.

Seven Truths to Consider When Defining Your Foundation's Role

When you consider forming a school foundation or reflecting on the role it will play, it is vital that you understand the following seven truths that will limit and govern its role:

1. **Private fundraising will never be able to replace or match public tax dollars.** Nor would you want it to. Public schools belong to the public and should therefore be funded by everyone through tax support, not just by those who can afford charitable donations. No school or district will ever be able to raise enough private funds that will reduce the tax support paid by citizens.

2. **The most important costs of a school system will always find their way into the school district's tax budget.** Therefore, by definition, privately raised funds will never be used to fund those things considered primary or essential.

3. **A school district does not need a foundation to raise private money.** Donations to public schools are already tax deductible, and school districts are perfectly capable within their existing framework of pursuing, managing, and spending private funds. Indeed, some school districts have "development departments" (along with education foundations) to attract private dollars.

4. **Public schools already raise plenty of private money.** If yours is like most public school systems, you have parent organizations that raise money, student groups that hold fundraisers, booster clubs with many activities, and youth and civic organizations which support different aspects of your educational program. Teachers write grants. Businesses support your school publications and sports teams through advertising. Parent committees raise funds for graduation night parties and

scholarships. And the list goes on and on.

5. **A school district can have a very successful foundation even if it raises very little money.** Some of the country's best school foundations are involved in many activities, bring numerous community leaders together to support student progress, but raise limited funds.

6. **The purpose of a school foundation is no more to raise money than the purpose of a school district is to collect taxes.** Money simply provides one tool to help a foundation achieve its goals.

7. **Your school foundation will develop its reputation — and define its role — by what it makes happen, not by how it raises funds.** Every school foundation should spend as much time determining its unique role as it spends planning fundraising efforts.

If raising money were the sole need of your school system, it would be more cost effective for your district to simply employ a professional grant writer or to set up a development department with trained fundraising staff that would not need to lose time answering to a citizen board of directors. However, your school district can reap benefits through an education foundation that will help you achieve your organizational goals. In addition, your foundation's board of directors can become your secret weapon and greatest ally.

Start Your Foundation with Research and Planning

Time spent doing research and analysis during the beginning phase of your foundation will pay dividends in the years to come. It will help you not only "do things right," but will also ensure that you "do the right things."

The following are the essential steps of establishing a foundation:

Step 1: Convene a planning committee

The planning committee should probably contain high-level school district administrators, possibly some school board members, and citizens who are familiar with nonprofit organizations and your community's philanthropic profile. This committee will determine if your schools might benefit from forming an education foundation and whether to move forward.

Knowledgeable committee members should understand and explain about your state's nonprofit corporation laws, what paperwork will be required, the fees involved, and the accounting system that will be necessary.

Meanwhile, the committee should ask the school district to compile a report of all private revenue sources that it already receives. Some of these amounts might already be reflected in your school district's annual audit, such as fundraising by student clubs and sports teams, grant funds awarded to teachers, and fundraising conducted by schools. Other sources of support — such as from parent organizations, booster clubs, and scholarship funds — might not be a part of your district's audit and will need to be researched to be included in the report.

This report should include the source of the private and donated funds, how the funds are spent, how funds are raised, and when funds are raised. Knowing this information is vital if your foundation is to differentiate itself from other existing fundraising efforts for your schools.

Step 2: Determine how to pay the bills

As an independent corporation, your foundation will generate expenses beyond the money it disburses to aid your schools. Some of these expenses will be one-time, start-up costs, while others will be annual and ongoing. Researching and compiling these costs will help your foundation develop an operational budget for its initial and first few years. The following are some of the expenses of a foundation:

■ State fees to incorporate your foundation including the initial filing fee, plus possible annual renewal fees

■ Internal Revenue Service fee to file and obtain your IRS 501(c)3 status

■ Possible legal fees to pay a knowledgeable professional to draft

and file these documents and help get your foundation started

■ Annual costs to pay for insurance for your foundation such as directors and officers (D&O) insurance, liability insurance and bonding

■ Possible banking fees to set up bank accounts

■ Possible broker fees to manage your foundation's investments

■ Printing costs to print foundation brochures, image pieces, gift acknowledgements, and board and financial reports

■ Postage costs to mail everything from board reports to fundraising solicitations

■ General operating costs for items such as office space, supplies, telephone calls, and post office box

■ Possible cost to obtain a separate computer, printer, and software programs for your foundation's own use and recordkeeping

■ Start-up costs to fund expenses for any type of special event your foundation may wish to sponsor

■ Annual expenses pertaining to your foundation's board of directors such as meals, training, travel, and out-of-pocket reimbursements

■ Costs associated with having a foundation staff member such as salary, benefits, training, travel, and professional fees

As you can see, the list is considerable and this is only the beginning. It is possible that you might be able to get some of these costs and services donated. Moreover, most school districts are willing to help cover some of these expenses. In many instances, the school district assigns a paid staff member to assist the foundation either part-time or full-time. In other cases, the foundation has to fund the costs of its own employee, or do without the benefit of paid staff. When funding these costs, your foundation can look to the following possible sources of money:

■ **Funding from a percentage of all donations** received by your foundation. Your donors — and the IRS — will want to know what percentage of donations supports your educational mission, and what percent goes toward "overhead."

■ **Funding from part or all of your foundation's investment earnings.** This income source has the benefit of not being tied to a particular donor, but your foundation will need to amass investments before this becomes a viable option.

■ **Funding derived from the proceeds of special fundraising events or sales.** Like the option above, this source has the benefit of not being tied to a particular donor.

■ **Funding from direct "underwriting" of your foundation's administrative expenses.** Your school district may absorb some of the costs. Your foundation board members and other

community leaders might be willing to designate their donation toward operating costs rather than educational programming.

Estimating all of these anticipated costs and determining sources of funding for them will go a long way toward establishing your foundation's first budget.

Step 3: Determine who will do the work

As with other endeavors, foundations are groups of people who combine their efforts to work toward a common goal. Your foundation's activities will create work, and getting the work done will be a major factor in its success.

The most effective education foundations have the benefit of paid professional staff, even if it is just a single part-time person. Usually, this position is paid for by the school district. While this approach may be controversial, realize that the school district will derive far greater benefits from having a foundation than a staff position will cost. In time, the foundation may be able to pay for its own staff expenses when it succeeds in securing more resources.

If a staff position is created for the foundation, a job description should be written and foundation board members should play a role in selecting the candidate. You should try to hire someone with nonprofit and fundraising experience.

Whether or not your foundation has a paid staff position, you will need to have a board of directors. Board members will be expected to bring their "wealth, work, and wisdom" to the board.

Board members should also have job descriptions. The planning committee should begin the process of recruiting persons to comprise a diversified board of directors who will represent all aspects of your school district. Some planning committee members may wish to serve on the initial board of directors and some may not.

Step 4: Determine a unique role for your foundation

After reviewing the fundraising report prepared by your school district, you are now in a position to define the unique role your foundation will play. You probably do not want to duplicate efforts that are already being successfully addressed by other groups, nor should you go into direct competition with other fundraising arms of your school system.

Your foundation can differentiate itself from other school fundraising entities by choosing distinctive approaches in the following areas:

■ What do you raise money for?

■ Whom do you raise money from?

■ How do you raise money?

■ When do you raise money?

If other school groups are raising money for classroom equipment and sports, perhaps your foundation should raise money for library books and the arts.

Most school groups raise the bulk of their funds from parents so your foundation should probably focus on the two-thirds of your community who do not currently have children in school. If other groups raise money through bake sales and golf tournaments, perhaps your foundation can sponsor cookbook sales and dinner dances.

Moreover, try to schedule your fundraising activities at different times than the other school groups so as not to compete with them for the same pool of donors.

Above all, your answers to the first question — what do you raise money for? — will help define the role and image of your education foundation. This limited range of needs to support will begin to shape your foundation's mission statement and may even suggest various fundraising methods and prospective donors.

Step 5: Determine your foundation's name, mission statement, and vision statement.

Step 6: Obtain a taxpayer identification number (TIN) for your foundation

With this number, you can open bank accounts and deposit initial donations needed to pay for filing fees and start-up costs. Any bank can help you file for a TIN.

Step 7: Draft your foundation's articles of incorporation and bylaws

Develop the articles of incorporation and bylaws according to the laws of your state or province. It is advisable to obtain the assistance of a lawyer or other professional who has done this before for other nonprofit organizations. File the articles of incorporation with the appropriate state or provincial authorities.

Step 8: Apply for 501(c) 3 tax exempt status from the IRS or equivalent Canadian authority

This process can take several months. You can raise money during this period because the tax exempt status is retroactive when it is granted.

Step 9: Convene your first board of directors meeting

Your initial board should approve the bylaws; elect officers; establish regular meeting dates, times and places; recruit additional members to the board if there are still vacancies; establish committees; and begin the process of designing a logo, letterhead, and other "image" pieces for your foundation.

The needs for various kinds of insurance for your foundation should also be discussed.

Step 10: Make plans for future foundation operations

As your foundation's board of directors gains experience, it will also need to adopt an accounting system, develop investment and money management policies, and create a strategic plan for the foundation.

This strategic plan should include fundraising strategies, a disbursement plan, a public awareness plan, a donor recognition plan, and administrative policies.

Beware Obstacles That Could Hinder Your Success

The path to a successful foundation is fraught with possible obstacles. Foundations that fail to live up to their potential often find themselves the victims of one or more problems. All are avoidable with advance planning.

Avoid these potential problems when planning a foundation:

- Setting unrealistic goals

- Trying to do everything the first year

- Spending a lot of money on information you can get for free

- Spending a lot of money trying to raise money

- Inactive, uncommitted board members or board members seen as "figureheads"

- Misunderstanding the role of your foundation

- Misunderstanding your community

- Lack of direction

- Lack of leadership

- Over-reliance on unqualified staff

- Over-reliance on a single donor or source of funds

- Fighting over money after it is raised

- Political meddling, or getting involved in controversial issues

Your foundation board of directors should conduct an evaluation at least annually to determine if any of these or other obstacles might be hindering your success. If so, seek professional advice and training. Evaluation is the key to continual improvement.

Pursue Partnerships That Could Increase Your Success

In today's philanthropic world, partnerships are key. Before giving you money, many grantmakers, corporations, and major donors want to see that you have formed strategic partnerships with groups beyond your school district. To be successful, your foundation should not operate in a vacuum.

The benefits of forming partnerships are many and powerful. Your foundation can reach out to groups which previously had no involvement in the educational system. You can make new friends and allies for your school district.

Your combined voice will be louder when advocating for children and you will find synergy — your collective efforts will be greater than the sum of the parts.

From these partnerships, your foundation might obtain information, ideas, advice, resources, assistance, volunteers, money, and potential new board members. You will greatly increase your chances of achieving your goals.

Your foundation can partner with others in several ways:

- You might conduct joint fundraising if you are partnering with another nonprofit group. You might share mailing or donor lists, or you might split the proceeds from a joint fundraising event.

- If both your foundation and your partners have financial resources, you might create a funding partnership in which each partner contributes toward the cost of a joint educational project which benefits your students and teachers.

- Consider a program partnership, where your foundation provides the funding and your partner provides the work and expertise to achieve the educational goal. Examples of this could include funding the Red Cross to teach students basic first aid skills, or working with your local chamber of commerce to start a Junior Achievement program.

The following are a few examples of organizations that could be potential partners with your foundation:

- PTAs or other parent groups
- Senior citizen groups such as AARP and retired teachers clubs
- Alumni associations
- Fraternal organizations
- Civic groups such as Rotary and Kiwanis

- Youth organizations
- Churches
- Unions
- Business and trade associations
- Arts organizations
- Environmental organizations
- Volunteer organizations
- Neighborhood associations
- Fire departments, police departments and Red Cross agencies
- City and local governments
- Local foundations
- Other charities and nonprofit groups

Many of these groups will likely be eager to partner with your foundation to benefit the local public schools. They are just waiting to be asked.

Successful Fundraising: It's Who You Know

As stated earlier, your foundation should define its role and determine what it is raising money for before deciding how and from whom to raise money. This is because the projects you wish to fund will likely suggest possible donors interested in these matters as well as potential methods of fundraising.

An old but very true cliché in the world of fundraising is that "people give to people." They don't give to institutions; they give to people that they know, like, and trust. Likewise, you will not be raising money from corporations or foundations. You will be raising money from people. Individuals will make the decisions whether to invest in your education foundation.

For large gifts, you need personal contact.

It is important that your foundation board is composed of individuals who personally know people with the means to give such as corporate officials, foundation officials, and high net-worth individuals. Most school districts are not in regular contact with such people. Your foundation board members will help open the doors.

Most education foundations will raise money through direct mail campaigns by mailing solicitation letters to a list of potential donors once or several times a year. This may be part of an annual fund appeal or membership drive. While such appeals may increase your donor base, keep in mind that few people make large donations through mailing campaigns. For large gifts, you need personal contact.

Your foundation should maintain a list of 25 to 200 potential major contributors. Form this list through research and the suggestions of your board members.

Your foundation must develop an ongoing relationship with these individuals through frequent communication and personal contact. At least once a year, solicit them for a donation. Such people may be willing to write a check, to discuss a planned gift, or to make a multi-year pledge to a capital campaign.

Remember, if you can find 200 persons willing to donate $1,000 a year into an endowment fund for a period of 5 years, at the end of that time you will have 1 million dollars.

Like other charities, your foundation board may feel the need to conduct a special event to raise funds. Such events can be a mixed blessing, usually taking a great deal of work and often raising only modest amounts of money. But they can bring your organization a lot of much needed publicity and also serve as a "gathering of the faithful." Such events can include formal dinners, concerts, dances, talent shows, auctions, golf tournaments, and other sporting events.

Your foundation may also sponsor a raffle or develop a product such as a calendar, cookbook, or limited edition print that it could offer for sale. Keep in mind, whether you are selling a cookbook, selling a raffle ticket, or selling a ticket to a concert, the success of all such activities will depend on the diligence of your "sales force" — your board members and other volunteers. Tickets don't sell themselves.

The following are a few fundraising ideas to be considered to raise funds for a school foundation:

■ Create a payroll deduction program for employees

■ Put a donation line on all student registration cards

■ Put donor cards in all publications and in prominent locations

■ Attach donor cards to gift receipts for future donations

■ Put donation canisters in various locations

■ Investigate corporate matching gift programs

■ Investigate school "scrip" programs and corporate "partner cards"

■ Allow donations via your schools' web sites

■ Initiate a memorial gift and "tribute gift" program

■ Encourage donations in honor of retiring employees

One of the most fulfilling ways for your foundation to earn income is to fund an educational project which makes money. For example, your foundation might provide a grant to a teacher whose students will create a performance or a product such as art or photography pieces, doll houses, or a cookbook, and these will be sold to the public. Your foundation is fulfilling its mission by funding an educational project, students are learning skills, and income from the project is enriching your foundation. It doesn't get much better than that. Invest in your foundation with enthusiasm, and your schools will reap the rewards.

Mark M. Havens

Mark M. Havens has worked in the areas of public relations, fundraising, and organizational development for more than 20 years. A lawyer by training, Havens served for 16 years as the community relations director for the Lewiston Independent School District, Lewiston, Idaho, and the executive director of the Lewiston Independent Foundation for Education, the first school foundation program in Idaho.

Havens served as the NSPRA Northwest Region Vice President from 1994–1997. He is the author of NSPRA's book, *Dream Big: Creating and Growing Your School Foundation.* He is currently serving as the executive director of the Gritman Medical Center Foundation in Moscow, Idaho.

The One-Person Public Relations Office

By Joe Krumm, APR

Running an effective school public relations office can be especially challenging for a professional working alone in a school district. Many professionals do all the public relations work for their district without any clerical or other support.

Those working with limited or no assistance can feel isolated because the pressure to implement the communication program can be intense.

Many challenges are unique to a one-person office. This chapter examines several topics covered in previous chapters, but puts them into the context of the one-person office. In addition, topics unique to the one-person office are also included.

A comprehensive communication plan is especially valuable for the one-person office because it helps direct and focus your work.

Assess Value of Public Relations Function

Many one-person offices are run by school public relations professionals who are relatively new to their positions. In addition to the pressure of operating a one-person office, people who are new to their positions also have the challenge of learning the school public relations function.

Whether you are new to school public relations or have been functioning in a one-person office for several years, it is valuable to assess the value and role of the public relations office in your district. It is important to know:

■ how the public relations role is defined

■ what communication strategies are in place

■ how the district as a whole views public relations

Explore both the areas of support and possible barriers to growing a successful public relations program. Part of this research includes having candid conversations with the superintendent, other key leaders, colleagues, and school board members.

The clarity that comes from this research will help you develop a comprehensive communication plan for the district. A comprehensive communication plan is especially valuable for the one-person office because it helps direct and focus your work.

When a plan is comprehensive and strategic and supports the essential role of the district, it acts as a guide for the practitioner and other leaders. The plan can also serve as a way to respond to those who recommend their "good ideas" about how the public relations office should do its job. You can weigh the suggestions as to whether they fit the plan or the overall direction of the district.

If various departments have common goals, it's easier to find ways to work together.

Building Alliances with Colleagues

A one-person office is often too small to do all of the important work needed to accomplish the communication goals outlined in the communication plan. Alliances with other departments in the district can be the answer.

Building an alliance starts with understanding the core mission of the school district. If various departments have common goals, it's easier to find ways to work together. Connecting with another office or department in the district can help align staff and financial resources in the same direction. The best alliances will come with people who understand the tie between their office work and improved communication.

Alliances are usually formed around shared projects. For example, the finance department may be interested in creating greater understanding of the budgeting process among community members and parents. One of the goals of the communication plan may be to implement a public engagement initiative. This would be a perfect opportunity to work together to schedule community conversations about the district's budget.

Other possible projects for building alliances with other offices or departments include:

■ Parent support classes

■ School orientation fair for new residents

■ Developing crisis response methods

■ Employee orientation sessions

■ Curriculum review nights at schools

■ Campaign to boost school attendance

Dozens of topics can bring the public relations office together with another department. Alliances are an opportunity to combine resources and, because a one-person office has limited resources, they give you a way to accomplish work by using the resources of other departments.

Some departments may resist such alliances and it may not be beneficial to force a relationship. However, in some cases, it may be necessary to insist on being involved in an initiative where public relations help is needed. In other words, you may need to "crash the party."

Show up, be polite, and ask to sit in with a key committee so you can learn more about what they do. When appropriate, contribute to the group and speak of the value of communication to address their interests. This will quickly get you connected with other departments and staff members for other alliances.

It is important to act professionally and be seen as someone who can be trusted.

Increasing the Status of Public Relations Office

The value of the public relations office often depends on how other district leaders perceive the public relations function. The following are ways to elevate the status of your one-person public relations office:

■ Act professionally.

■ Serve as the district's conscience.

■ Do a good job and do more than was requested.

■ Tell people about how you can help.

The most important part of elevating the perception of the public relations office is to act professionally. People who may not understand the need for communication may better understand after they develop a relationship with the professional in the office. Do whatever you can to work with other departments and to be seen as an important part of the district.

Act as the district's conscience.

The success of the one-person office will depend on your integrity, character, judgment, leadership, counsel, reliability, accessibility, and responsiveness. It is important to act professionally and be seen as someone who can be trusted.

The next way to elevate the perception of the public relations office is to act as the district's conscience. Developing this role involves being an ethicist, an historian, a current affairs expert, and a futurist. It is one thing to say that the district should "do the right thing," but it is another matter to develop the judgment and experience to know "the right thing." Nevertheless, counsel on the right choices should reflect what will be defensible, and even understandable, with the community.

You should share the community's perspective while deliberating issues to help others consider the implications of a decision. Understanding your district's history can help the public relations professional provide counsel on past issues and decisions. Studying current education issues can help you and the district prepare for emerging issues. Further, anticipating future trends can help the public relations office to be at the center of planning.

Do a good job is the third way to elevate the perception of the public relations

office. People will gain confidence in you if your office provides tangible resources to other departments. These actions will help others see your value to the district and demonstrate what you can do:

■ Have systems in place to respond to crises.

■ Know research techniques and apply them to make programs more effective.

■ Know the community and have the connections with other organizations.

■ Demonstrate how to effectively communicate about key issues.

■ Develop and demonstrate a skill that no one else can do.

■ Provide perspective on key issues.

■ Offer training on communication-related skills.

■ Counsel principals on media interviews.

The final way to elevate the status of your public relations office is to "tell people about it," or make sure others know how you can assist. Most educators do not have a background in public relations or communication and do not fully understand the role of a public relations office. Part of your role as the district's public relations professional is to teach others what you bring to the district. Marketing on behalf of the department should be part of the weekly to-do list as well as an aspect of annual planning.

Developing Leadership

Developing and demonstrating leadership can and should be an important attribute of any school public relations professional. This is especially true with those in a one-person office. By assuming a greater leadership role, you have the opportunity to offer options for consideration and to function more as a strategic advisor.

Because having limited time is often an issue in a one-person office, it is important to be able to quickly frame issues and provide advice to other leaders. Consider these steps when providing perspective on an issue:

■ Describe the problem clearly.

■ Analyze the problem.

■ Present options.

■ Make a recommendation.

■ Describe impact.

■ Evaluate and debrief.

One way to develop your leadership skills is to find ways to serve as a leader. Opportunities can come with local service clubs, local NSPRA chapters, national NSPRA committee work, or community organizations. Many local chambers of commerce also offer classes in leadership. This can lead to greater connections with current and future leaders.

Avoiding Burn-out

The very nature of running a one-person office can lead to burn-out and a sense of isolation. It is important to connect with other professionals to get another perspective on your work.

Without feedback, self-perceptions can swing wildly about the quality and effectiveness of one's work. One can become overcritical or oversensitive to the sways of the day. It is important to have a colleague nearby or reachable by phone or e-mail to provide some balance to your perspective.

The following are some causes that can lead to burn-out for the professional in a one-person office:

■ Overwhelming amounts of work

■ Never-ending loop of deadlines

■ Monotony and repetition

■ Little, no, or poor direction

■ Answering to many stakeholders

■ Lack of appreciation

■ Little control over external forces

■ Not enough time to complete long-term projects

■ Budget cuts — never enough money

■ Difficulty finding balance

Draw a clear line between work and home to avoid becoming overtaken by the work load.

The work in a one-person office can be overwhelming. Consider these few ideas to not let the work load take over your life:

■ Practice self care and balance work with other interests.

■ Be patient — you will not reach your goals overnight.

■ Limit things that distract from your work.

■ See situations clearly — don't exaggerate or minimize situations.

■ Be willing to step out of your comfort zone and try new things.

Satisfaction in work comes from getting regular breaks from it. It is one thing to "not take work home" by leaving the laptop at the office, but don't let the issues of the day dwell into the evening. Professionals in a one-person office need to draw a clear line between work and home to avoid becoming overtaken by the work load.

Managing Time and Routine

Professionals in a one-person office need to have adequate time to work on the major communication issues of the district. Yet, a great deal of time can be taken away by clerical and other tasks that do not fit with the goals of the communication plan.

The mundane must be managed effectively or it can sap the necessary energy and time needed for more important tasks. The following are ideas for managing time and using it more efficiently:

■ **Analyze the situation.** Any plan to improve the management of routine starts by understanding how you work best. Do you move from working on a major project to mundane work without prioritization? Do you compartmentalize and prioritize your work? Do you create lists of tasks to organize your work? What is the combination of approaches that works for you?

Evaluate where you spend your time effectively and where you waste it. Break down the task lists, the calendar, and the time spent on items. Look for efficiencies and where to set aside specific times for specific purposes without interruption.

■ **Employ some tricks.** Some members have had success making a stack of the routine items that can wait for a time when they can be done all at once. This might include the multiple quick tasks, like writing a press release, fixing web pages, or returning phone calls. There may be certain times of the day when you can do these basic routines most effectively and comfortably. Declare Friday afternoons as your time to complete clerical tasks and busy office work.

■ **Getting efficient.** When writing materials, use an item for several purposes. Never write anything for just one purpose. Reuse it and adjust it for the media, the web site, key communicators, internal and external newsletters, and the e-mail news list.

■ **Prepare templates and drafts ahead of time.** Write drafts of letters and other materials that you will likely need throughout the year. Letters in response to crisis situations are good examples. You can write the basic outline of the letter ahead of time and edit it to reflect specific details.

■ **Follow the plan.** Communication plans will help establish priorities. Put those priorities on the office wall. Then as new ideas and suggestions come in, you can weigh whether they move you toward your goal or if they will be a waste of time. Another way to look at this is to evaluate all tasks as an A, B, or C priority. Do the As. Forget about the Cs and force the Bs into either one of the other piles.

■ **Borrow from colleagues.** School public relations professionals readily share work samples and ideas. Rather than re-inventing something that someone else has already done, get ideas from others to get a head start on your work.

Building the Size of the Department

As you experience success in your one-person office and demonstrate what you can provide to the district, there may be a desire to expand the department or provide you with more resources. This desire to expand the office is more likely to come if you have demonstrated leadership skills and had success in creating a comprehensive communication program.

The following are some possible options for increasing your one-person office:

■ Part-time or full-time clerical assistance

■ Part-time or full-time communication specialist

■ Part-time or full-time technical assistant

■ Part-time or full-time position focused on specific projects

■ Contracted consultants to complete specific projects

When the opportunity to add a staff member arises, it is important to assess the areas where you need the most help. The first instinct may be to ask for clerical help. However, that may not be the most efficient use of a second person's time. The department's needs may require more special skills than those offered with a clerical role. It may be best to seek someone with more advanced skills to go along with the clerical duties, such as writing, layout, web page management, or design.

Be ready to manage the larger office.

If a full-time position isn't supported, it may be appropriate to consider a part-time, shared, or pool position. It may be possible to connect with colleagues in other departments to share a position. It may also be possible to get some clerical assistance from a receptionist or technical assistance on the web site from the technology department.

Another approach is to look for a vacant position in the district and develop an argument for adding the position to your office. This may be a grant consultant, foundation executive, volunteer coordinator, or other position. Push to put this person in the public relations office so some of the work that matters to both positions can be shared. These positions also lend themselves to being addressed through a personal services contract rather than through an outright hire. If the person works from home, that person may be able to take some public relations tasks at an hourly rate.

When you have the opportunity to add staff to your office, it is important to be ready to manage the larger office. It is helpful to clearly outline the duties for the new position. You will need to practice your delegation skills to spread the work. It may also be necessary to learn some management and supervisory skills so you can effectively guide the work of others.

No matter whom it is, being able to share some tasks and projects with someone can be a relief and it can begin to break the sense of isolation that can exist in a one-person office.

Build relationships and stay focused on your goals.

Final Thoughts

In a one-person office, creating a position that is productive and fulfilling may seem simple, but it is likely to take time and patience. When the work is so overwhelming, it can appear difficult to believe that it will ever be under control.

Practitioners who stand for something have the most value to the organization. Identify issues and causes that are important to you. When the right issue or person comes along, be prepared with skills, plans, wisdom, judgment, process, and vision. Build relationships and stay focused on your goals.

If you wait to be "ready" to take on a greater role in the district's work, the wait could be considerable. With confidence and the right skills, you will find success at the core of the district's mission.

In a one-person office, there will be things left undone. Don't worry about those things. A lot of energy can be wasted by being distracted by the to-do list or by the thoughts about what needs to be done. Remember, plan, prioritize, be on purpose, and focus on your plan.

Resources to help

NSPRA can be especially helpful to the one-person public relations office by providing:

- Information and resources that you can use every day

- Shortcuts to understanding breaking issues

- A communication audit that will demonstrate the importance of public relations to your community and the value of the work you do

- Study help to earn an accreditation to increase your professional development

- Research from the Communicating Accountability Project (CAP) that will provide evidence to build your program

- An opportunity for service at the chapter or national level

- An opportunity to grow teaching skills by conducting workshops at NSPRA

- A network of NSPRA colleagues

- NSPRA awards to earn recognition for your communication program

Joe Krumm, APR

Joe Krumm, APR, is the director of community and government relations for the North Clackamas School District in Milwaukie, Oregon.

He served as NSPRA Northwest Region Vice President from 2001–2004 and is a past president of the Oregon School Public Relations Association. He has also co-chaired the NSPRA Environmental Scan Committee for several years.

Krumm currently serves on the North Clackamas County Chamber of Commerce Executive Board and is active with the Leadership Clackamas County program and Youth Leadership Project. He recently was named Volunteer of the Year by the chamber.

Krumm regularly presents seminars and classes on many subjects including media relations, lobbying, beating burn-out, crisis communication, effective school communication with a small public relations office, and how to create videos to support staff morale.

His expertise in operating a one-person public relations office comes from experience in his district. Many of the techniques described in this chapter have come from personal trial and error. After using approaches discussed in this chapter, his staff is now larger and more effectively serving the needs of the district.

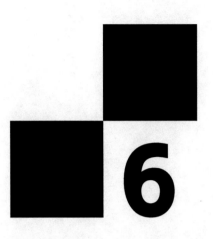

6

Appendix

What Is NSPRA?

Since 1935, the National School Public Relations Association (NSPRA) has been providing school communication training and services to school leaders throughout the United States, Canada, and the U.S. Dependent Schools worldwide.

NSPRA's mission is to advance education through responsible communication. We accomplish that mission through a variety of diverse services that we provide to our members and to other school leaders who contract with or buy from us.

With over 70 years of experience, we have a reputation in the field for practical approaches to solving school district and agency communication problems. We have useful communication products, offer workshops and seminars, maintain resource and research files, have contacts and resources within the corporate communication industry, and have 32 chapters throughout the country that provide local networking opportunities for members.

In keeping with our mission, NSPRA provides workshop assistance to school districts, state departments of education, regional service agencies, and state and national associations. For many of these groups, we have completed research-based communication audits to analyze the communication flow, targeting, content, and effectiveness of their communication messages.

The NSPRA National Seminar, the most comprehensive school communication conference anywhere, is held each July. This 4-day conference offers more than 70 topics on a wide array of school communication issues. The 2007 Seminar will be held in Phoenix, Arizona.

 NSPRA's monthly membership newsletter *Network* is a communication resource for school leaders, not just our members. Each edition tackles a major problem and explains how communication can play a vital role in solving it.

 *PRincipal Communicator* is our monthly building-level PR newsletter which provides practical help to school principals and other building-level leaders. The planning calendar and a variety of communication topics are helping many to effectively improve communication at the community level.

Our four electronic newsletters, *NSPRA This Week, The NSPRA Counselor, NSPRA Alert,* and *Opportunities* provide summaries of breaking national education news, in-depth studies of issues and trends, and updates on seminars, products, and services available to educators.

 *Communication Matters for Leading Superintendents* is an e-newsletter targeting issues and topics related to communication for school leaders.

The Flag of Learning and Liberty is a national education symbol, developed by NSPRA in its 50th Anniversary Year. On July 4, 1985, the Flag of Learning and Liberty flew over the state houses of all 50 states to launch the rededication of America's commitment to education and a democratic, free society.

NSPRA is a member of the Learning First Alliance (LFA), a coalition of the leading 17 educational associations in the United States. In addition, NSPRA is a founding member of the Educational Research Service (ERS).

The association also sponsors four national awards programs to bring recognition for excellence in communication to individuals, districts, and agencies.

NSPRA Resources

School Public Relations — Building
Confidence in Education is only one of
many excellent resources available from
NSPRA. Listed in this section are other
products that school public relations
professionals and other education leaders
will find invaluable in addressing
community relations needs.

For more information about NSPRA
services and products, visit the NSPRA
web site at **www.nspra.org**.

The Complete Crisis Communication Management Manual

Packed with updated information and
real-world insights, this manual provides
step-by-step directions and
communication techniques
to prepare for and react to
issues ranging from child
abuse to chemical spills.
Included are dos and
don'ts of working with
the media. Also available
on CD-ROM.

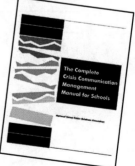

Dream Big: Creating and Growing Your School Foundation

 Learn how to develop and maintain strong relationships with businesses, community leaders, and government organizations — relationships that can reap dividends for your school or district. Topics include fundraising, critical administrative and legal steps for nonprofit incorporation, and tips to make your foundation prosper.

Flag of Learning and Liberty

Raise the Flag of Learning and Liberty to dramatize the links connecting education with your community's ideals. Indoor, outdoor, and classroom flags, as well as lapel pins, are available.

Fundraising Tips and Tactics: A Practical Guidebook for Developing New Funds

 Boost your schools' bottom line. This guidebook offers many useful ideas on partnering PR and fundraising, planning, preparing proposals, budgeting, managing ethical issues, targeting prospects, and linking with businesses.

A Guidebook for Opinion Leaders/ Key Communicator Programs

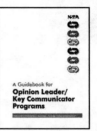 Keep those who shape opinion in your schools and communities among your strongest advocates. An information-packed guide, this publication will take you step-by-step through creating, nurturing, and growing your key communicator network into one of your most valuable public relations and engagement activities. Also available on CD-ROM.

Making/Marketing Your School the School of Choice

One of NSPRA's most popular resources, this handbook enables education leaders to win public support by helping people understand what's working and why. Here are just a few of the important topics covered:

- research on why parents choose schools,

- techniques to become a customer-friendly school,

- how to involve staff and students in marketing efforts, and

- how to engage community members in defining your school as the school of choice.

Making Parent Communication Effective and Easy

Give your teachers and principals what they need to be outstanding communicators. One of NSPRA's newest resources, this practical guide and accompanying CD-ROM provide tips on communication activities, making the most of parent-teacher conferences and open houses, using online grade and planning books, and dealing with difficult parents.

Included are a classroom newsletter template, PowerPoint presentation for open houses, sample welcome and appreciation letters, and many more adaptable communication tools.

Mastering E-Newsletters

Another of NSPRA's newest products, this guidebook and accompanying CD-ROM are helping school leaders communicate effectively using electronic newsletters, e-bulletins, web offerings and more. Scores of tips and ideas are provided on finding the right technology; getting a grip on costs; and designing, delivering, and tracking your e-publications. Also included are sample publications and documents.

NSPRA's Pat Jackson Collection on Public Relations

This collection captures the wisdom of one of North America's most respected professionals in the PR field. His passion for education and appreciation for school PR brought him to many NSPRA seminars, where his sessions were always packed with veterans and newcomers. The entire collection includes more than 15 hours of Pat's timeless and practical advice that has inspired thousands.

NSPRA's Scenario Collections

Take advantage of the professional insights of school communicators on the frontlines. In these two books, covering more than 40 case studies, you'll find out what works, what doesn't and how to avoid the pitfalls of school communication. Here are just a few of the wide range of issues covered:

■ dealing with budget critics,

■ bomb threats,

■ changing school boundaries, and

■ working with a new superintendent.

Powerhouse PR for School Leaders

This training kit empowers school leaders to meet today's communication challenges with marketing, engagement, media relations, and management approaches that work. Some of the many valuable tools included: a guide packed with basics of good PR for administrators, workbook with directions for conducting an effective school communication workshop, reproducible materials and handouts, PowerPoint presentation, and CD-ROM with all materials — plus it's rewritable so you can add your own slides and handouts.

Principals in the Public: Engaging Community Support

The research is clear — public engagement is a must for successful school leaders. This book and accompanying camera-ready worksheets and handouts give principals the tools they need to reach and involve parents and community members. Included are tips and scores of ideas to build community support, conduct research, communicate more effectively, develop a communication plan, use technology, address diversity, and find additional resources.

Practical PR for Principals: A Handbook to Help You Build Support for Your School — Second Edition on CD-ROM

Updated and revised on an easy-to-use CD-ROM, this popular NSPRA resource provides building leaders with the essential tools to develop and maintain a communication program that will exceed parents' and community expectations. Included are:

■ more than 100 PR ideas,

■ "fillers" and quotes to add pizzazz to publications,

■ a sample parent survey,

■ advice on parent communication, and

■ techniques on staff training.

Unlocking Sensational Service: Tools for Tapping the People Power in Your Schools

Bring customer service to life in your schools with this vital collection of tools and tactics. This user-friendly CD-ROM has everything needed to launch a customer-service program that meets your demands.

The choice is yours — create workshops, daily meeting starters, ongoing training sessions or other activities using sample texts, handouts, discussion outlines, PowerPoint presentations and more.

Election Success:
Proven Ways to Win

NSPRA's update of the blueprint manual of *Win at the Polls* provides the know-how and tools to win your next finance election by mobilizing community support. Save time and money, and win at the polls with 300 pages of tips, tactics, and approaches that work.

Included is information about getting organized, learning about your voters, conducting community research, evaluating past elections, techniques that persuade, and targeting your messages. Available on CD-ROM.

The ABC Complete Book of
School Marketing

Meet the school-choice challenge with marketing ideas from best-selling author and school communications, expert Dr. William J. Banach, APR.

Packed with time-tested and proven marketing approaches, this guidebook provides strategies to overcome resistance to change, concepts of targeting and image-building, public engagement tips, a process for planning at all levels, and reproducible forms to chart plans and strategies.

The ABC Complete Book of
School Surveys

Being armed with data explaining teacher, parent, and community member perceptions allows school leaders to take control of public dialog and advance school needs. This resource guides you through every aspect of surveying.

Some of the many topics include:

■ how to create and administer your own survey,

■ 18 essential steps in every survey project,

■ how and whom to sample,

■ types of questions to ask and how to frame them, and

■ reporting on and using results.